THE FLYING LIFE - II

more stories for the aviation soul

BY THE SAME AUTHOR

The Flying Life: Stories for the Aviation Soul

If Airplanes Could Talk: The Pilot's Book of Wit and Wisdom

Man Things: Equal Time for Men

THE FLYING LIFE – II

more stories for the aviation soul

Lauran Paine, Jr.

CASCADE PUBLISHING

SALEM, OREGON

Portions of *The Flying Life – II: more stories for the aviation soul* originally appeared, in somewhat different form, in EAA's *Sport Aviation* magazine.

Printed in the United States of America

Published by Cascade Publishing

Salem, Oregon 97304

www.thunderbumper.com

Paine, Lauran, Jr.

The flying life – II: more stories for the aviation soul

Private flying – Anecdotes, facetiae, satire, etc./Lauran Paine Jr. – 2nd ed.

ISBN: 978-0-9657607-6-8

for my bride of fifty-two years,

and to our grandchildren,

Trystan, Colin, Maryn, and Carys,

who give special meaning to the words “joy” and “pride”

CONTENTS

INTRODUCTION

Not quite sure how I got to this point, publishing another book of aviation stories. Aside from growing up on a cattle ranch, about all I've ever done is fly airplanes. I certainly never imagined myself as a writer. I once got a B+ in high school English…highest grade I ever got there. And that, I figured, was that. Done!

But, over the years, stringing words together has become this: a connection with all of you 'aviation nuts' out there. What a fun and magnificent group you are…each in your own way.

Aviation provides satisfaction and adventure….and stories. It's been my good fortune to be able to tell some of those stories. And I say this: if you have a story, write it down and save it. Sometime, somewhere, somebody's gonna a get a kick out of it. It's all very much a part of this big aviation world we inhabit.

Good days and good flyin' to y'all! Thank you for flying and reading……

Lauran Paine Jr.

1

NEZ

Our youngest son, Darin, a member of the Texas Air National Guard (ANG), was called to active duty recently to help during the COVID crisis. He wrote me about it.

"All of us on the local area deployment were Drill Status Guardsmen - which means we were all 'part timers' with separate lives outside of the military. I had the tremendous privilege to meet so many others on the base I would not normally interact with. We have different backgrounds, different ethnicities, different ideologies, come from different parts of the country but we share one common belief: accomplishing the mission. Primarily we worked rather mindless but often demanding manual labor at a foodbank warehouse with limited A/C. We made boxes; we stuffed boxes full of food and supplies; we sorted boxes; we broke down boxes - over and over and over. We passed no judgement. We did not question anyone's motive. We simply gave out food to those who were hungry. And it was tremendously rewarding. Providing hundreds of thousands of pounds of food to those in need is what kept us going—that and a wide-ranging variety of music depending on who was in control of the Bluetooth speaker. We also felt the welcome Texas hospitality. One of the foodbank volunteers is a special needs woman – she became like family to us. We would go out to lunch and people would pick up our tab without saying a word to us – just telling the server to thank us. To those who we provided food for we heard "thank you" and "God bless you." It wasn't about politics or accusations - it was about doing what we were asked to do. We are mothers and fathers, sons and daughters – one team, one fight. If you want to make an impact do what you can to help your neighbor. Spread the good just by doing your part."

***

One of the fellow Guardsmen my son met while on duty was Nezabian Thomas. "Nez" for short. He had a story that 'perked my ears up.' (My Mom used to say that all the time.) I have to tell you about it.

Nez is currently serving in the Texas ANG as an Intelligence Analyst with the 147th Attack Wing, Ellington Field Joint Reserve Base. He is a Staff Sergeant. He's also attending LeTourneau University, Longview, Texas, majoring in Mechanical Engineering.

Nez grew up an only child. His mother passed away while he was in high school. He was sixteen years old! That's tough going. He said, "I made up my mind that I had to do something with my life." And he has. But there were yet more bumps in the road to endure/overcome.

He always had a "thing" to fly. He wasn't sure why; he just did. He built paper airplanes and such. You all know about the "aviation calling."

After high school he enrolled in Texas Southern University to study Aviation Management. Then he enlisted in the Texas ANG. There you get discipline, educational benefits and a strong sense of belonging. And he started flying lessons.

Nez, after some study, chose Light Sport. The school had Tecnam P-92. It just seemed to him like a good place to start. Then came the accident. It was a dual lesson. He had five hours of flight time. The weather was good. Nez made the takeoff with the instructor following through. After rotation he felt what he described as a "funny response." His instructor told him to get back on the centerline. The next thing he knew, the nose plummeted. His first memory after that was being back on the ground, upright, but on fire. *He* was on fire! Flames up and down his left arm! He tried to open his door. It was jammed. His instructor was slumped over in the right seat, head down. Nez managed to get the right-side door open. He had to crawl over his instructor to get out. (Nez physically winced telling me that part of the story.) He was still on fire. He began looking for some grass to roll in. Somebody behind him said, "Get in that ditch over there." So, he did and doused the flames. Life Flight came and airlifted him to the hospital. The airplane was a total loss. The instructor perished.

The next six months—six months! –were spent in the hospital. Some of the time Nez was in an induced coma. He said, "The people were nice but a burn unit is just not a pleasant place to be." Healing from burns is laborious…..and painful. Family and friends and members of his Guard unit came to visit him. He says, "I had a lot of time to think. I vowed to make something of myself."

What happened? It's a little murky to me. Nez didn't read the accident report until a long time after but when he did it said "power-on stall." Hmmm. I don't know of a CFI who would let a five-hour student over rotate on takeoff. But I don't want to judge. Flight control malfunction? Dunno. The mangled remains of the crash would make that a difficult determination. Like I said, murky. But it happened and the aftermath was Nez's mountain to climb.

There was a passage of time…..obviously. But, somehow, this young man still wanted to fly. Inner courage? Inner drive? Both? Don't know. But whatever it was, it remains admirable.

Nez signed up for a Discovery Flight in a Cessna 172--- a plebeian airplane with a lot of class. He said he was really nervous. And it was bumpy. He held the yoke…with both hands and a very tight grip. A lot was going through his mind. He said, "It was a short flight but I took some comfort in it." Next, he signed up to fly a Diamond DA-40, saying, "I always wanted to fly one." His instructor was demonstrating traffic patterns and landings when he took a cell phone call. (That's a new one for me!) Nez took the controls. He says, "I watched everything he'd been doing." The instructor kept talking on the phone and kinda waved his hand forward, indicating 'go ahead.' So, Nez landed. He said, "That really got me kinda fired up again. I was thinking 'I can do this!'" (My question: was it a fake phone call to get Nez to take over? Don't know. That's a new technique on me but, whatever, it worked.)

Nez went on to solo in a Cessna 172. He took an on-line ground school course and is now a Private Pilot and checked out in the 172 in Houston and Grand Prairie, Texas. All that isn't just an admirable journey; it's a motivational journey, too. Nez….as humble as he is…..probably doesn't even know how much his story inspires others. But it does.

To our conversation, Nez brought and introduced me to his cousin, Joel. Nez's mother and Joel's dad were brother and sister. Joel said, "I was an only child for ten years. Nez and I spent a lot of time growing up together. He's five years older and has always been a big brother to me." Mighty fine big brother, I'd say.

Joel enlisted in the Army National Guard and became an 11B (Eleven Bravo). That, in Army talk, is basic infantry. Tough duty. He also was called-up to serve in the Covid relief effort. He's now enrolled in college and ROTC and wants to get his commission and fly. That's what you call "focus."

I asked Nez what he wanted to do in aviation. He said, "I want to make a difference." I've asked a lot of kids that same question and none ever gave me that answer. But, with Nez, I get it. He doesn't just want to fly; he wants to contribute to the profession. And he has, for sure, the intellect and passion to do just that. His National Guard unit flies the RC-26. National Guard units are traditionally offered slots for military flight training. I can think of no better candidate for them that Nez Thomas.

Nez lives in the Houston area; Joel is in the Dallas area. When they get together in Houston, they spend time at their grandmother's house. I can only imagine how proud she must be of her grandsons. And I can also imagine what a wonderful lady she must be.

So, here I was, sitting at the kitchen table and talking to these two young men and, well, (I don't know any other way to say it) a feeling came over me: I was just deeply touched by their drive, their intelligence and their class. It gave me a good feeling about our country's future. I couldn't help but contrast it to the barrage of negativity the media drums up every day. The media's approach is wrong. There are so many fine young people out there dreaming and working and making their way. I know, I just spent an afternoon talking to two of them.

2

OLD AIRPLANES

We've all checked out in different types of airplanes. It's a familiar process. You learn the different systems and switch positions, stuff like that. But when you move the controls forward, the nose goes down, back, and the nose goes up and left is still left and right is still right. That part remains pretty much the same. Okay, I'm over-simplifying but you know what I'm saying. You do what you gotta do to learn what you gotta learn.

But I want to talk about checking out in the *old* airplanes, say a Stearman, AT-6, or DC-3. Those are different animals….for a lot of reasons. And these days, since many don't get the opportunity, it's becoming a bit of a lost art. But if you do get the opportunity, there are some things you need to know…..and *accept.* One, wear old clothes. The old airplanes seep and leak and have grease and oil all over the place. The radial engines have gallons of oil in them, not quarts. So it's like this: If you don't get grease and oil on you while doing the pre-flight, then you didn't do a proper pre-flight. Oily handprints on your trousers are a mark of thoroughness. An oil drip on your head means you walked underneath the engine, unaware. That identifies you as a rookie.

Don't expect comfort or ergonomics. The old airplanes were meant to work, not coddle you. Sitting in them you'll see stringers and floorboards and wires and tubing and bell-cranks, not color coordinated frou-frou. And the pilot seat isn't some multi-adjustable form fit thing; it's generally canvas or old leather sewn around some sort of padding. And a lot of people have sat on it over the years. The place where your butt goes generally has no cushion left at all. And the airplane instruments are in no particular order. They are here and there and everywhere. Locate oil pressure and airspeed. Those are your primary flight instruments. 'Glass' is reserved for the windscreen. Do not ask about heat, air conditioning or pressurization. If it's cold, dress warm. If it's hot, crack the canopy (AT-6) or open the side window (DC-3) or just strap-in (Stearman). Only the guy with the oil drip on his head would ask about pressurization.

Of note, the old airplanes have tailwheels. Five hours in a Citabria won't help you. So you not only need quite a bit of tailwheel time but you need to *understand* tailwheels. They can bite you. Just having that awareness and appreciating it is a big step in the right direction.

And don't expect good visibility. On landing, the back seat of an AT-6 has the same visibility as if you were driving down the freeway with your car hood up. With the Stearman in the flare the long nose blots out the Universe so having eyes like a chameleon helps: see both sides of the runway at once to make sure you're straight on the runway. Land cockeyed and suddenly you are a cat on a hot tin roof. The visibility out the front of the DC-3 isn't too bad but the windshield is seemingly about six inches from our face. A hard landing can bang your head (or knock your headset off....don't ask me how I know that). And, with no hydraulics, the flight controls tend to be heavy. Anticipate inputs so you don't get into a wrestling match that you'll lose.

So far you're still hanging in there with me, right? You gotta *love* the old airplanes. Some don't. 'Course most of those are pampered children enamored with technology and comfort but completely missing out on the romance of aviation. (Did I really just say that??!!??)

Here's something else you need to do: start the radial engines. In a jet you push a button and maybe move a lever at some % of rpm and the thing starts. Not so with the round-motors; starting them is like building a house. First you have to prep them for start, outside. Make sure there's no oil pooled in a bottom cylinder, maybe pull the prop blades through a few times, things like that. Now…now!....sit in the seat and twirl your finger to signal start. Here we're talking DC-3/C-47: no ignition key, just start switch, mags, mixture, primers and such. And you have to manipulate them all in the right order at the right time and be ready to jiggle and cajole some of them while starting, depending on what you're seeing or hearing from the engine: master on….toggle start….engine grinds and whines……look outside and count eight blades….mag on…..mixture up…..nothing….hit a little prime….cough….sputter….mixture back…..another cough…another….mixture back up…doing this by engine sound now….sput…sputter….sputter…cough….and, finally, a puff of smoke and a low rumbling idle. The sweetest aviation sound on planet Earth. Now start the other engine. It's a little more difficult since now you can't hear it as well, what with #1 engine already running. So now you have to *feel* the start. #2 starts and now you're sitting in living history. It's a mighty fine place to be.

Now fly it. (This is just me talking but I'm not one to get in the pilot seat of a flying airplane and take the yoke and say I 'flew' such-and-such airplane; no airplane goes in my logbook unless I trained and/or qualified in it.) I went to C-47 training at England AFB, Louisiana while in the Air Force in 1970. (Yeah, I know, that was a couple years ago.) It was the first propeller driven airplane I'd ever flown in the military.

At first I thought it was a crap assignment but it turned out that I was wrong about that. My first training flight was September 17th; my final training flight was September 30th. In the eight flights I flew during that time I made seventy-nine landings. That's how you learn to land the beast! On October 28th I was flying passengers and cargo and mail to various destinations in Korea, some paved, some grass and some sandy beaches. That's how you work an airplane. On December 2nd, I flew from Okinawa to Guam (7+45); on December 3rd, Guam to Wake Island (9+15); on December 12th (after time out for a mag repair), Wake Island to Midway (6+50); and the next day, Midway to Hawaii (7+45), our destination. Then it was back to Korea to finish my tour of duty.

And that, m'friends, is how you go about learning, training, qualifying in, enduring, appreciating and, most importantly, bonding with an old airplane. And I wouldn't trade for an hour of it. For the experience, I am forever grateful.

3

DOOLITTLE RAIDER

Today you are a Doolittle Raider. Buckle in!

How you got here is pretty much a result of the accident of your birth and cascading world events. You were a teenager in the late 1930's; you lived in a small town; you attended school; you worked in your father's machine shop after school and on weekends; you had Model T Ford that you could drive if you could keep it running. Hard work was the norm. That's just the way it was. Germany was creating some havoc in Europe but all that seemed so very far away. Scuttlebutt around the shop and on the street was that someday America would eventually become involved. Still, it all seemed far away. The Model T occupied most of your thoughts. Well, it did until December 7, 1941 when President Roosevelt said on the radio, "This is a day that will live in infamy."

That day of infamy would change the course of your life. Though it seemed a little surreal at first, you didn't dread the change; it was simply a call to duty for able bodied young men…..of which you were one. You weren't alone: America felt the call to duty! American's arose, not yet ready for war but with the belief that soon they could be. It was good vs. evil and America was the good.

You-- and many others --went to military recruiting offices. You wanted the Army; they had airplanes. You'd always been fascinated by airplanes, ran outside and watched every time one flew over the machine shop. You liked things mechanical. It was exciting to think of someday being able to fly one!

You went to military basic training. There you learned to march and shoot and wear the uniform. You got yelled at a lot but whatever you had to do to get to flight training, you were willing to do. Something else you learned at basic training: camaraderie and teamwork.

The day you were selected for flight training was a good day indeed. You reported for primary training in California. It was tough; many washed out. But it wasn't too tough if you wanted it bad enough. You wanted it bad enough.

The day came when you pinned your pilot wings over the left pocket of your uniform. You stole many a glance at those wings. You then wrote your girlfriend back home and said, "I'm a pilot. Enroute to 17th Bomb Group. Meet me in Reno." She met you in Reno and you got married.

The 17th Bomb Group had the new B-25 medium bomber. What a beauty! Big and powerful! You couldn't wait to fly it. After qualification training you flew many coastal patrols looking for Japanese submarines. Then you were transferred to South Carolina. There, your Squadron Commander called everyone in and spoke of a hazardous mission that was being planned. Then he asked for volunteers. You volunteered. Those who volunteered were then transferred to Florida. There you were told you were a part of a "Special B-25 Project." This was getting to be quite a whirlwind!

You started training for the "Special B-25 Project" but still didn't know what it was all about. You were told not to talk about it….to *anyone*. A month after training started you were once again called in for a briefing. In walked Lt. Col. Jimmy Doolittle! Wow! Everyone had heard of him; he was already a legend. This was big! He explained that the mission was a hazardous one and only volunteers would take part in it. Then he said, “Some of you will not be coming back.” The room was silent. Then he added, “Any of you can withdraw now, no questions asked.” No one did.

The training began in earnest. Still, all you knew was that it was “hazardous.” All excess weight was stripped from the airplanes; extra gas tanks were added. The lower gun turret was removed along with the big liaison radio. The tail guns were removed and replaced with two broomsticks painted black. The range of the airplane was effectively increased from 1000 miles to 2500 miles. You still didn’t know why.

Then a Navy pilot joined the group. His job was to teach short field takeoffs and shipboard etiquette. Hmmmm. Short takeoffs were full power, full flaps, stab trim three quarters up, yoke back and lift off with the tail skid about a foot off the runway. Then relax. Easier said than done. It was unnatural at first but later you got into competitions. One crew stalled and crashed and was eliminated from the mission. You also flew multiple day and night low level practice bombing missions. Doolittle again asked if anyone wanted to drop out. No one did.

On one cross country you were able to visit your wife again. You couldn’t tell her where you were going; you didn’t know. As you walked back to your airplane, you took a longing glance at her. She was pregnant.

Upon returning to base after the cross country you were abruptly told to pack your bags. You were heading for California, low level all the way. You alarmed a lot of farmers on the trip. Of the twenty-two airplanes that made it, those who reported no mechanical problems were told to continue to Alameda Naval Air Station, Oakland, California. On final approach into Alameda, below you, was an aircraft carrier.

The thing was huge! On the deck were two B-25's! After you landed, a jeep met you and whisked you and your crew away. You glanced back at your airplane and Navy crews were already attaching cables to aircraft lift points.

The next day you left San Francisco Bay on the USS Hornet, along with a task force of other ships, passing slowly beneath the Golden Gate Bridge. People on the bridge stopped and waved.

Once well out to sea, Doolittle called the group together. He announced, "Gentlemen, your target is Japan." A cheer exploded among the men! The ship's Captain made a similar announcement to the ship's crew. Another roar went up throughout the ship. Doolittle continued, "The Navy will get us as close as possible and we'll launch our planes. We'll hit our targets and continue to airfields in China." Then he asked, once again, if anyone wanted to back out. No one did.

On the ship you bunked with two Navy pilots from Torpedo Squadron Eight. All of their airplanes were below deck because the top deck was full with sixteen B-25's. The Navy guys were great, doing their duty just like you. (You heard later that both were killed at the Battle of Midway.)

The routine while at sea was to check your airplane daily and to study the mission plan and your targets over and over and over. You had it all memorized. Every day there was a call to "general quarters" where you ran to your airplane from wherever you were on the ship. You did *not* want to get lost somewhere on the ship when THE call came. You felt great purpose but you also felt some tension as you steamed closer and closer to Japan. You had a change of clothes and some candy bars packed for the "trip" but that was about it; no identification cards or letters were allowed. And your airplane was loaded with four 500 lb. bombs and 1450 rounds of ammunition. Two more days to scheduled launch….when you were approximately four-hundred miles from Japan.

The next morning at breakfast you notice the ship really pitching and rolling. Then comes the call, "General quarters. General quarters. Army pilots' man your airplanes." THE call! Breakfast trays crash to the floor and you run to your airplane. Your crew is all there. Someone asks, "What's going on?!?" Someone else said, "I think an enemy trawler spotted us! We've been found!" The ship was really pitching; waves are crashing over the bow and washing over the deck. This is bad! And you're too far out! Airplanes in front of you are starting engines; you start your engines. All planes are then hastily loaded with an extra ten 5 gal. gas cans. You notice your heart pounding. This is the real thing! Good chance you won't make China now. Damn!

The airplane in front of you is a scant few feet away. Your tail gunner, separated from you by the rubber long range gas tank, remarks over the interphone, "Can't wait to use my broomsticks!" The ship seems to be full speed ahead, the winds gale force; your airspeed indicator is registering nearly thirty knots sitting still! Waves and water are crashing across the deck. You strain to see around the airplanes in front of you. This is it! You glance at your co-pilot; he glances back. Knowing glances; no words are spoken. The deck officer has to time the releases: deck down….go…..so lift off occurs as the deck pitches up. The deck appears to be pitching nearly sixty feet. You've never taken off from a moving runway before.

The deck officer waves Doolittle….in the lead….to go. He moves….seemingly so very slowly at first…..then gains speed. The deck pitches up a little and he is airborne! He made it! Your co-pilot yells, "Yes!!!" The second airplane appears to stall, nose high, and sink toward the ocean. Then you see it staggering upward once again. The third airplane does the very same thing.

Your turn. Mind racing, engines racing, deck pitching, one-way trip, people on board the ship waving, you push the throttles forward as far as they will go. You keep you left main wheel and nose wheel on the white lines painted on the ship for you. A little too far left and you're off the deck; a little too far right and you smack the ship's island. The sea is swirling and spitting all around you. Noise, concentration, vibration and adrenaline. You think, "This is my job; this is my duty." You release brakes. You begin to roll….so slowly, it seems. The deck pitches down and you're looking straight into the water! Faster now, the deck now rising. The plane lifts…ever so little….then more. You're airborne! The crew lets out whoops and hollers. Relieved, you mutter to yourself, "That was short!" As briefed, you level off low- level over the water, joining loosely on your mates. You can see the whitecaps below. You will stay joined until you reach the Japanese shoreline, at which time you will all break off toward your individual targets. It's 0900. Five hours to Tokyo.

Your tail gunner is emptying the extra gas cans into the long-range tank and then tossing them overboard. You are so low that occasionally there is ocean spray on your windscreen. The sense of speed down low is actually exhilarating. You feel the will of your country pushing you. You feel some nervousness but, curiously, you don't feel fear. There is a lot riding on this mission.

Nearing your estimate to see landfall….Japan!.....you spot some ships. That ups the level of intensity. Sighting land you stay low and you can see people waving! Beautiful countryside. But from your target study you know you are well north of where you should be. You climb to two-thousand feet to get a better look. That's when you see the anti-aircraft fire. Off to the right is billowing smoke. Some of your comrades have already been here! You drop back to low-level and head south. You find the torpedo factory you're looking for, increase speed to 200 knots, then pull up to fourteen-hundred feet and open the bomb bay doors. Anti-aircraft bursts are everywhere now. You fly through them. Bombardier yells, "Bomb's away!" Shortly thereafter the broom-stick-tail-gunner exclaims, "We got it!" You turn hard left and strain to look behind you and see a crane blow up and fall over. "Take that!" There is a lot of clapping and yelling in the airplane. Time to get out of the area…right now! You head back out to sea. You take one more look over your shoulder and see smoke rising. You think, 'We…did….our…job!' Now you have to find a place to land…..somehow, somewhere. But *not* in Japan.

You fly south once again until the navigator tells you it's time to turn toward China. You glance at the fuel gauges; up until now you hadn't much wanted to think about them. From how far the navigator said it was to China, well, it didn't look good to make it! Maybe, just *maybe*, however. The radio beacon you had been told would be there to home-in-on never materialized, try as you might to find it. Perhaps it had been destroyed by the invading Japanese. It is getting dark now; you figure….hope….you're at least nearing the coast of China. You climb to hopefully clear any mountains. It's totally dark now. The fuel gauges are bouncing around on empty. You tell your crew, "We're probably gonna have to bailout. Gather what you need." You're at 6500' now. Fuel gauges are no longer registering anything. You engage the autopilot. You all gather around the escape hatch, the order of exit having previously been briefed. You've never done this before; might be time for a little fear. You open the hatch: nothing but black, cold nothingness below. First guy jumps.

Then the next and the next and the next. You reach up and pull the throttles back and then jump.

You pull the parachute rip-chord and…..wham!....you get jerked hard as the chute opens. Overcast above and no lights below…very disorienting….but you figure your feet must be pointing toward the ground. The silence is eerie after thirteen hours in the airplane. Then you hear a crashing sound and see a ball of fire. Your airplane! You see the sheen of water. Not the ocean! You're supposed to be over land! Then you hit hard and crash to your side: a rice paddy! You bury your chute and get out your compass to walk to….where? You don't even know where you are! One thing for sure: You want to be found by Chinese, not Japanese.

It's wet, cold, dark and lonely. Stumbling around you eventually find another crewmember! Then all of them! Alive! All have some injuries; none complain of them. You wander toward some dim lights….a village? Or a Japanese military encampment? Turns out to be a Chinese village. With great risk to themselves and with the help of some Catholic missions along the way, eventually the Chinese help you get out of China.

True to Doolittle's words, some crewmembers did not make it back. Some were captured by the Japanese, some were executed, some were imprisoned, some escaped through China. All sixteen B-25's were lost. Doolittle at first thought the raid was a failure: It was not! It was a huge morale boost for America and it caused Japanese military planners to re-position military assets from the Pacific to closer to home. America was rising!

You did not make it home in time for the birth of your child. In fact, you ended up flying B-29's from the Marianna's on bombing raids to Japan. You fired the first shot on Japan; you very nearly fired the last.

After the war you came home and worked in an auto supply store, staying close to 'things-mechanical' that you always enjoyed. Your wife taught school. Together you raised two sons. You never considered yourself a hero but often said you served with many.

4

AUTUMN MAGIC

(*the paragraphs in italics are my bride's*)

Over morning coffee my bride said, "Let's go flying today." She doesn't say that just every day. She likes to fly but she doesn't *have* to fly. I *have* to fly. If I go for a stretch of days without flying I get, well, you know, itchy. My bride doesn't get itchy. She just picks her days….the nice ones….and then says, "Let's go flying today." But when she says that I'm all over it like grease out of a hot skillet. She's been my best buddy for forty-four years and we share everything and I especially enjoy sharing flight with her.

Into the '64 VW Bug we jump and head for the airport. The Bug just sort of sets the tone. When we got married, I had a Bug. It's simple (doesn't buzz when you open the door with the key in the ignition), functional (two knobs on the dash, one for wipers and the one for lights), basic (one AM radio), easy (heater is one knob that you turn), and fun (you roll up the windows and shift the gears by hand). It's kind of simple in the manner that the relationship with my bride is simple, consisting of two main ingredients: love and trust.

It was a nice day at the airport but it wasn't a deep blue day. It was a hazy day. But it was rock-solid calm so I knew it would be smooth. My bride likes smooth. She's not much into turbulence and strong winds and such. She also prefers no more than 5° of pitch or 10° of bank. I respect all that and try mightily to accommodate. This trip is to enjoy the purity of flight, to experience the wonderful magic of two little silver wings being one with the air. And to enjoy the fall scenery around our home of long standing.

Rain was in the near forecast after a superb span of sunny fall days. AirVenture always gets me in the mood to go flying, but summer activities had kept me busy. Today looked like a perfect day to enjoy a flight with my favorite pilot.

I preflighted. We have this little secret thing that we do during the preflight. We did it every day, before every flight, to and from Oshkosh. I still do it even when preflighting alone. It involves something we touch on the airplane. But that's all I can tell you. (It's a secret, remember?) But it works for us so we keep doing it.

Our little airplane started right up and purred like it always does. But, somehow, it seemed like it knew this was a special day. It was like a hmmmmmmm that you could hear and feel, like it was saying, "Not to worry. I'll take good care of you." That kind of hmmmmmmm. At the end of the runway, after the run-up, I asked, "All set?" Bride answered, "Yup. Er…roger!" I held up my right hand, palm facing back, and she gave me a "high five." We always do that.

I had been watching the geese in their V or "delta" formations and as we taxied the plane out, I commented to the pilot "we need to watch for geese today". Being the consummate pilot and gentleman with thousands of hours in his logbook, he just said "Okay."

On takeoff the airplane performed like the RV that it is: quick and wonderfully agile. Straight-out departure, about 4° of pitch with 0° of bank and, yup, the air was smooth. Not a ripple; only ambiance. It's was as smooth as our mood was good. First thing we see on climb out is the island in the Willamette River where we once sought refuge while kayaking. We're generally mountain lake kayakers (read: calm water) but one day we decided to try the river close to our home. In we went and the paddling was easy. It was easy until we realized that, just before reaching the island, we were paddling with a subtle but strong current. We sought refuge on the island to better assess the situation. We formed our plan and launched upstream. My bride is from Texas, is pretty darn strong. It was slow going fighting the current but we made it. Another story; another memory. From aloft, the island looked quite benign. It was a nice contrast to our previous memory. Flight does that: smooth's rough edges and lends itself to more gentle perspectives. I like that about flight.

As we lifted from contact with the earth, my whole perspective changed. Seeing where we live from the air makes me realize the abundance of nature's gifts in our valley. The rivers catch the sunlight and reflect their serenity. The fields are laid out with a sense of order and offer up a promise of harvest created by hard work. The coastal range mountains are gently covered by a soft blanket of fog. Just beyond the mountains lies the Pacific Ocean and the coastal villages where the fisherman bring in their catch of the day.

The plan was for a long and lazy circle around the Willamette Valley that we've called home for the last twenty-five years. We flew over Monrovia Nursery. It's huge and the foliage colors of many different species of plants made it look like a giant quilt. Then over the Evergreen Air Museum, where a Boeing 747 sits on top of a building, now a *giant* water slide. My airplane lends itself to just looking outside; I engineered it that way. Yeah, I flew airliners with all those TV screens in the cockpit. And, yeah, I know they call them PFD's and MFD's and EFIS and HUD's and CRT's and such. Whatever. They were still TV screens to me; I'm old. But here's the deal: you can't enjoy fall foliage on a MFD. Not possible. So when

I level off at a couple thousand feet AGL, I check the oil pressure (75 PSI), the oil temperature (180° C), airspeed (140 KIAS), and fuel (FULL). The only knobs I have to touch and turn before landing are the two on my VHF radio. So I simply look outside and fly. Flickering electronic displays with a jillion options and buttons would detract from that. Don't beat me up too much about my airplane, okay? My airplane is what I want it to be; I like it that way and I'm too crotchety to change.

My bride says from the back, "You're really happy when you're up here, aren't you?" I reply, "I am." Then we fly over the Old Mill Feed and Garden store in Dallas, Oregon where we buy our animal feed. It's an old feed mill, complete with creaky wooden floors, loading docks and nice people. From the air the steep roof shows lots of rust. It's old, too. Then we're over the rectangular patterns that mark what's left of Camp Adair, a former WWII encampment. My Uncle, my Mom's brother, was stationed there towards the end of WWII. He told the story of leaving there a few days before he was supposed to; he badly wanted to reunite with his family. He said, "I'd already landed at Omaha Beach and been a POW. What were they gonna to do to me?" They didn't do anything. Then we flew over Reser Stadium, Corvallis, Oregon, home of the Oregon State football Beavers. Both our sons graduated from there; we've been to many games and tailgate parties there. We bleed black-and-orange. Even from the air, the stadium radiates the passion that is college football. More memories.

Then it was time for my bride's recurrent training. I asked, "Wanna fly it a little bit?" "Okay," she said. The airplane wiggles ever so slightly as she holds straight-and-level. Then she said, "Okay, that's enough." Straight-and-level is sometimes her job when we're flying cross country and I have to fold or unfold a chart. Why? You know why. You *know* I wouldn't let an autopilot come within one-hundred feet of my airplane. When an autopilot is on, you sit; when you don't have an autopilot, you *fly*! Just sayin'.

If there is one single thing I've learned about flying from my instructor at the controls in front of me is that the best results are achieved by making gentle movements and corrections with the stick. I practice that so that he will be impressed. He compliments me on being smooth and I am pleased that my few minutes of flight are well executed. I watch the throttle position to the left of my armrest as we take off and land. The only controls I have in the rear seat are the throttle and stick. But I take note, knowing that in a real emergency I would have little control. But I might still have a little control.

We fly on. Lazily we fly; happily we fly. Rock solid air; rock solid airplane. A steady hmmmmm from our 180 hp friend up front; very slight and wonderful vibrations come through the seat, the rudder pedals and the throttle. All combined with a mix of scenery and memories. We are one with it all and one with each other.

The landing? Squeaked it right on. (Yeah, it was still calm.) From the back seat I heard, "Nice." I just smiled. I just didn't feel the need at the moment to add, "And lucky." We taxied in.....slowly....savoring the last drop of flight. We shut down, I rolled the canopy back and we did another "high five." Then I logged another 1.0 in the books. A very special 1.0.

We touch down ever so gently and are reunited with the ground. I feel very lucky to get to spend some time flying in the fall sky like the geese I love to watch. Soon it will be dark and rainy and windy and I will think back on this glorious day in our little silver bird with my life's partner. We slipped the surly bonds and we will tuck this memory into our treasure chest of good and unexpected adventures.

Before I got out of the airplane I glanced down at my kneeboard and these were the words I had scribbled in flight: "simple/pure/clean/sight/sound/feel/values/random thoughts/memories." Yup, all of the above.

Life is good. It's even better when you fly.

5

HONOR FLIGHT

It was my privilege to participate in the "Honor Flight," so named to honor WWII veterans, that took place during AirVenture 2010. Its purpose was to fly eighty of those veterans from Oshkosh to Washington, D.C., to visit the WWII Memorial, a place they might otherwise never see. The memorial was built in their honor, so it was fitting that these members of "the greatest generation" visit it.

Fair warning: it was a day of deep emotions.

But first, some perspective. Seventy years ago, these men were eighteen, nineteen and twenty years old. And their country-- the United States of America --was being drawn into a war that had global implications, from Germany to Japan. It was quite clear to see: other countries with evil intentions had to be stopped in their tracks. And Americans answered the call. In droves. My friend, Jack, said that when he went to sign up the line was so long at the Army recruiting area that he went down to the Navy office and signed up for flight school there. Life is often a matter of timing: wrong place at the wrong time; right place at the right time. This was simply "America's time." And America rose to the occasion in a manner never to be forgotten.

When I say "America rose to the occasion," I mean *all* of America. Soldiers signed up, for sure. But, too, women went to work in aircraft factories, there was rationing of commodities to help the war effort, there were civil defense drills and the call "Buy War Bonds" rang out. And women served in the military as nurses and the WASP's (Women Airforce Service Pilots) flew and ferried military airplanes (and recently, finally, got there just due for doing so). It was to this national backdrop that American soldiers marched to foreign shores……where 400,000 of them lost their lives. It was about duty, honor and country. And America met those standards on all counts. Wars since have been more political than global but GI's, from Korea to Vietnam to Iraq to Afghanistan, still answer to the call of duty, honor and country to the standard set by the WWII vets. And those veterans, too, have succeeded. They always have; they always will. And, believe me, that fact is not lost on "the greatest generation:" they honor *all* veterans and those currently serving. But WWII remains the one time when the nation stood as one against global enemies in the name of our most endearing cause: freedom.

Imagine now, for a moment, some of the reality, the nitty-gritty, that the WWII veterans went through. They landed at Normandy, jumping off landing craft into deep and unfriendly waters and clamored up sandy beaches into blistering volleys of small arms and artillery fire, feeling the clatter and din and confusion that comes with close combat. And their fellow soldiers and buddies were falling all around them. And all so far from home. And they did the same thing at Iwo Jima and Guadalcanal. So far from home. And they served on ships, heaving through stormy seas, into huge waves and splashes of salt water, all the while scanning the horizon for enemy convoys. And imagine the sweaty, thick air in a submerged WWII diesel submarine, running silent to avoid detection, hoping not to feel the blast of depth charges, meaning they'd been discovered. Or the bitter cold in a foxhole in Germany, hungry, fingers numb, just yards away from the enemy, summoning courage, one more time, somehow, from somewhere, to keep going, day after day after miserable day. So far from home. Or the sweltering sands in Morocco. Or jumping from a C-47 with a parachute, a rifle and a few rations. Or flying a B-25 or P-47 or B-17 or P-51 or B-24 into the throes of anti-aircraft fire and swarming Focke Wulf's. All so very from home……but a home that held them in their thoughts daily. Yet, through it all, they did not falter. They marched forward with bravery and purpose and the American flag. The banded, bonded and won. They proved to the world that this relatively new American concept-- freedom --was something worth fighting for.

Not all soldiers went to the front, of course. Many were cooks, worked in supply, were mechanics, instructors at home in infantry tactics, artillery and flight schools. But they served. They did whatever they were asked to do. As always, it is the sum of the parts that makes for a successful whole. Their support, on all counts, was vital.

And then, battles won, honor intact, freedom preserved, they came home. They married, raised families, and went right to work building America: roads, schools, bridges, businesses, hospitals, and factories. And set the standard, once again, for what's right and good about America: hard work and freedom equals opportunity and happiness. Their America *remains* the example of what America is truly about. Work, don't whine.

Back at Oshkosh now, eighty of these veterans, all in their 80's and 90's, gathered in the airport terminal at Wittman Regional Airport to go through security screening and get seat assignments for their flight to Washington, D.C. But the gathering quickly became more than that: it became a gathering of soldiers who served seventy years ago. "How you doin'? Where'd you serve? When?" And exclamations like, "I was there, too! My brother flew that airplane! Boy, that jeep was really something, wasn't it!" And, "My cousin lost his life in that battle." Shared hardships and sacrifices form everlasting bonds.

I imagined them, seventy years ago, in similar gatherings, perhaps at a train station, asking "Where ya headed?" and exchanging rumors about how the war was going. Maybe they had been dropped off by a parent, a wife, or a girlfriend. But not today. Today a veteran was dropped off by his daughter, who gave him a hug and said, "Have a great day, Dad!" And then each veteran was greeted by their assigned "guardian," who assisted the veteran throughout the day.

A word about the "guardians." All were volunteers with some past or current military connection and their task was to accompany and assist their veteran for the day. They did yeoman's duty (many of the veterans were in wheelchairs) and thrived on it. Many wore shirts that said "It's never too late to say thanks." The entire operation is impeccably organized and operated by "Honor Flight." They don't mind the publicity--they want to do other Honor Flights and need your support to do so --but make no mistake, the bright shining light, the focus, is squarely on the veterans themselves, right where Honor Flight wants it to be.

Each WWII veteran was given and wore a light green polo shirt with the words "Honor Flight" embroidered on it. Some wore their military uniforms, complete with their stripes and badges. Many wore their airborne insignia and combat infantry badges. One, who wore his uniform, said, "Weighed one-sixty-one then; weigh one-sixty-one now." But it was their ball caps that told so many different stories: "1st Marine Division, 738 MP Bn., USS Redfin, USS Ponchatoula, USS Santee, Purple Heart, USS Flasher, Navy, Army, Air Force, Coast Guard." And the pins on their hats: a B-25, military wings of many aircrew specialties, a P-47, jump wings, infantry badges, various military medals, and unit pins. Many wore their VFW (Veterans of Foreign Wars) and American Legion hats. It was plainly obvious that those two organizations mean a lot to them. Bottom line, they stood out; they stood proud. Age may have robbed some of them of their agility but every ounce of their pride was still intact.

Buses were then boarded and the veterans were driven to AeroShell square, basically the center of the universe at AirVenture. There an enthusiastic and flag waving crowd met them. Parked there, also, was an American Airlines 737, N905AN by registration number. Printed in large letters on the side of the fuselage was "FLAGSHIP LIBERTY." Below that it said "in support of those who serve." The airplane a donation by, you guessed it, American Airlines. As the veterans got off the busses and walked towards the airplane, music played, Civil Air Patrol cadets stood at attention and saluted, as did current military members and people dressed in period military uniforms. Many of the veterans saluted them back. Enthusiasm and thanks abounded. There were brief speeches of thanks, a moment of silence for the fallen and then taps was played. I dare say there's not a military member alive who does not remember some sacrifice and is not moved when taps is played. As we boarded the airplane, a disabled veteran sat in his wheelchair at the base of the loading ramp. He had no legs. He shook the hand of every person boarding that airplane.

We hadn't even left yet and I was already tearing up.

The flight to Washington, D.C. was immediately memorable in its ambiance: it was a noble cause for noble people by a grateful people. Of note, every member of the crew on that airplane was also a volunteer. They flew this trip on their days off or on vacation days. Every one of them had a military connection and got on the PA system to share it with us. One pilot had flown F-14's; another B-52's. Flight Attendants had fathers and brothers and husbands and sisters who served. It was yet another special touch....one of many, as it turned out, on this day.

As we neared our gate at Reagan National Airport we received a water cannon spray salute by two fire trucks. The ground guides on each wingtip waved American flags. As the veterans deplaned they were greeted....again....by music, saluting members of the military, and a clapping, cheering and flag-waving crowd. The WWII veterans, ever humble, saluted, mouthed "thank you," and smiled. They were deeply touched...you could tell. *This* is why Honor Flight exists.

Inside the terminal...Gate 30, to be exact.....the entire concourse, from the gate to the sidewalk where the busses were waiting, was lined with another continuous crowd of clapping, flag waving people. One young Marine, who looked like he'd been chiseled from granite, pushed the wheelchair of a WWII Marine. The "weighed one-sixty-one" veteran had his picture taken with three young female military members. Americans were honoring their WWII heroes. Big, cold, political Washington, D.C., for this moment, at this time, had turned warm.

Buses were boarded once again....with a squad of current military members standing at attention and saluting....and headed to the World War II Memorial. Upon arriving, it is readily apparent that this is a special place, especially to the veterans. It is big, bold, symbolic and every state is represented, with flowing water adding flavor and life. Over one pool are four-thousand gold stars, one for every one hundred American lives lost in the war. One veteran sat in his wheel chair and wept. Another said, "I never thought I'd live to see this." And another said, "My brothers would have liked this." He lost two brothers in the war. Another laid a wreath with a picture of his wartime buddy on a wall. His buddy was to accompany him on this trip but passed away two months earlier. Another had to sit down because of the heat…it was 90 degrees temperature with 90 degrees humidity…..but rose saying, "I didn't give in in 1940; I ain't gonna give in now." Another said, "I never felt this special before." Figuratively, the memorial was built by these veterans; it was their service and sacrifice that inspired it.

Then the veterans gathered at one side of the memorial, some stood, some remained in their wheelchairs, but they all saluted the gathered crowd. They were honoring the country they served….once again.

Aboard the buses again, we drove by the Korean War Memorial and the Vietnam Wall. It was obvious, once again, that these guys honor all veterans. I was wearing my "Vietnam Veteran" hat. One WWII veteran leaned over toward me and said, "Arizona had a deal honoring you guys. The guys there got the homecoming they never got before." It was a poignant moment for me, especially coming from him. He then asked, "Do you know guys on that wall?" I said, "Yes, I do."

We then toured more of Washington, D.C. by bus, seeing the Capitol, White House, Lincoln Memorial, Jefferson Monument, along with various other federal buildings and monuments, each special in their own way, all part of the nation protected and preserved by the WWII veterans visiting today. And then we drove by Arlington National Cemetery. It got very quiet on the busses. The somberness and respect for the moment was palpable.

The flight home to Oshkosh was yet another treat by the special American Airlines crew. I've ridden on many airliners, usually tired, crowded, with a "just want to get there" attitude. But not today, not on this airliner: it was full of good feelings, nose to tail. It was noticeable and it was special. Enroute, a "mail call" was held for the veterans, each veteran receiving a large envelope full of letters from family and friends. I watched them read; I watched them wipe tears. One veteran then stood and talked on the airline PA system in a slow but loud and deliberate voice, "I want to thank you all, we all do, for this day. And I want you to drive home *s l o w l y*, so that you'll arrive *s a f e*."

Landing at Oshkosh, we were greeted once again at AeroShell Square by a flag waving crowd. As the airplane taxied in, the pilots were taking pictures out their side windows. And the crowd was taking pictures of the airplane. A fitting display of mutual respect for the veterans of WWII who set the standard for service to their country. Afterwards, the veterans were treated to dinner and music and reunited with their families. It was a special day for a special group of people.

Were the veterans tired after this day? Probably. But, like seventy years ago, they did not falter, they did not complain; they did, once again, what they set out to do. They helped make America great; they're still making America great.

It was an honor to be among them.

6

ONE MODEL AT A TIME

It was rather an accidental happenstance. A lot of times, life is like that, isn't it? But it was a good happenstance.

I was babysitting my eight-year-old grandson, Trystan, after school. On the nice days he usually plays outside with his neighborhood buddies. But this wasn't a nice day; it was an Oregon day…..rain, rain, and more rain. In that case he usually plays video games (of genres unknown to me) or watches cartoons on TV. And he's happy doing that and, on days when I'm busy with something else, so am I. You know that drill! But on this day he asked, "What else can we do, Papa?" Hmmmmmm…..good question. On a nice day we might go to the hangar and putz-around, drive the tractor, stuff like that. But this wasn't a nice day. I sort of mumbled, "Build a model?" He said, "A what?" I said, "A model. You know, like an airplane model." (Somewhere in the foggy recesses of my mind, I seemed to remember having some in the garage…somewhere.) He was all over that with, "Yeah, let's do that!"

Okay, I opened my mouth; time to back it up. Out in the garage we went….to where the dusty boxes are…..and found one labeled "MODELS." Hmmmmm…..again, 'Wonder what all is in here? It's been a while.' We opened it and….voila!....there were airplane models inside. Lots of them. Most were still in their boxes but lying on top was a partially completed balsa wood fuselage of a P-51. In the model boxes? A couple OV-1's, a Beech T-34, a couple F-105's, and a smallish, yellow P-51. I recognized them all as airplanes I always favored. And there was a KC-135 model. I pulled the KC-135 out, figuring that would be a good one for Trystan to start on. It was fairly large and didn't have a lot of parts. The top of the box was labeled "Boeing KC-135 Jet Stratotanker." The airplane on the box said "US Air Force" on the side but there was no boom-operator refueling pod or refueling probe. Probably the model maker sold the same model with different markings as a Boeing 707. Also depicted on the box top were two F-86's flying alongside the KC-135. (Note to graphic artist: F-86's didn't have air refueling capability.) But, hey, it was a model in a box and it was time for my grandson and me to build it.

Back in the house we gathered some paper towels, found a tube of plastic glue and placed it all, with the model box, on the kitchen island. Good place to build, right? Then we opened the box. And right on top where the directions: "© 1963, Aurora Plastics Corporation, West Hempstead, L.I., N.Y." Yup, guess I've had that model for a while, huh! On the directions, a tube of glue was advertised for 10¢. On the back, Aurora advertised other models they made. Under "MODERN DAY FIGHTERS" was listed F8U-1 Crusader, B-47 Stratojet, Grumman F9F-6 "Cougar," Convair F-102 "Dart," F9F Panther Jet, Convair V.R. "Pogo," and North American F-107A. Under "WORLD'S FIRST MANNED SPACE SHIP" was listed X-15 Sateloid (that's what it said!) Rocket Plane. Under "GIANT BOMBERS" they listed B-58 Hustler and Russian Nuclear Bomber. Under "SUPER MODERN JET AIRLINERS" was listed Pan American Boeing 707 and TWA Boeing 707. Ah ha!! I thought so!!!

Under the directions were airplane model parts and.....hey!....decals. Cool! I asked Trystan, "Ever build a plastic model before?" He said, "I don't think so." He has great parents, but they're both professionals and busy. "Papa," on the other hand, is "old" and has the time to do such things. Of course Trystan, like seemingly all kids nowadays, has all manner of electronic stuff to play with. But electronic games don't require glue. That's where I come in. Oh, he has Legos, too. But those don't require glue either. And he's put stickers on things but never decals. (Would the decals still work after forty-years? We were fixin' to find out.) Okay, so all grandparents don't have forty-year old models lying around to build but, hey, you work with what ya got!

Well, guess what? When we opened the box, parts were missing. Not surprising, I suppose, given the passage of time. Some of the main landing gear parts were absent. So, okay, we'll build it 'gear up.' Problem solved. Some engine cowlings were also missing. Hmmmm....we'll deal with that later. Still, we had enough parts to get started.

Model building revealed some cultural gaps between Trystan and me. He's more accustomed to starting and finishing something in the same day, like video games and Legos and such; in my day, you glued something and often had to set it aside to dry, oftentimes waiting until the next day to resume your project. Patience was a different concept to the two of us. But he got the gist of it when I showed him how to glue the two fuselage halves together: trial fit first to make sure the parts go together easily and correctly; then dab a *little* glue here and a *little* glue there; then put the two parts together and hold them together, patient-like. New concept! He'd hold the nose and let go of the tail end and the tail parts would separate. I taught him 'the rubber band technique.' You wrap rubber bands around the fuselage to hold it together while it's drying. That way you can move on to other parts. He liked that concept, thought it was pretty cool. New learning! And, yup, in case you were wondering, he got glue on his fingers and fingerprinted the fuselage with his gluey fingers, like model building kids have done since time immemorial. It's a right-of-model-building passage!

Then Trystan started on the wings. I stood back. Then he started on the engines-- the two we had, anyway. He trial fit, glued, held, fingerprinted, rubber-banded and set 'em aside to dry. Then he asked, "What do we do now?" I said, "Wait. We'll build some more tomorrow when you get home from school." So much for instant gratification.

Next day, first thing he asked when he walked in the door was, "Can we work on the model?" I said, "Yup, we can." We got everything out again and he took all the rubber bands off the parts and all the glued parts stayed together and he found that very satisfying. Then he went to work putting the wings and horizontal stabilizer on the fuselage. Couldn't use rubber bands this time. Glue-and-hold only. We talked about dihedral and getting it right. So he trial fit and glued and held and sat and looked at me with the 'how long is this going to take' look. I answered his non-verbal communication with, "Hold 'em until they're dry enough to stay in place. Dihedral, remember?" Two seconds later I got (and you *knew* this was coming, didn't you?), "How much longer?" Some concepts you have to learn the hard way; I think I spent half my model building life holding drying parts. Then, mercifully, I said, "Here….let me show you another trick." I had him set the fuselage down. The wings, glue not dry yet, started to droop. I said, "Here….put these little blocks under the wing tips to hold the wings at the correct dihedral. Now let the thing dry." More non-verbal communication: he looked at me with the 'why didn't you tell me that before' look. Sneaky Papa! Then he said, "I like the tricks." And asked, "What now?" I said, "Decals….tomorrow."

Same as the day before, after school Trystan burst through the door and asked, "Can we work on the model?" Same answer from me, "Yup." He said, "Decals?" I said, "You got a couple small parts to do first." He said, "But they're so small I can hardly hold them in place with my fingers." I said, "New trick!" He liked that. So I showed him how to hold the small parts in place with tweezers until the parts dry. That took a little coordination but he got the hang of it.

Okay, time for the decals. (I was still wondering if they'd work.) I had him cut the individual decals apart with scissors while I got a cup of warm water. I said, "Now take one decal and put it in the water." He did.....intrigued. Then I told him, "Watch it curl up." And it did...after forty-years of being in the box! Then I told him, "When it starts to uncurl, take it out of the water, slide the decal off the paper and carefully put it in the correct place on the model." And he did all that....and the decal promptly stuck to his finger, then to the airplane, then back to his finger, then tore in half. One decal down. Rookie mistake. I told him, "Slow, careful, keep it wet, slide it on easy, *ease* your finger off." Second decal he did all that and....victory! He grew to like 'the decal concept.' One small victory for a boy.

But we still had the 'engine issue.' I would have put the two engines we had on the inboard locations. He wanted to put them on the outboard locations, saying, "It'll steer better that way." Well, alrighty then! So be it!

Trystan took his model home that evening. Bedtime is 8 PM but he stayed up until his Dad got home at 8:30 PM because, "I wanted to show my model to Dad." That's a concept we understand perfectly, isn't it? Be it a model or a homebuilt airplane!

What does all this mean in relation to the totality of the universe? Not a whole lot. What does it mean to a grandchild and his grandpa? Well, to grandpa it means offering new knowledge about old ways; to grandchild it was probably not nearly so symbolic.....it was mostly just new learning. But that's kinda the key, isn't it? We elders plant the seed-- one model at a time --such that perhaps someday, somewhere, sometime, somehow, Trystan will have just enough 'airplane spark' within him to go to an airport, preferably one that doesn't have a chain link fence around it, and experience some of the happiness that airports have given me in my life.

I'm already planning our next model projects: a Guillows balsa wood Aeronca Champ, like the first airplane I taught his Daddy to fly, and a Lear jet, like his Daddy is flying now. My aim, now that Trystan has model building skills, is to personalize the hobby. Obviously, Trystan will find his own way in life; I just want to make him aware of a possible path.

One model at a time......where else are they going to learn about things-aviation if they don't learn it from you and I?

7

WHEN RETIRED PILOTS MEET

I recently attended a gathering of old retired airline buddies. As you might imagine, there was no shortage of conversation. It was what you might call a "target rich environment" for stories!

There was a dozen or so of us gathered around the table representing, roughly, 250,000 hours of flying time. It was basically burgers and beer, befitting the simple taste of a bunch of simple guys. Turns out some of the stories are printable. I'll tell you about the printable ones and leave the others to your pilot-imagination.

First, a little background to set the stage: I don't know that there is a typical airline career; most all, these days, have lots of twists and turns. Those twists and turns tend to shape perceptions which, in turn, shape stories. I started out with a commuter called Air Oregon, flying Navajo's. There were twelve of us in the beginning. They called us "The Dirty Dozen" which was probably appropriate since they didn't pay us enough to afford hot water for showers. Some of those same twelve guys were sitting around the table, thirty years later. We know each other well. Some went on to other airlines. Some didn't. Some other pilots came that are still working (flying), presumably to see what airline retired life is like. It's like this: burgers, beer, and lies. It's a good life.

Air Oregon was purchased by Horizon Air, founded by the enigmatic and loveable Milt Koult. It's a regional airline that survived, grew and did well. Horizon was then purchased by Alaska Airlines. So, from being hired by an airline headquartered in a double-wide trailer after a five-minute interview while dressed in a smelly National Guard flight suit, I worked six months as a co-pilot and twenty-five-and-half years as a Captain for three different airline companies and never missed a paycheck. All I had to change was uniforms (and I still have a closet full of those). Typical? Maybe. Maybe not. But I ended up having a lot of fun.

What I'm saying is that the guys around the table cut their "flying teeth" in the Pacific Northwest, flying into all manner of coastal, mountain and windy flatland airports. They stared down many a thunderstorm, shed lots of ice, landed on many snow-covered runways, did a thousand non-precision approaches following a radial that took them up canyons below the ridge tops so that they could break out at 300' AGL to land to the tune of a thirty-knot crosswind. And they've been number ten in the holding stack at Seattle and Los Angeles and Salt Lake and Denver. And they flew on lots of clear and beautiful days when the Pacific Northwest mountain ranges shown like snow covered gems. All of that is a part of their flying soul. In other words, they've been-there-and-done-that in the airline business. But guess what? That's not what they talked about when they first sat down.

The first thing they talked about.....after the initial insults, anyway, like, "Geez, you look older'n dirt!".......was their health: hearing, eyes, heart, melanoma. That stuff is "big deal" to pilots; it's all about the medical! The retired guys rather roll with it; the working guys worry about it. It's very much a part of the flying life.

After the second beer, "pilot personalities" began to emerge. Warren walked in sporting a very gray beard. He was greeted with, "Hey, Warren, does the glue hurt that you glue your beard on with?" And from Reese, "Warren, you remember the time you gave me a check ride in the sim (simulator) and you failed an engine on the first takeoff and I never got it back for any of the other approaches?" Warren gave the head down shoulder shrug that said, 'Aw, shucks…sorry.'

And, "Hey, Greg, remember the time you put the HELP WANTED sign in the cockpit window while parked at the gate? And the fake baby diaper you used to pick up off the floor and put on your head to the gasps of the Flight Attendants?" Greg, nodding and smiling, said, "Yeah, I got 'the call' on a couple of those."

Then Greg told the story of flying with Ron's (another retired Captain) daughter as First Officer. They were holding short for takeoff because there was another airplane on the runway awaiting takeoff clearance. Once the airplane on the runway got clearance for takeoff and started to roll, Greg started inching forward. Ron's daughter then looked over at Greg and said, "What is it about 'hold short' that you don't understand?"

Stan chimed in with, "Remember going to the sim in Charlotte, we asked the cab driver how far it was to Kitty Hawk? The cab driver just kept saying 'Kitty Hawk, Kitty Hawk.' Finally I said you know…where the Wright Brother's first flew?" And the cab driver said, "Don't know no Kitty Hawk. Guess they ran that right by me in school."

And, "Hey, Stan, remember that guy who was having trouble with steep turns in the sim and you reached over his shoulder from the instructor station and rolled the sim into a forty-five-degree bank and the altimeter never moved? Did you ever tell him you had the altitude hold on back at the console?"

Reese added, “I remember asking So-and-so….don’t remember his name…..up ahead of me how the weather was. He answered, ‘It’s blacker’n the inside of a cow.’”

It was about this time that a couple of complete strangers walked up and asked, “Who are you guys? You’re having too much fun! How do we get in your group?” They smiled and moved on but they would have been welcome to listen in. But to be fully accepted into the group you have to have shed some ice and seen lightening inside a thunderstorm at night. That’s the fraternal bond.

Then someone asked, “BJ, remember when so-and-so was asking you about the airplane’s wingspan, length, height of the tail and stuff like that during an oral exam?” I remember your reply: “They pay me to fly the things, not build boxes for ‘em.”

Tom, our favorite ground school instructor was at the gathering, too. He lost his medical early on but was a gifted instructor so conducted many of our ground schools over the years. It was good to see him. He told of the time he had one of our resident-rebel pilots in ground school and the guy had a burr under his saddle about some procedure and would *not* let it go. Finally, Tom pointed at him and said, “You! Come with me!” With that, Tom walked down the hall and into his office, the rebel following. Tom then *kicked* the door closed and said, “Let it go! Don’t you *ever* try to hijack my ground school! Ever!” Then they both walked back into ground school and all was well. Problem solved. Tom commanded respect, but mostly because he knew his stuff and presented it so well. He had a way of stuffing stuff into our brains without us even knowing how it got there! One of his favorite expressions, after describing a particular system, was, “It’s EWOD…..Either Works Or Doesn’t.”

How many of the guys are still flying? Not many. Some lost medicals; some just wanted to try something else; some were burned out. Some still fly: I count myself among that fortunate few. Two are aircraft homebuilders.

There were a lot of "What ever happened to so-and-so?' questions. Once in a while you got shrugs but, usually, someone had the answer. When asked what ever happened to so-and-so management pilot, Stan said, "I think they made him Manager of Complacency."

Veteran pilots understand and other pilots are getting the drift: This was not a gathering for the thin-skinned. You can't be thin-skinned and be a professional pilot. It's part of the pilot ethos. Inch of ice on the wings? You don't whine about it; you make a decision and hang tough. Most of these guys are what some would call politically incorrect. And if someone did call them that, it wouldn't bother them one iota. No Pollyanna here; it's just the way it is. But here's the deal: If you are ever in a foxhole, these are the guys you want with you.

As you might expect, there was talk of the old vs. the new technology (read: glass cockpits). The consensus seemed to be that the glass stuff can do some pretty magnificent things but it was a lot more fun "being a pilot rather than a systems operator." Just sayin'.

The gathering was to set to begin at 1 PM. True to form, about half of the retired Captains arrived late. They walked in to, "Still runnin' late, huh? Nuthin's changed!"

We're meeting again next month. C'mon down! You'll recognize the place: a little grungy, neon signs on the walls, a big table, burgers and beer, guys sitting around with their hands waving every which way and a waitress with a good sense of humor. Don't hang your hat on everything that's said but I do guarantee you this: You will break a smile.

8

RETRACING STEPS

I'm not a big bucket-list guy. I've always just lived my life doing what I wanted to be doing, where I wanted to be doing it, all the while enjoying family and making friends. And that practice hasn't left me many gaps: I'm happy. But there has always been this one thing, in the back of my mind, that I've wanted to do: retrace the steps (in my homebuilt RV-8) of my very first airplane ride ever. I really wasn't quite sure what to expect from doing so but I just wanted to do it. So I did.

My first airplane ride ever was from Montague, California to Medford, Oregon…..in a DC-3. (Are you remembering your first ride now?) I certainly remember the ride itself-- quite vividly, in fact --and some of the details about how it came about but I can only bracket the year. I piece it together like this: I know we were living on our cattle ranch at the time. We moved to that ranch in 1953. My best guess is that the airplane ride happened a couple years later, in 1955 or maybe 1956, when I was eleven or twelve years old. I'm guessing that because at that age I was really into Little League baseball and there was no time, ever, when I got into a car that I didn't take my baseball glove with me. But that one day, probably because of the excitement of going to the airport, I forgot my glove! I still remember that stricken thought passing through my mind.

How the ride came about is also a little incongruous to me, at least in retrospect it is. I had gotten sick with what-I-don't-remember but it was a sick-in-bed type of sick. One morning my Dad came into my room and said, “When you get well, we’ll go for an airplane ride.” I remember that! But here’s the incongruous part: My Dad was not a soft, sentimental-type guy. Not by any stretch of the imagination. Before that it was always, if you fell down, broke something, scraped something, bent something, it was just, “Hey, shake it off and get back to work.” That’s just the way it was on the ranch. Certainly it wasn’t “….get well and we’ll go for an airplane ride.” Besides, even though I had airplane models all over my room and hanging from the ceiling, airplanes were just not something we talked about. Airplanes were my own private dream. But, hey, never mind because there was one other thing that went with living on a ranch: Your word was your bond. If my Dad said it, he’d honor it.

I eventually got well and the day for “the airplane ride” came. It was a big deal because my Mom ironed a shirt for me, one that had a collar with those big pointy tips. I only wore that kind of shirt on Easter, Thanksgiving and Christmas. The rest of the time is was t-shirts, blue jeans and black, hi-top Keds. Montague Airport was about five miles from our ranch. Montague was another small town but had a pretty big airport, left over from WWII. The air was thick with excitement that day. At least it was for me.

We drove into the airport on a small gravel road to a large parking lot. There was a three feet high chain link fence with gates wide open, a large empty expanse of concrete-- the ramp --and a building off to the left. It had a wooden porch on it. I remember that because I remember clomping on it. We walked up to the counter and my Dad bought some tickets-- round-trip, Montague to Medford and back to Montague. An airplane ride. Did people even make reservations in those days? I suppose they did. But how could we have? We didn’t even have a phone until we got electricity and that wasn't until about 1957. (I know, difficult for young people today to even comprehend that scenario.) Anyway, we got tickets!

A little while later a big airplane….a DC-3…..landed and taxied up, rumbling beautifully, rocking along, glinting in the sun, propellers slapping the air. My eyes went wide and my mouth fell open. Next thing I knew I was standing at the bottom of some stairs near the tail of the airplane. A lady in a dress and wearing a hat (my Mom only wore a hat on Easter, unless it was a cowboy hat while herding cows on horseback) stood at the top of the stairs and said, "Welcome!" Up I went, clomped up the aisle-- what a magnificent cocoon! --and sat on the right side of the airplane, towards the front, next to an engine. My Dad sat across the aisle from me. To this day, I can't remember the name of the airline. I guess it didn't matter much to me; it was an airplane and I was going for a ride in it. That's all that mattered.

Soon the propeller next to me started to turn, then turned a little faster, the engine let out a little puff of smoke and then the prop spun into a blur, accompanied by that magical rumbling noise again. Holy happiness! Never in all my eleven years had anything ever been so immediately captivating. I was lost in magic. (And, though I didn't know it at the time, hooked by it, too.)

We ambled along a taxiway and then turned onto the runway and the noise and rattle increased greatly as the airplane gained speed and then-- I felt it! --lifted off the ground. The Earth fell away and I was riding on wings and air. There was nothing to say; there was much to see and feel. The experience somehow had the feeling of warmth and satisfaction of home to me, the thing I loved most in life. I reasoned that this was a place I very much liked to be. Yeah, right then, right there, eleven years old, I wanted to be a pilot.

We sauntered along, rocking gently and sometimes jolting in the light turbulence, wings flexing, engines in a low roar, the two guys up front looking about, occasionally touching levers and switches and such. I could see the bend in the river that partially framed the biggest hayfield on our ranch I saw Black Mountain and Pilot Rock and the town of Hornbrook. Then, seemingly just like that, the airplane sounds changed and we were slowing and descending and then we touched down at Medford Airport. Just like that. When you are lost in magic you are also lost in time. How long the flight? Maybe thirty minutes. Not sure. But, just like that, I was smitten.

In Medford we got off the airplane and lingered by the tail of the airplane while it was being refueled from a truck. A guy in a uniform with some stripes on the sleeve came up and patted me and asked, "How ya doin', son?" And then we re-boarded and repeated the procedure back to Montague and experienced yet more magic. I wasn't just smitten by then; I was changed. One flight!

Long story short, I went on...very single mindedly and without ever so much as a doubt.... to become a pilot. I never forgot the DC-3, of course, but never had much to do with it either until, fifteen years later, I got a type rating in it. I then flew it all over Korea and once ferried one, island happing, across the Pacific Ocean. There I got to look out the same windows and fiddle with the same levers and switches that my very first pilots did. Full circle, I guess you could call it.

That's the memory. If I retraced the steps of my first flight, what would I feel? Don't know! But I wanted to find out.

RV-8 and I landed at Montague (now KSIY) early this year and parked on the ramp. The *same* ramp. And I was the only person and airplane on it. There was silence all around. There were some buildings/hangars to the south, with maybe some people, but not where I was. I was alone, completely alone, with my thoughts. The road we drove in on in 1955? Still there. The parking lot? Still there. The chain link fence? Still there. The gate? Still there….and open. The terminal? Well, there was one old wooden building with peeling paint. Same building? Don't know. But it had a wooden porch on it so in my mind, that day, I made it to be the same building. I looked about and the scenery, the mountains, were the same. Heck, the sky was the same; the temperature was the same; the breeze was the same. Even the time was the same. I was lost in a time warp and loving it.

I walked from the parking lot, to the wooden porch, to the fence, through the gate and across the ramp to my airplane. It was time to fly to Medford (now KMFR). I taxied out…same taxiway….and onto the same runway and pushed the power up, recreating, fifty-seven years later, an indelible personal memory from my childhood. It was a good beginning.

Straight-out departure, gentle climb, light turbulence…same magic! I again saw the bend in the river where our big hay field had been, only now it was dotted with recreational vehicles. I flew by Black Mountain. I took a lingering look at Hornbrook, where I attended grammar school. And, like many pilots before me, spotted Pilot Rock. The time warp continued; it was a good feeling difficult to describe. It was just one of those "within you" type moments. And then, there I was, on final to the Medford Airport again. The tower said, "Experimental 214KT, offset to the right and let faster jet traffic pass. He has you in sight." Wasn't much else to say but, "14KT, roger." My time warp? Poof! Gone! My first-flight-pilots from fifty-seven years ago certainly didn't have to deal with faster jet traffic! Time marches on and I had just marched right back into it.

After landing in Medford I didn't linger, just asked to taxi back to the active, taxiing by a huge (tall) control tower, a big terminal building bustling outside with several large airplanes and, well, I was suddenly surrounded by "progress." "Progress" was not what I was looking for this day. I took off and headed northbound for home, Salem, Oregon. In the air once again, I was able to recapture some of my mood. I landed in Salem satisfied with my mission: retracing early steps. The memories both filled and satisfied me.

I'm not some deep philosopher or anything like that, but I came away from the day thinking, 'Ya know, a faster life is not always a better life. There's a lot to be said for simpler times. Not having electricity for a part of my youth was not an altogether bad thing. And bonding with a DC-3, in 1955 at age eleven, was, indeed, a very good thing.'

9

THERAPUTIC FLYING

In between straight-and-level travel/sightseeing-type flying and competition/airshow aerobatics-type flying, is a place for us all to dwell, a place for us to spice-up and more thoroughly enjoy our flying. It's a place I go often. I fact, I go there *every* time I fly alone. It makes me happy. Where is it? It's a place in the sky; I go there to play. And it's *very* good medicine.

Here's how you play: you climb to a safe altitude in your favorite practice area, far from airways and cities, and do a couple steep turns. That allows you to "clear the area." But here's the deal: If I don't like the steep turns I did, I do them again. And again, as necessary, until I do them to the standard I've set for myself. And that's the idea: Today we're going to fly to *our own* standards, not someone else's, not to some agency standards, but to the ones you've set for yourself. (Hint: set your standards high.)

Okay, you get the idea. Now do some slow flight. Don't do it to some vague reference from some training manual in your past. Do it like this: Start at 90 KIAS. Then slow to 80. Then to 70. Now to 60. And I mean *do it*; don't just slop through it. Nail it! Whatever speed you are at, put the pointy tip of the airspeed indicator needle smack in the middle of the index marker on the airspeed indicator and keep it there. Settle for nothing less. And do not let the altimeter move, or the heading. Can you always keep everything perfect? Of course not. But you should always be trying. And guess what? The more you do it, the better you'll do it. Guaranteed. And note how the closer you hold your tolerances, the smoother you must be. That's always a good thing, right? You're not doing this for anybody else or for some check ride; you're doing this for *you*. And the better you do it, the better you'll feel about your flying. And that, exactly, is the point. Plus, it's fun!

I don't need to remind you to keep looking outside, right? Good. That's part of the exercise, too. Don't fixate on the instruments: feel the airplane, listen to it, note the position of the nose on the horizon. The better you read *all* the clues your airplane is giving you, the better off you are.

Now…before you jump up and down on my head about telling you how to fly…..I'm just telling you some of the things I do. Period. Take them or leave them. But continually practicing the little things always makes me feel better about my flying. Too, there are a lot of different skill sets in aviation: IFR, aerobatics, military-type flying, and formation, to name a few. Here I'm talking about the basic VFR flying that a lot of us do in our homebuilts and Cessna's and Piper's and such. I'm just trying to spice it up a little with some small challenges.

Okay now, while you have that airspeed indicator *pegged* at 60 KIAS, do a 180° level turn. Don't let the long needle on the altimeter move. Look outside. Note your radius of turn. Feel it; enjoy it. After that, do another one-eighty in the other direction. Nail that one, too! You're starting to feel pretty good about it now, right? You're perfecting the little things.

Now, pull the power off and hold the nose on the horizon, straight-and-level. The airplane will eventually stall, right? About as simple as it gets. But don't recover right at the first beep of the stall warning horn (if you have one….I don't). Just let the airplane go a little deeper into the stall: check the feel, hear the airplane, check for wing drop. Then recover like you know how. Do it again. Do it in a turn. Do it until you feel really comfortable about what's happening and how you are recognizing/handling it. This isn't flying by some rote, memorized numbers and procedures; this is flying by understanding and knowing. *Your* understanding and knowing.

Okay, spins. All manner of apprehension and hangar-talk about them, right? A lot of it from people who have never done them. But, hey, if you stall and yaw at the same time, i.e., an overshot final, there's a good chance you'll enter a spin. If you've practiced spins, it's more likely you'll know how to recover from one. It's an age-old argument, I know. Just sayin'. (And, of course, never do them in an airplane that's not certified for spins.) Bottom line: in a spin, you lose altitude at a pretty rapid clip; that happenstance close to the ground is bad. If your defense is to be able to recognize stall and yaw and not let them inadvertently happen to you, fine. I respect that.

Another one for fun: establish a climb at climb power and climb airspeed. Now, pull off the power and do a 180° turn. Note your altitude loss in feet. Good info to have in your pilot-bag-of-tricks.

A couple more 'for fun' things. Never mind the names--Chandelles and Lazy Eights and all that. Just maneuver the airplane to your comfort level. Nose up, slow, 45° bank or so, turn, let the nose fall through the horizon and then roll out 90°-- exactly --from where you started (use a road or something). Do it again the other way. What's the purpose? Just to explore and become comfortable with what your airplane will do. And here's the deal: the more you do it, the more you'll do it. Proficiency and comfort increase confidence. You'll become a little more adventuresome each time; you'll want to better your performance. And you can because you *know* you can--

you've done it before and are comfortable with it. And that, basically, is what this discussion is really all about.

This was taught to me early-on at Sean Tucker's aerobatics school, Tutima Academy, in the Pitts. Because aerobatic pilots so often have no horizon, they have to be able to reference a point in space. Here's what you do to practice that: pull the nose of the airplane above the horizon and scribe a square in the sky with it. As in: nose right (rudder), nose up (elevator), nose left (rudder), nose down (elevator), then nose back right (rudder) to where you started. Now "draw" a triangle. Now a circle (that's a little trickier). Make the airplane do what you want it to do with the precision you demand of yourself. It's about practice and it's about pride.

My airplane (RV-8) will do recreational aerobatics so I do them. (None of the twisting, tumbling, gyroscopic stuff, like the Pitts does, of course.) I'm not going to go into a dissertation about aerobatics; I'm not qualified to do so. I just want to mention something I do for fun. I'll come out of a loop with excess airspeed so I like to bleed off the speed by pulling the nose to the vertical, slow, then "walk" the nose around with the rudder to a vertical down line and pull out again. And I'll just keep doing that two or three times in a row. What's that called? Not sure. It's not really a "hammerhead," per se. It's just something I do; it's dancing....one, two, three.....float up, over and down. It's just fun. And you can't do it in an idiot automobile. But I digress.

I'll add this, though: When you want to do an aerobatic maneuver to a standard, check out the International Aerobatic Club (IAC) website. Lots and lots of good stuff there about standards, aerobatics, and flying in general.

Back in the traffic pattern now, pull off the power opposite the touchdown point and see if you can touchdown on a preselected spot on the runway. I know, sometimes traffic doesn't allow, but when you can, practice it. It's a very good skill to have come engine failure time. Note how fast, if you find yourself ending up short of your touchdown point, the ground is coming up at you when you can't add power. The *tendency* is to pull back on the yoke....and you know that's not right. Just make a mental note of that. Not for an exam, for *you.* That way you're less likely to be surprised and more likely to do the right thing should, someday, power be lost.

Just throwin' it out there, m'friends. Stuff to do, stuff to practice, stuff to think about. One thing's for sure: The more you practice, the better you'll fly. That's just how it works. And you may not be able to fly all you want but you can sure make the best of the flying you do. Too, it's about feeling good about your flying.

10

AND NOW THERE ARE THREE

This is a story about the B-29 "Superfortress" and the women who have qualified to fly it. Hint: there are but a few. Okay, to be exact, there are three: two in WWII and, of late, one more, an EAA member. Note I'm not talking about women since WWII who have sat in the seat and taken the controls and "flown" the B-29 (under supervision). I'm talking about full ground and flight training, check rides and official and accredited qualification.

First, some background: The need for a big, fast, high altitude bomber with a large payload capacity was recognized early in WWII. With the war in the Pacific looming, the new bomber needed to have a long range and to be able to fly higher and faster than the fighters of the day. Meanwhile, in Europe, B-24's and B-17's were carrying out the bombing missions and it was tough duty mixing it up with the enemy fighters. The B-29 came into service late: 1944. Some say it was rushed into service. Maybe it was; maybe it wasn't. But it did have a lot of new technology for the time and new engines, too, so it had a lot of problems in the beginning. Engines were overheating and catching fire and the new fire control system was also problematic. New mods were coming so fast that it was tough for the service mechanics to keep up with them. Reliability suffered. While still in high school I worked on a ranch for a man who had flown B-29's. He often said, "Something went wrong every dang time we flew 'em." The all too frequent engine fires gave the airplane such a bad reputation that pilots were refusing to fly it.

In 1944, Paul Tibbets was a twenty-five-year-old Lt. Col. in charge of B-29 training. He believed in the airplane. He also had a bigger picture in mind: He knew there would be "teething problems" but he also had confidence that they could be overcome and that the airplane, mastered, had huge potential. Turns out he was right on all counts. Still, he had to overcome the bad reputation stigma. He came up with an idea: He would teach two women to fly it. Today that'd be no big deal; in 1944 it was a bit of a big deal.

By 1944, the WASPs (Women's Army Service Pilots) had already proven themselves by flying and ferrying all manner of military airplanes with great success. Lt. Col. Tibbets selected two from among them to train and qualify in the B-29: Dora Dougherty and Dorthea "Didi" Moorman. Dora said, "I'd never even seen a four-engine airplane before." When Tibbets' flight engineer first saw the two women, he said, "What are those?"

Dora and Didi began training and received a "no slack" checkout in the B-29. On one of the training flights, they had a #3 engine fire. They handled it by the book. Tibbets himself was the check pilot for the final qualification ride, which was administered by the CAA (Civil Aeronautics Administration) since the WASPs were not officially military pilots.

After qualification training Dora and Didi flew a B-29 named "Ladybird" to several bases and then spent time giving demonstration rides to pilots, navigators, and flight engineers at Alamogordo, New Mexico. In a maintenance bulletin issued by the Air Ops Director of Maintenance, it was written that the female crew was "carrying out some tests on engine heat and what have you....quite a big job for two delicate dishes of femininity."

As the demonstration flights went on, gradually the men stopped complaining about the B-29. The program, however, was halted, basically because of politics, after only two weeks. A staff general wrote Tibbets that the women were "putting the big football players to shame." Too, it turns out, he was terrified of what might be the repercussions if an accident happened. It was concluded and written that "the B-29 is a safe aircraft and even a woman can fly it." Dora and Didi went back to flying for the WASPs, mission accomplished. Boy-howdy, was it accomplished!

(When the WASPs disbanded after the war, Dora had been checked out in twenty-three different military aircraft. She later taught flying at the University of Illinois and earned a Ph.D. in Aviation Education and Psychology from New York University. She set the bar high.)

Okay, that was your brief historical trip down "B-29 Lane" in 1944. Now leap forward nearly seventy years and meet the *third* woman to be officially trained and checked out in the B-29: Debbie Travis King. Debbie is a member of the CAF (Commemorative Air Force) and is the daughter of Tom Travis, American Airlines, retired, and also a member of the CAF. Debbie is trained, qualified and current on the CAF's B-29, "FIFI."

Some time ago, Debbie applied for and was selected for B-29 crew training. I don't think anyone in the class tried the "delicate dish" line or asked, "What are you?" But there *were* some glances around the room. After all, for the last seventy years, no other women had qualified on the B-29. It helped, at this point, that she had already qualified on the CAF's B-24. Regardless, no way around it, she was under the microscope.

How did Debbie get to this point? Her Dad took her for her first flight in a J-3. Then, in the mid-80's, he soloed her in a Cessna 150 and gave her dual through Private, Commercial and CFI. After that, they owned and flew a Cessna 140, her Daddy insisting, "You're gonna learn to fly one with the little wheel in the back." (I understand: I did the same thing with my son, teaching him in a Champ.) Later, she and Tom went through Falcon 20 school together where she earned her ATP and Falcon 20 type rating. She's had corporate jobs flying a Westwind and a Citation and also taught Advanced Airmanship at SimuFlite. Today she's a simulator instructor for the Falcon 900 at SimuFlite. In between all that, Debbie became involved in the CAF and became the third woman in US history to formally qualify on the B-29 "Supefortress." Dora set the bar high; Debbie has kept it there.

I want to say this about flying and qualifying in the WWII-type, historical airplanes: To do it you have to *want* to do it. They're not like the push-button airplanes of today; you have to fly them, every inch of them. They're not about creature comfort; they're about function. You work at it-- from engine start to engine shutdown, and very little of the fancy stuff you learned previously applies other than be knowledgeable, aware, and ready for anything. They shake, rattle, roar, and rumble. Debbie will tell you, "Flying the B-29 is like wrestling an elephant." If that sort of thing doesn't appeal to you, you're in the wrong flying pew. In the end, however, it's something very few people get to experience in this day and age. And to think the twenty-year olds in WWII flew these rumbling treasures almost every day, sometimes five and six hours at a time, in *combat.* It gives you an appreciation of the price that's paid for freedom. And that's the point of flying them still: preserve the knowledge that freedom isn't given…it is won and preserved.

I once said to Tom, "You must be kinda proud of her." He said, "Well, yeah, considering I knew her before she could walk…….maybe just a little bit proud."

11

HANGAR ETIQUETTE

When it comes to hangar etiquette, there are few rules. At least not in the low places where I hang out. And especially not written rules in the manner of Emily Post. (The young people reading will probably have to Google Emily Post.) Most matters of hangar etiquette are simply just *understood.* And there's only one way to learn: by hanging out.

Let me make it clear that I'm not talking the big, spotless, polished-floor hangars where the shiny jets that don't leak anything reside. That's where Emily Post hangs out. I'm talking about the places that have a little grime and a lot of patina. That's where I and my peers can be found.

How do you enter a hangar where Hangar Bums reside? If the door is open, you walk in. Knocking not required. Hollering a mild insult as you enter usually gets the conversation started, "Don't appear to be much work goin' on in here." The snappy retort might be, "Ain't supposed to be." (Hangars are no place for the thin-skinned.) If the hangar door is closed but the resident Bum's pickup truck is parked outside-- common in cold weather --you give a rap on the side door, walk in and then holler your insult. If the response is unintelligible it usually means the Bum's head is under a cowling or he's prone in the tail cone checking a control cable. Oh, and don't park in front of an open hangar door; that immediately reveals you as an imposter.

So here's the deal about the above: There is no rule that a Hangar Bum has to stop what he's doing when you walk in. If he's in the tail cone, then that's where he'll stay while you're talking. If he's up to his elbows in ProSeal, which has a cure time, he'll keep doing what he's doing. Take no offense at that; to do so would expose you as a Hangar Rookie. The Bum will still talk to you but be prepared to talk about what he's doing at the moment because *that* is where his mind is. Most Hangar Bums have very short attention spans but when they are focused on some airplane thing, they are *focused.* Never interrupt a good airplane trance.

Hangar conversations are pretty free-wheeling. Do not, however, speak of the latest fashion trend or daytime TV: Those two topics will get you the 'what-planet-are-you-from' look. Political discussions are generally lively and Hangar Bums can routinely solve most any mess Washington, DC can make. If only Washington, DC would listen. Airplanes are, obviously, the most frequent topic of conversation. Any and all types of airplanes; all are free game and heartily discussed. Conversations about family are also frequent and they are sacred. And practically everybody at the airport is family. Hangar Bums *care.* They just do. I like that about them. Advice comes freely and in many forms. On one very cold day I put the key into my hangar door lock and it wouldn't turn. Locked out of my own hangar! I tried a little WD-40. Still nothing. I wandered on down to Guy's hangar, rapped on the side door and hollered a suitable insult. He had just passed his IA exam the day before so was feeling rather buoyant. It was appropriate I asked him a mechanical question. I asked him about my lock situation. He said, "That wasn't on my test." I said, "Well, it shoulda been." He said, "Hold your hand on the door knob until it warms." Well, I about half believed him but since he didn't tell me to put my tongue on the stupid door knob. I thought, 'What the heck, I'll give it a try.' So I did. I held the door knob while my hand froze and the door knob slowly warmed. I again put the key in the lock and....voila!....it worked. Who'd a thunk it! There is definitely a body of knowledge at the airport. Some of it is even useful! One more thing: money is seldom talked about. And it's not because money is no object. It is. It's just that passion rules what goes on in hangars and money is just an irritant that you sometimes have to have. Better to talk about passion than irritants.

Here's something else permissible while in hangars: Feel free to check 'em out. They might have some neat workbench or lighting system or a space heater you haven't seen but now surely need. Or a new type of tow bar. Or a new tool. And the Bums will surely tell you if the item is worth a hoot or not. Too, you need to know who has what tools, especially the homemade kind fabricated for a very specific airplane purpose, because you need to know where to go to borrow it when you need it. And if you're a bona fide Hangar Bum, properly certified in the ways of grime and hanging out, you can borrow any tool at any time, no questions asked. Just like in the olden days. It's called trust.

Here's something you don't talk about in hangars: décor. That's because there is none. There is what's called "accumulation." There's the couch from a living room past, possibly a yellow refrigerator, a bullfighter-on-velvet wall hanging, and a well spattered microwave. Each item comes with a story; you have but to ask. And there are all manner of airplane parts that have been removed in favor of new ones and then put on a shelf. And there they stay. Forever. Sometimes one part is moved slightly to make room for another old part. The more the better. That's the genesis of "accumulation." And then something magical happens: Years of accumulation ultimately turns to.....drum roll......*treasure.*

It don't hardly get no better than rediscovering something really cool that you forgot you had!

Cleaning is something else you don't talk about. No need to. The physical rules of dirt are, as are the physics of flight, ironclad: dust settles, grime goes where it needs to be, grease spreads, shavings and filings, left alone, drift of their own free will. Allow it all to assume its natural state. A once yearly brandishing of the leaf blower is elegantly sufficient. 'Nuf said.

Notice I haven't mentioned attire. That's because it's not an issue....ever. Unless you walk in with a white shirt and necktie in which case you might as well have a rotating beacon on your head because you are proclaiming, "I ain't from around here." Bringing the point home, my bride recently asked me to trim some shrubs in the yard. I brought my Carhartt coveralls from the hangar because the canvas-stuff they're made of is great for wading into the pucker brush. I put them on in the garage and my bride said, "Those need to be washed." What?!!?? I couldn't even speak! I finally mustered, "They've never been washed." That earned a one word response, "Obviously." I knew this was an issue I wasn't going to win but I did manage, "No Hangar Bum has ever told me they needed to be washed." That earned me an eye roll but with a slight smile as she replied, "Well, yeah, I'm quite sure that's a true statement." I did the yard trimming and then managed to whisk my coveralls back to the hangar where they are, once again, safe.

There's something else you need to roll with when visiting old hangars: They don't just have airplanes in them. They have old tractors, old cars, boats, motorcycles and rusty lift trucks, stuff like that. Things mechanical, usually in various states of repair. Bums are generally attracted more to things old than things new. I mean, hey, if you have an empty corner and your tools are there, that's where that stuff needs to be. (Some airports are "sensitive" about that, but from my soapbox, it's keeping old equipment alive and there's not one thing wrong with that.) Now, if you really want to get a Hangar Bum talking, ask him about one of his projects and then sit down and listen for the next hour while he tells you. In detail. Great detail. If he's working on an old Volkswagen Beetle he'll tell you the amount of torque required for the castellated nut holding the rear brake drum and the size of the cotter key used with the castellated nut. And he'll tell you about mistakes he's made on the project. Listen closely; you can really learn stuff during this phase of the conversation. At no time yawn or roll your eyes. One, Bums don't understand subtleties and, two, if you're bored, the door that let you into the hangar is also available to let you out. So, if you're in a hurry (which you should never be when you're in a hangar) don't ask questions unless you are fully prepared to listen.

Here's something not to do when you enter a hangar: brag. Hangar Bums have heard and told many tales-- that's part of the culture --but bragging does not fit and they can spot it a mile away. My hangar faces, and is about a hundred yards from, transient parking and the self-service fuel pumps. Often, when the hangar door is open, pilots wander over and wander in. And about 95% of them are welcome, polite, fun and interesting. But the young fella in the white shirt and tie with the shoulder epaulettes who crawled out of a Citation and wandered over and saw my collection of grime and tractors (and my coveralls) and one homebuilt airplane, well, he knew he was talking to a bumpkin. He then proceeded to tell me all about how high and fast the Citation would go and how much jet time he had. Okay, I have no problem being a bumpkin-- I am one --but was thinking, 'You wandered over here to tell me how wonderful you are?' But what I *said*, while pointing to my visiting Hangar Bum friend, Doug, who was sitting on the hangar bench, "Doug here has seven-hundred-fifty Atlantic crossings with Pan Am." That served to subdue the Citation guy a bit. Okay, so what I said about Doug wasn't true but, hey, the statement served its purpose. Point being: don't underestimate grunge. If you come in a-braggin', some of those wily old Bums are likely to toy with you.

Here's another hangar behavior to know: Bums may be opinionated, grungy and sometimes full of hooey, and they may hang out in musty places with rusty and not-so-rusty stuff, but bring a kid or a grandson or a granddaughter into their hangar and they turn to putty. They will drop everything to talk to a kid; they'll show-and-tell anything in the hangar. They'll let kids sit in their airplanes, on their tractors and they'll answer questions all day long. Hangar Bums can be all gruff and goofy but when kids enter the picture they're all about giving and caring. It's really a neat thing to witness.

Okay, so now you know how to behave in the lower level hangars, the ones like me and my Hangar Bum buddies have. It's not rocket science: just be real and never mind the dirt.

12

MILESTONE

Indulge me, please. I recently passed an aviation milestone of sorts.

It was July 11th-- my birthday. Seven-eleven. The year was 1967. I was twenty-two, going on twenty-three years old. And I was in U.S. Air Force pilot training at Webb AFB, Texas and on the scheduling board for two "area acro solo" flights in the T-38. I was where I worked for twenty-two years to be and doing exactly what I wanted to be doing. And today I was going to be doing it alone in a cobalt blue sky in an airplane that knows few limits. Happy birthday.

I can still remember the sequence: check the schedule board and get the tail number and the row where the airplane was parked. There was no ignition key to get; it would be ready when you walked up to it. At the allotted time, you would go to the equipment room, slap your g-suit around you and zip it up, throw your parachute on your back, grab your helmet, oxygen mask, kneeboard and gloves, check your oxygen mask at the test station on the way out the door then walk into the sunshine. There was a tram to shuttle you to your airplane but I usually just walked if the airplane wasn't parked in 'the north-forty.' I liked the walk-- I was a knight, suited up and marching to my steed. (Gimme some slack here: I was only twenty-three, remember?) At the very least, it was my time to get into character to strap on my mini-rocket ship. I *loved* the anticipation.

There it sat, on "G" row, tail #834: sleek, proud, powerful and fast. I was thinking, "You and me, buddy. Let's defy gravity in every axis." Acknowledge the crew chief (they are, after all, the ones who keep these airplanes flyable), check the Maintenance Log, pre-flight, pull gear pins and ejection seat safety pins, and finish fastening your parachute. Then climb up the ladder and settle into the seat. SETTLE INTO THE SEAT! This is home; this is happiness; this is adventure. The airplane surrounds you. You connect to it: to the ejection seat, plug into the g-suit and oxygen systems, and strap on your kneeboard and pull on your gloves. Then run the checklist-- caress the switches, throttles and stick. The anticipation builds. Then you pull on your helmet, slap on the oxygen mask and lower the helmet visor to mute the sun. Then you raise your gloved hand and give a little twirl of two fingers to signal the crew chief: starting engines. Push the start switch, advance the throttle to idle at 14% RPM, and watch that the EGT doesn't climb past 890 degrees. You can *feel* it; your steed is coming alive. Then you do the same thing again for the left engine. Then you put your fists together, thumbs out, and pull your fists apart: pull the chocks. Then the crew chief out front raises his arms and motions you forward. Power up, the jet moves. You roll forward a little then check the brakes. Tap them firmly and bounce the nose strut a little-- it's just *so* cool to do that.

Taxi to the run-up area, run more checklists and, after being cleared onto the runway, check mil (100%) power: this horse wants to *run.* You're cleared for takeoff-- for more fun than a human being should be allowed to have. Canopy down/locked/light-out, power up, light the afterburners and it's a RACE!! Focus ahead; vision to the side is a blur. Rotate, positive rate, gear up, flaps up and pull the nose up. *Way* up.

Waaaay up. And the ground falls rapidly away. At the top of the climb, roll inverted, let the nose come back to the horizon, roll upright and head to your practice area. Happy birthday.

Now for the next hour or so it's just you and your fighter, a match made in heaven. Loop. Straight up. Straight down. Split-S: straight down is *soooo* much fun. Immelman: from top to bottom, gain 10,000' and roll out on top of the world. Roll rapidly three times left, then one to the right-- to get your eyeballs centered again. Roll, pull, sweat, grunt-- this is joy personified. Twenty-three years old today. Thank you, Mom.

Back to the traffic pattern, up initial at 300 KIAS, pitch-out mid-field, haul the stick back, make the oxygen mask sag and the g-suit inflate and wing-tip vortices come off the wingtips. Do it with panache; fly it with spirit! Gear down, flaps. Fall "off the perch," 180 degree turn to final, and get "in the groove" on final at 155 KIAS. Plunk! Nose high for aerodynamic braking-- fun to do that! Then slow, clear the runway, raise the canopy, feel the breeze and taxi slowly back to "G" row to savor the experience. Park, shut down, listen to the engines whine down, get the 'chocks-in' signal, savor the ride some more then unhook and unbuckle and climb out. Sign the Maintenance Log, "Flight O.K.," thank the crew chief and head back to the line shack. Happy birthday.

Now drink a bunch of water, eat a bag of peanuts and an hour or so later, do it all over again. Except, this time, go to "F" row and fly #594. Happy birthday, again.

Was I tired after all that? Not one iota. I was twenty-three years old; I could have done that all day long. But tonight I had a dinner date with my girlfriend, Kay Lyn Statser. She gave me a present at dinner. It was a book, "The World's Fighting Planes," by William Green. Inside she inscribed, "To

Lauran with love-- but be careful flying these things! Kay. 7/11/67."

It's now July 11, 2007-- forty years later, a milestone of sorts. It's also two careers-- one military and one airline --seven type ratings and nearly 20,000 hours later. It's also.....some really lousy weather, a couple near misses, four engine failures and a couple stupid things later, too. And my "fighter" is now piston powered-- an 0-360, to be exact --and I built it myself, an RV-8. I painted it military style. It completes me. It takes me back to where I started this aviation journey: sitting astraddle the airplane with a canopy overhead and a stick and throttle inside. And it is here that I *continue* to experience the joy of aviation. I've worked hard to be where I am but fully realize I've been propitious in genetics, lucky in the happenstance of life, and fortunate in marriage. And I give thanks for these things every day.

So, forty years later, July 11, 2007, it's time to commemorate the journey. The anticipation builds as I drive to the airport. There I open the hangar door and push my little fighter into the sunshine. It glints proudly. I preflight and climb in. I *settle* in. It's home-- airplane cockpits have always been home. But this one I designed and built myself; it is every inch what I want it to be. I strap-in, hearing the buckles snap. I like the sounds. They signal the beginning of the flight. I do the checklist, holler "Clear!" and start the engine. The airplane comes alive; I *feel* it come alive. I like it alive. I call for taxi and amble toward the runway. Ambling allows me to savor the experience.

Cleared for takeoff, I roll: tail up, light on its wheels......airborne! Forty years later to the day. Not as high, not as fast, not as far, not as many g's, but with the *same* joy. *Still* the same joy. Aviation is a good life.

I climb on silvered wings and fly to my practice area. There I roll and loop and roll some more and remember the day forty years ago when I flew in kind. And somehow I also think of the pilots I've known who also loved the sky, who once touched it but now do not. My pilot training classmates: Steve, who is now recovering from a serious heart attack; Ken, who fell ill while flying 0-2's in Vietnam and now spends most of his days in a wheelchair; and Gary, who called everybody "Silly Savage," who now has a brain tumor. These rolls are for you guys, because you've been there and the sky will always be a part of you. And the loops, the climb, the top, the dive, the pull at the bottom, commemorative for Bruce, who hit the ground in an F-4, Guy who also hit the ground in another F-4 and Harold who did the same in an A-7. Did these guys want to die flying? Of course not. Did they want to be doing what they were doing? Yes, they did. And all of them once had "area acro solos" in the T-38 and there, I'm quite sure, felt the joy. They wanted to fly and fly they did. Their careers were shortened but their stars burned bright. I rolled and looped and looked at my wings in the air and thought of such things as I flew along forty years later. Bittersweet thoughts on a happy birthday.

I didn't want to land. I wanted to stay in the air and fly forever. But forever is not for mortals. So it was back to the traffic pattern for an overhead break to a landing and taxi-back, canopy open, to the hangar. Mixture to lean and the prop stopped. Switches off and I sat there. Just sat there.....for a long time. Time marches on but time is still good. And, yes, I'm thankful for that, too. Was I tired? A little-- forty years later my 'abs' are a little more 'rounded,' there being forty more years of wear on the body. But the aviation joy is the same. Still the same. I climbed slowly out of the cockpit. I had another dinner date with Kay Lyn --now-- Paine, same girlfriend, forty years later. At dinner she gave me an Oregon

State polo shirt: after family and flying, our other passion is college football. And a card. Well, actually, two cards. One card was inscribed, "Still loving you forever. Katie." The outside of the second card said, "It's your birthday! Get yer motor runnin'! Head out on the highway!" Inside it said, "Pick up bread and milk. Then come home again!" The inscription read, "Sometimes I crack myself up. Love you always-- Katie."

Aviation milestones are a time to reflect: reflect on the joy of aviation, the joy of life, the rewards of persistence, the fruit of hard work, on love and on another very happy birthday flying.

13

TYLER'S FLIGHT

(*the paragraphs in italics are my bride's*)

Have you had any bad days lately? Perhaps a fender-bender at a residential street intersection? Dog dig up the new flower bed? Hot water heater stop working? Sorry, but those aren't bad days. I'll tell you what a bad day is: cancer. And my friend Tyler has it. He's seventeen years old. He spent two-hundred days in the hospital last year. He's out now and one of the things he wanted to do was go for an airplane ride. An EAA member, Mike Rhodes of Chapter 902, who knew of Tyler's plight, called and asked, since I live nearby, if I'd take Tyler for a flight. I guess we all know the answer to that question.

Before I go one inch further I want to re-phrase something. I said Tyler has cancer. But what I want to say now is that Tyler *had* cancer. He's had surgeries and has completed chemotherapy and, right now, the cancer is past tense. As you might imagine, he's on "close watch" so goes back in a couple months for another check-up. Now that I know Tyler-- we flew together! --I know he's a fighter and the cancer is going to *stay* past tense. I'm bettin' the house on it.

Every day we hear of sad and tragic events in our world. We process the news and put it away where we don't have to think about it. It doesn't affect us directly, though we empathize for those affected. Well, young Tyler, handsome, tall and lanky, walked up to me with a big smile, shook my hand, and put a face to an event I had heard about. We have a "cancer cluster" in West Salem. It is frightening in that it has affected 7 people, all but one are kids. Three have died. They have developed osteosarcoma, a rare type of bone cancer.

The EPA is investigating and we are all anxiously awaiting the outcome of their studies, which center on a middle school, high school, park and baseball fields. Causes can be high levels of radon, fluoride and dioxins. All that aside, these kids are real. They are our neighbors, our children's and grandchildren's friends. It is right here in our everyday world.

While Tyler and Lauran were preflighting, Craig, his dad, was updating me on the situation. He is a loving dad, a caring person, easy to talk to and very open about what has been going on with Tyler. He tells me that Tyler is a fighter. I have no doubt. He spent 200 days in the hospital last year and will still graduate this spring with his senior class. He and Lisa, another cancer victim, were named Homecoming King and Queen at West Salem High School. That speaks volumes about this senior class. Sadly, Lisa passed away shortly after she was crowned.

Tyler lost his much-loved grandmother this same week. It was unexpected. He pondered canceling the flight. He didn't. I told Craig that flight can allow you to, at least for a time, literally leave all our cares and worries on the ground. He was hoping this would be true for his son.

I contacted Tyler's dad, Craig, and we began the process of meshing schedules. Of course, best laid plans this time of year (January and February) in the Pacific Northwest are often foiled by weather conditions: rain, more rain, fog, and more rain still. And that's what we had for about three weeks straight. It was frustrating but we wanted to do the flight right and safely. Finally a day dawned without rain and without fog, but with an 1800' solid overcast. Craig called and asked, "Okay to fly today?" I replied, "Yeah, it's okay but not ideal. We can scoot around under the clouds but won't be able to get over the hills to the coast or on top to see the snow-capped mountains." He said, "Well, this is a once in a lifetime deal for Tyler. I'd just as soon wait so we can do it all and make it special." The weather was forecast to get better in the next few days so we set Friday as the day to fly. Thursday morning Craig left a message on my phone. I didn't check messages until late that afternoon. His voice sounded flat as he said, "It's about the flight." I called him back. He said, "Tyler's grandmother (Craig's mother) passed away last night. At first Tyler didn't think he could do the flight, but now he does." I said, "It's his decision. We can reschedule. I understand either way." He said, "Let's go ahead. That's what he wants to do." On Friday the fog lifted at 11:00 AM and it was clear above. The perfect day had finally arrived; perhaps it was his Grandmother's blessing.

Craig told me the whole story while they were in the air. He has two other sons, 14 and 21. He will be married this fall to his junior high "crush". He has held his family together through this ordeal. He is warm and kind and strong. He is hopeful that the EPA findings will have positive results so that other kids and parents don't have to endure what he and Tyler have. He is as excited about this flight as Tyler. I promised him a flight too, as soon as the sun shines again. He has shouldered an enormous burden and is still smiling, still positive. Everyday heroes.

On Friday we all met for the first time in the airport restaurant parking lot, Craig, Tyler and I. I liked them right away. Easy to talk to, very grounded, very real. Tyler is tall and thin. Chemotherapy will make you thin. Before the disease he was a strapping 6'1" filled-out high school athlete. Thin or not, he still has the spirit and competitive nature of an athlete. He wants to *do* things, probably one of the reasons why he was at the airport this day. You could feel that about him: a fighter.

We wandered over to my hangar. I had "Ohh Kay!!" out front, preflighted and ready to go. My bride had made Tyler a gift basket: an EAA shirt and hat, some aviation magazines, a couple of my books and, yup, some homemade chocolate chip cookies. As is my custom when giving a ride, we never just hop in and fly. We talk about it first. I showed Tyler pictures of the boxes that my airplane came in. Then, with some scrap aluminum, we squeezed a couple rivets (never does a new rider leave my hangar without having learned the word "cleco"); then we listened to the ATIS on the handheld radio; then I laid out a sectional, showed him where we were and asked him where he wanted to go. He pointed to the coast and the mountains. I then got out my little wooden model airplane and showed him which controls do what and showed him some maneuvers and said, "It'll be smooth and clear. We'll only do what you want to do."

We climbed into the airplane. Tyler wound his long frame into the backseat and fastened his harness and belts. I showed him how the headset worked. Then the cameras of the people standing around came out. A few of the regular Hangar Bums wandered up, too. I hollered to Craig, "These are Hangar Bums. You couldn't get a nickel for the lot of them down at the street corner. You don't have to talk; all you have to do is listen. But don't take notes because nothing they say is important." (Hangar Bums love it when you talk like that.) Then I told Tyler, "If you're in an airplane and the cameras come out you have to give the "thumbs up" signal. It's aviation lore." He did and a fine "thumbs up" it was!

As the plane lifted off, there was a gleam in Craig's eye and joy in his heart. We talked the whole hour and a half they were gone. He talked of Tyler's character. Of homecoming and graduation. Of the loss of his Mom the past week. And of what this flight meant to Tyler. I had no doubt, it meant as much to Craig. He thought that maybe Tyler would become interested in learning to fly. He has some physical limitations due to a new knee and rod in his leg. But nothing that would keep him from flying. He has plans to be a river rafting guide this summer. He wants to take a trip to the Great Barrier Reef for his Make-a-Wish dream. This young man, with his easy smile and his thumbs up, is inspiring. We left that day knowing that we got as much or more from this experience than anyone. Thank you, Tyler and Craig, for sharing in your journey.

I hollered "clear" and the crowd stepped back and the airplane started right up like it always does. Sound and vibration: now we're talkin'! At the end of the runway I explained everything I was doing during the run-up. I dialed in tower frequency and asked Tyler, "All set?" He said, "Yup." And with that we were off. A straight out departure allowed us to look to the left and see where he lived and also to get a glimpse of his high school. A little further north and off to the right was where his grandmother had lived. On takeoff, Tyler had emoted with a "whoa" and a "wow;" over his grandmother's house he got quiet. It was a quiet moment and a reflective moment…from on high. I said, "This is your day, buddy. Up here you are free to do and think and feel as you please. The sky is yours." He nodded.

Then we were over the Evergreen Aviation and Space Museum, where a Boeing 747 sits on top of a building, now a big waterslide. Tyler asked, "Is that a real airplane?" I answered, "Yeah, it is. Or it used to be." Then I said, "Okay, here's where you do the flying." I had him take the stick and wiggle it to get the feel for what he had control of. Then I pointed out front and said, "The ocean is right over there." He didn't jerk the airplane around; he just nudged it along. Nice touch for a newbie. Arriving at the coast he nudged the airplane to the left and flew along the coastline. We flew over where Craig's old high school buddy has a lake house and loaned it to Craig and the boys for a long stay. I asked Tyler if he liked the coast. He said, "Yeah, I really do."

On the way back from the coast we flew over Beaver Stadium, the home of his favorite college football team. He looked outside a lot during the flight. He grew up in this part of the country so pretty much knew what he was looking at. I had worried some about Tyler's stamina, given all that he had been through. I asked him if he was comfortable. He said, "It's a little cool." I turned on the heat. And the headset seemed to be bothering him some; I think it was pressing his sunglasses a little too tight against his head. But there was never a hint of complaint from him. He was glad to be flying and he was making it work. Next we headed for the mountains and skirted the edge of them. The peaks were resplendent with their fresh snowcaps. I said, "Sometimes when I'm doing this I don't want to come down. You're in control and there are no strings." He said, "Yeah."

As we headed back towards the airport, Tyler asked, "Can we do a flip?" I said, "Okay, but first I want you to feel some g's. I'm going to do a steeper banked level turn and when I tell you "when" I want you to lift your arms. They'll feel heavy. That's g." We did all that and he said, "Whoa! Cool!" Then I told him he's going to feel that again and I talked him through and did a "flip." About halfway through, he said, "Yeahhhhowwwiiiieeee!" Straight and level again, I asked, "Doin' okay?" He said, "Yeah, that was awesome." As we were heading back to the airport again I asked, "Is there anything else you want to do?" He said, "Another flip." So we did.

On the forty-five to the downwind we flew, closer this time, by his high school, easy to spot with the black turf in the football stadium, home of the West Salem Titans. We entered traffic and landed and were barely off the runway when he began thanking me. I said, "Thanks, buddy, but it was a pleasure for me, too. I can tell, you 'get' the flying thing and it's fun to share with people like you, who 'get it.' Too, I know a bunch of pilots who would do for you what I just did. It's a fraternity and you're now a part of it."

We taxied back to the hangar where his dad waited. We shut down and rolled the canopy back. Tyler was a little tired, I think, but he was happy with what he'd done. So was I. I hollered to his dad, "Hey, this boy's got the touch. And he's good at navigation, too. When he got to that big body of water he immediately knew it was the Pacific Ocean." That got a laugh. I told Tyler before he left, "The weather gets better in the spring and good in the summer. Any time you want to go again, we'll go." When we do, I'm calling it a new beginning because Tyler deserves one.

14

MYSTERY AIRPLANE

You and I have been on a few journeys in this column over the years. I want you to go on another one with me. This one is a little different. At least it was for me. I'll ask you along the way what you would have done. All I can say is that this one drew me like a magnet, yet it took me a few years to get up the nerve to act upon it.

Okay, look at the photo on the title page of this column. Look at it closely. See the airplane silhouette? Unmistakably, it's the shape of a DC-3. Or some variant of a D-3. In any case, it's the silhouette of a widely recognized, historically significant airplane. And it's located just a few miles southwest of my home airport. Every time I fly in that direction I fly over it and every time I do I wonder about it. And I've been doing that for about, oh, seven years now. Almost every time I circle and take another look. Yup, sure enough, it's a DC-3 parked in a farm yard with no obvious runway about. Curiosity often takes me a little lower for a better view. After all, I flew the DC-3 (well, the C-47) in Korea and once ferried one, island hopping, across the Pacific Ocean. I have a soft spot for the Gooney Bird. Historically, it's an aviation icon. Descending a little lower now, it's *still* a DC-3. But how? Why?

What are you thinking right now?

I'm feeling pretty safe loitering about the location; I'm thinkin' plenty of other airplanes have circled this guy's place, too. How can you not?? Remember, for sixteen years in the National Guard, I was a reconnaissance/surveillance pilot. It's in my aviation blood to find things from above and sort them out. Of course, in the OV-1, I had Side Looking Airborne Radar (SLAR), infrared cameras, conventional cameras and a team of analysts on the ground to interpret what's what. Now I just have a lone RV-8 and one set of eyeballs.....and a lot of curiosity. Too, I have this soft spot in my heart for airplane people, whoever they are, in whatever pasture they may be in, with whatever airplane. I'm sensing a bit of a character here and I like characters.

Looking for more details in my lazy circling, I see a big shop-type building, a home, a small pond with something in it, another much smaller airplane silhouette, various pieces of equipment and machinery, and some cars, one seemingly the shape of an older Volkswagen Beetle. Just your typical barnyard, right? But with a DC-3 centerpiece. I also made a mental map of the roads and lanes and driveways I'd have to travel to the get to the place. Should I, that is, ever get up the nerve to drive there.....uninvited. Curiosity killed the cat, ya know.

I also mentally rehearsed the first thing I'd ask after I drove up. Something like, "Hi, uh, are you aware that you have a DC-3 in your front yard?" Or, "Is this the next airplane to Tulsa?" Don't like either of those? Okay, what would *you* first ask him?

I also managed to get some approximate coordinates (remember those?) for the place. At home, I and Goggle worked on them and, lo and behold, after some roundabout computer pathways new to me, came up with.......an airport! OR-39 to be exact. Public knowledge. "Flying Tom Airport" by name. It's not on the sectional but it's in the FAA's "official books." I thought to myself, 'Well. I'll be a switch tailed heifer!' Along with other official stuff about the airport was the owner's name: Kevin. After that, getting a phone number was relatively easy. Getting the nerve to call Kevin....I'm shy....was not so easy.

Finally, one fine day, I pulled myself up by my bootstraps and said to myself, 'You just need to drive there. How bad can it be? It's airplane people. It'll be okay.' So that's what I did....almost. There is a small country store just before you get to the lane leading to Kevin's place. I stopped and asked if they knew anything of the DC-3 on the hill. They did not. I then asked the beer truck delivery driver who happened to be in the store the same question. He drives the hiway that goes nearest to Kevin's place nearly every day. (You can see the DC-3 from the road if you know where to look.) He denied all knowledge of any DC-3. Okay, what's going on here??!!? Am I the only airplane nut? Or am I the only *stupid* airplane nut? (Never mind. Don't answer that question.)

From the country store I head down the hiway and turn onto the lane that I knew, from my aerial reconnaissance, lead to Kevin's place. It's a nicely graveled, tree-lined lane. Quite inviting.... right up until you spot the black sign nailed to a tree that says, in bright florescent letters, PRIVATE PROPERTY – NO TRESPASSING. Uh-oh! I can't quite turn around on the narrow lane so I keep going....albeit a little slower....and come to another sign near a railroad track. This sign says, "PRIVATE RR CROSSING – NO TRESPASSING." I'm beginning to get the hint but still don't have room to turn around. I drive a little further to a bend in the road where I can finally turn around. In the turn I looked right up the driveway that leads to the barnyard and the DC-3. So close, yet so far. I chickened out and headed for home with more questions than answers.

Okay, Tough Guy, what would you have done?

At home, somewhat emboldened by my near brush with danger (in my mind, anyway), I picked up the phone and called Kevin. Got the answering machine. I left a message, a rather rambling one: "Hi, Kevin. My name is Lauran and I fly out of Salem and, for several years now, have flown over the DC-3 parked in your yard and I used to fly DC-3's so am curious about your airplane and was wondering if I could maybe stop by for a visit or something like that sometime?" How's that for rambling? Then, at the last moment, I thought I'd better close with a caveat: "But, hey, if you don't want to talk about it, I can certainly understand that, too." Then I hung up and the wait began. Would he or would he not answer?

And I waited and wondered some more.

The next morning I was sitting at my desk and the phone rang. I answered and the voice on the line said, "Hi. This is Kevin."

Yo! I briefly thought of opening with the "next airplane to Tulsa" line but then thought better of it. I said, "Hi. My name is Lauran and I fly out of Salem and can't help but notice that you have a DC-3 in your front yard. Is that something we can talk about?"

Kevin says, "Sure." And then, long pause, he says no more. I sense that Kevin doesn't waste a lot of words.

I open with, "How did it get there?"

"We flew it in."

"I didn't see a runway."

"It's right next to the driveway. It's pretty nice when it's all mowed."

We're on a roll now so I ask, "How long ago did you fly it in?"

"About twelve years ago, right before 9/11. We flew it to Salem in 2001 for some radio work."

I mention, "It's probably got quite a history. All DC-3's do."

"Oh, yeah. It was once a government sprayer. Then the Cummins Engine people had it. Then Indiana University. Then it flew car parts for a while. It's got the modified cowl and gear doors so it goes pretty good."

"When'd you last start it?"

"About four or five years ago."

Okay, I'm thinking enough questions about the DC-3. It's Kevin's airplane and he likes it. I'm not one to pass any kind of judgment. I change the subject a bit with, "There appears to be something in the pond."

"That was my first airplane. I wasn't very good back then. It was wrecked so I put the fuselage nose down on a stump in the pond."

"On a stump?"

"Yeah, it was just something to do, I guess."

I reply, "Hey, if it works for you, it works for me. And under the wing of the DC-3, there appears to be another small airplane."

"That's an experimental. It's got an old EAA sticker on it."

"And a smaller airplane out in the open?"

Kevin says, "That's my P-51 weathervane."

"And one of the cars appears to be a Beetle?" I'm starting to feel like a nosey idiot now but I'm liking Kevin's honesty and spunk.

"I put in a septic tank for a college professor and he paid me with the Beetle. I think he got the better deal. Thing needs brakes. I got a couple 8N Ford tractors, too."

Ah, tractors are always good. I had to ask, "Flying Tom Airport?"

"Tom was a buddy of mine that was killed. It was pretty traumatic at the time. I wanted to remember him." I was beginning to think I'd bothered Kevin long enough when he added, "I liked Gordon Baxter."

I said, "Me, too. He was my writing idol."

"I know."

"You know???"

"I read your stuff."

Well, shut my mouth! Here I am circling Kevin's place for years and he reads my stuff. We're connected! I then said, "I'd like to meet you sometime. I like the way you roll. I started up your driveway once but saw the NO TRESSPASSING signs."

"That's new. Most people don't pay any attention to them. I work at various construction sites (Kevin has an excavating business) and the kids are teenagers so they're busy coming and going. There's usually somebody here. Come on up, anyway, though. Fine with me if you look around. Dog's friendly. We'll catch up to you one of these days."

So….finally….I went there, *all the way* there, right by a sign on an equipment shed that said "Taildragger Lane" and up to, yup, the DC-3. It was standing a bit weathered but still tall and proud as DC-3's tend to be. I knocked on the door of the house. No answer. Dog just wagged his tail. I felt a little awkward being there alone so I didn't stay long but the landscape was friendly to me now since I'd talked to Kevin.

There was a light breeze and it just felt good being surrounded by the aviation serendipity. I took photos. I now knew the stories that went with them. And now so do you.

So that's my little story of aviation intrigue. It was me long being curious about a DC-3 in a barnyard and Kevin nicely sorting it all out for me. I thank him for sharing his aviation world. I liked him. No nonsense. He likes what he likes and does what he does. I like people like that. I'm looking forward to meeting him. There'll be more stories, I'm pretty sure of that.

15

WES

Writing this column is a gift. I say that because through it I meet the best of people. Over the past several years I've told you about many of them. I want to tell you about yet another: Wes Schierman. His story is one of extreme courage and patriotism. And, yes, he's an airplane homebuilder.

The aviation connections and threads that bind us to this story are many. BJ Paine once wrote to tell me she liked something I had written. She also wrote because we have the same last name: Paine spelled with an "i" is not nearly as common as Payne with a "y." We compared relatives and came up blank but the bond began when she mentioned that her husband, Chuck Paine, flew B-24's in WWII and eventually retired from Northwest Airlines as a B-747 captain. His was a career that spanned the Golden Age of Aviation. When he passed away in January of 2009, the Blackjack Squadron-- a schooled and practiced band of pilots flying formation in Van's RV's --flew a missing man formation for Chuck's memorial. (I wrote a column about Chuck Paine's life in the June 2009 issue of *Sport Aviation.*) Wes Schierman, also a retired B-747 captain from Northwest Airlines, was the lead aircraft in that formation.

Wes Schierman is a story unto himself. He was a pilot for the Washington Air National Guard from 1956 to 1962. He also flew as a DC-4 co-pilot for Northwest Airlines, based in Spokane, Washington. In 1960 he was furloughed from the airline. In 1962 he signed up for a three year active duty tour with the US Air Force, first flying the F-100 and then the F-105. Jump now to August 28, 1965 and Wes Schierman is flying his 37th mission-- leading a flight of four F-105's -- over North Vietnam. As he rolled in on target he squeezed the trigger to fire his gun. The gun fired a short burst then stopped firing. Then Wes heard a "clunk" on the left side of the airplane, followed by a very large explosion towards the rear of the airplane. The gun had imploded. Then the engine ground to a halt. About this time his #4 man in the formation radioed, "Lead, you got a lot of fire coming out the back." Wes radioed back with, "I'm getting out." With that he raised the handgrips and ejected.....over North Vietnam.

The next thing Wes remembers was something hitting him. It was the ejection seat, which then became tangled in the parachute risers above him. He was still trying to hold the seat at arm's length when he hit the ground....hard! Stunned by the hard hit, he was relieved to discover that all his main body parts were still intact. He proceeded to conceal his parachute and flight gear as best he could and then headed for some cover. It was after that that he noticed he was bleeding profusely from his left wrist. He wrapped it as best he could. He contacted his flight using his survival radio and they told him a rescue helicopter was on the way. About five minutes later he heard voices coming up the hill. They turned out to be a platoon of North Vietnamese infantry armed with automatic weapons. They had found his chute and were combing the area. On about their fourth pass, they found Wes Schierman, thirty years old, a husband and father.

About this time the RC-54 rescue coordinator aircraft appeared overhead. The North Vietnamese became quite agitated and tied Wes's hands behind his back and looped the rest of the rope around his neck and began running and dragging him until they were concealed under dense jungle cover. Wes remembered thinking, "The very best I can look forward to is losing a couple years of my life." That turned out to be an understatement. (At that point in time, however, I don't suppose you'd really want to know that it would turn out to be nearly eight years!) After about a week of heavily guarded travel, Wes was delivered to Hoa Lo Prison, the "Hanoi Hilton, on September 3, 1965. When the steel gates of the prison slammed closed behind him Wes knew he was now in a different war: a war of wills, theirs against his. He made up his mind right there that he would rather not return home than dishonor himself, his family or his country. (Please go back and read that again....slowly.)

Wes was placed in a solitary cell and within a few hours the interrogations began. His captors threatened him; he stood by the Code of Conduct. His left wrist was now badly infected. His captors offered medical attention if he would answer questions. He refused. After about ten days he was thrown into another dank cellblock nicknamed "Heartbreak Hotel." This was the first he was able to communicate, between cells, with other prisoners. Those communications tuned out to be, as you can imagine, vital to prisoner survival. If you were down, there was always support! If they couldn't communicate by voice, they communicated by a tap code they had devised. At "Heartbreak Hotel" Wes found "Percy," whose memorial service he had attended since it was determined that he had been killed. He had not! All prisoners made a habit of remembering names in case someone escaped from prison they would be able to pass those names to families. At one point, Wes had memorized 368 names.

In late September, many prisoners were moved to "The Zoo." The "V" (as the prisoners came to call the North Vietnamese) were becoming frustrated with not being able to gather enough information so they worsened the living conditions. Imagine living in the dark twenty-three hours a day, often in leg irons. Thus began a system of torture that lasted 4 ½ years. The "rope trick" was one of those tortures. The V wrapped a rope around the biceps and drew the arms up behind the back while forcing the head down. Due to compression of the chest, breathing was greatly restricted. The worst part was when the circulation was cut off and "it felt like your arms were being thrust into boiling water." That was when prisoners found they could be broken. Knowing it was happening to others eased their guilt. The motto became: "Do the best you can. You're human. Just don't give them anything for free."

Enough. You get it. The courage of these men was monumental.

In 1969, for the first time, Wes received a package from home. In it was a picture of his daughter and son, now 8 & 7 years old, not 4 & 3 any longer. For the first time in captivity, Wes cried.

In late 1972 and early 1973, the "V" began organizing the prisoners according to their "shoot-down" dates. And the food improved considerably. The POW's sensed something different was happening. The "V" then gathered them in a courtyard and announced an "end to hostility agreement" had been signed. They mentioned nothing about prisoner releases.

On February 11, 1973 the POW's were issued a different set of clothes and told to change into them. Then they were bussed to the Gia Lam airport. US Air Force C-141's were parked on the ramp. Names were read and, one by one, the POW's were escorted to their C-141. The POW's remained subdued, almost disbelieving, until they got airborne and the gear came up. It was then that the cheering began. When the pilot announced they were "feet wet" and out of North Vietnamese airspace they cheered even more. “Freedom Day” had finally come true!

After the C-141’s lifted off from Hanoi, a listening-in, passing Northwest Airlines airliner asked an Air Force crew if they could get a message to Wes Schierman. The message was: “Welcome home, Wes. Thought you’d like to know your seniority number is 428 out of 1550. Sure glad to have you back, even though you are senior to me.”

After “family situation” briefings, all were allowed to call home. Wes’s family was still solidly intact. On February 16, 1973 they were reunited at Travis AFB, California. You don’t need me to tell you about that; you can imagine it. Wes was now home……after nearly eight years of unspeakable deprivation……with family and, apparently, an airline job. It was all a lot to take in.

After convalescent leave, Wes returned home to Spokane. He said he felt like Rip Van Winkle. He was starting life all over again. He had to get new everything! He wondered about the flying so asked for a ride in an Air National Guard T-33. He said he was obviously rusty but was pleased that he was able to control the aircraft fairly well.

Wes met with Northwest Airlines in May of 1973. He was afraid he wouldn’t be welcome; it had been thirteen years since he had worked for them, nearly eight of those as a POW. He later said he couldn’t have been more wrong. They worked with him at every opportunity. Wes was aware he was breaking new ground…..from POW to airline captain in pretty short order…..so he wanted to set a good precedent. And he did, which shouldn’t surprise you, now knowing the character of the man. Wes retired from Northwest in 1995 (age 60) as a Boeing 747 captain.

In 1988, Wes purchased a partially completed RV-4. In October he flew it for the first time. Then he began flying formation with a friend, Marty Foy, who also had built and flew an RV-4. Two old fighter guys returning to their roots. That union eventually led to the formation of the Blackjack Squadron-- the one that flew the missing man formation for Chuck Paine.

I communicated a few times via e-mail with Wes, mostly about the Chuck Paine story and the flyover. He genuinely enjoyed doing flyovers for fellow airmen. BJ Paine is forever grateful; it absolutely made her heart pound with pride. I once broached the POW subject with Wes, "I understand you were a POW." He wrote back, "Yeah, I was a jailbird." "Jailbird", indeed. *Hero* is a lot more like it!

Later, Wes built and flew an RV-12. He really enjoyed the building process, all over again. On the vansairforce.net community, Steve Rush wrote something that rather typifies Wes Schierman: "My dad and I spent time with Wes helping in the build of his RV-12 as we had already built one. He was always great to talk to, though he never mentioned his background to us. I flew with Wes a couple times in my RV-12 as he was preparing for the first flight of his. At the time I had no idea of his background. Now that I do, I feel like a total idiot for trying to tell him how to fly. He was very gracious and truly appreciated the time I spent flying with him." Ever the gentleman, it was typical Wes.

In 2005, Wes was invited by his former squadron, the 67th Tactical Fighter Squadron (now flying F-15's), to fly one more mission. The purpose was to get the final landing that he didn't get on August 8, 1965. He flew the mission and got the landing: mission complete.

A couple more connections: In 2008 I attended a reunion at my old US Air Force pilot training base (now closed) in Big Spring, Texas. The speaker was Julius Jayroe. He, too, had been a POW in North Vietnam. He spoke of the atrocities. He talked for approximately an hour and you could have heard a pin drop the whole time. Afterwards we all stood and sang "God Bless America." And sang it loud. Unknown to me at the time, Julius Jayroe had once been in the same cell with Wes Schierman.

Another connection: In November of 2012, I wrote "Flight of Forty," about the forty-ship flyover at AirVenture to honor Dick VanGrunsven. The leader of that flight was Stu McCurdy. Many years earlier, the Mig Cap leader for the Son Tay prison raid (where Wes had once been held) in North Vietnam to rescue POW's was Stu McCurdy. The raid was not successful but only because the North Vietnamese had recently moved the POW's to another prison. The POW's got word of the raid, however, and it was a morale booster just knowing that *someone* out there still cared.

Wes passed away in January 2014 after a short battle with lung cancer at the age of 78. He leaves his wife, Faye, three children (two of whom are professional pilots) and three grandchildren. And he leaves a legacy of character and heroism. He lived on a quiet but close knit cul-de-sac. A neighbor said, "It was an honor to live next to the Schierman's. He was the hero of the neighborhood. He never talked about what he went through. He was very humble." The neighbors set up a wonderful and heartfelt memorial in his front yard, replete with American flags. Another neighbor remembers once asking Wes how he was doing and Wes replied, "Anytime you can turn the doorknob and go outside is a good day." From Wes, that statement has special meaning. *Special* meaning.

For Wes: you are free to soar, m'friend, a shining example for us all. Fly high and fast, free forevermore.

16

APOLLO 13

We were sitting in a corner booth at Elmer's Restaurant in King City, Oregon. It was mid-morning. Around us, at the various tables, people were eating breakfast. Some had finished and were sitting contentedly with their fingers crooked through coffee cup handles, sipping. The air was full of morning talk, the kind where you're just starting your day, planning something or looking forward to something. Friendly talk; good talk.

I was there at the invite of my RV-8 buddy, Nel. Nel's barely worth 2¢. I know this because I once tried to sell him on a street corner and 2¢ was the high bid. But he said, "You gotta meet this guy. He was an engineer on Apollo 13. Talk about experimental aviation, those guys were at the tip of the experimental spear." 'This guy' was Larry McAlister, now 85 years old. He was very welcoming, humble, polite, sharp as a tack and still with a twinkle in his eye. He's also the closest I've ever been to Apollo 13.

You all know of Apollo 13, the explosion in the spacecraft, the suspense of the aftermath, the reconfigured, risky re-entry. It gripped the nation (and was later immortalized in a movie with Tom Hanks). Larry, sitting quietly before me in the booth, led the team that designed and built the backup computer that was largely responsible for getting the astronauts home safely. Apollo was built with a whole lot of talent and spirit of adventure. Larry was right in the middle of all that. It was an honor to meet him.

Of note, as we talked, Larry tended to deflect individual credit by mentioning again and again that it was a wonderful team effort. Larry was in California; Grumman built the Lunar Module in New York; the Command Center was in Houston. That kind of team effort: huge.

Larry's team was responsible for building the AEA and DEDA for the AGS. (Hey, this was NASA; you *knew* some acronyms were coming!) AEA (Abort Electronics Assembly); DEDA (Data Entry and Display Assembly); AGS (Abort Guidance System). Think back a bit now, like to 1970. Computers were large and slow by today's standards and memory was small. Yet, given the small confines of the spacecraft, they were to assemble devices that not only worked but could only be a little larger than a shoebox. This was their charge…..and challenge. And they were still using slide rules. They had to create, assemble, and test everything…over and over again. It *had* to work. As you might imagine, there were no naysayers on Larry's team; they *would* complete the assigned task, whatever it took. That was their attitude. Larry once discovered a small device that had been left out of their planning. That caused a delay. Larry cried that night. These people *lived* the job. Larry's team ended up doing it right and, as it turns out, we're glad they did.

To do what all they had to do, Larry arranged for engineers, manufacturing personnel and quality control personnel to all be in a room just a few feet from where the computer was being assembled. They dubbed that room the "Tiger Tank" to honor the dedication of all who worked there. Twelve hour days, seven days a week were the norm. That sort of work schedule, no matter how committed the workers, brought out both good humor and tempers. And some divorces.

Monumental accomplishments are seldom achieved without some pain. Friday afternoon was stress relief day: a three martini lunch at a nearby Chinese restaurant. A martini with the appetizer; a martini with lunch; a martini with desert. Three: no more, no less. No body called the "Tiger Tank" on Friday afternoon. They were not available.

To this day Larry waxes poetic about Mary Quist (later Rush), who was secretary at the "Tiger Tank." He said, "She kept that band of strong personality achievers on an even keel. I don't know how she did it but she did. It's hard to imagine what it would have been like had she not been there." After he said all that he closed his eyes and shook his head and softly said, "Whew! That was something how she did that." Ever heard the term 'unsung hero?' Mary Quist was one. Monumental accomplishments are seldom achieved without unsung heroes either.

Why all the dedication? They were young and inspired with "landing a man on the moon in this decade." That's why. Personally, I sometimes miss that single minded pursuit of a cause. I prefer explorative zeal to political quagmire. But that's just me talking.

Larry's journey to NASA is, in itself, a journey of dedication. He was born in Oklahoma. His father was a physician, his mother an accomplished pianist. It was expected in the family that Larry and his siblings would do well. Plus there was always music in the house. That's a nice combination: good parenting and music. His brother became a physician and his sister an opera singer. Larry always loved aviation and built many model airplanes. He graduated from the University of Oklahoma with a degree in Mechanical Engineering. Afterwards he entered the US Army and served in ordnance. After his military service, he went to work for TRW which had the contract that eventually led him to NASA.

Of note, Larry is on the Dawes Rolls in Oklahoma for being part Cherokee Indian. That's a big deal in Oklahoma. Is Larry the first Cherokee Indian to be involved in putting a man on the moon? Don't know. But it's a nice thought.

Back in Elmer's Restaurant now, we were still talking about his experiences. I was enthralled with the many stories about the Apollo program, involving pride and effort and brainpower, coming from this gentleman before me. About this time an older lady got up from a nearby table and walked over to ours. We glanced up and she said, "I don't mean to eavesdrop but I couldn't help but overhear some of your conversation. My husband, now passed, was one of the original fifty-two astronauts selected. Your conversation brought back a lot of memories from those times. They were exciting times." Wow—out of the blue that came. Wonderfully so. Connections! Then, almost as quickly as she appeared, she turned to leave, saying, "I don't want to keep you. I just wanted to share." Larry looked up at her and softly said, "Bless you."

The nice young waiter was standing by the table while the above exchange took place. His mother lives in the Pacific Pointe Retirement Inn, the same pace were Larry and his wife, Pat, live, so he knows Larry. The waiter said to Larry, "I didn't know you were a famous man." Of course, Larry doesn't see himself as that; he's too humble. Which is why he doesn't go around talking about it unless you drag it out of him, which is what Nel and I were doing. That's not to say he's not proud of his work with the Apollo program. He is.

I asked Larry of the explosion in the space craft. An oxygen tank exploded in the CSM (Command Service Module). (You remember the immortal line, "Houston, we have a problem.") It was determined the astronauts, to conserve power, oxygen and water, should relocate to the Lunar Module, where the

AGS was. Larry said, "Boy, that was all hand's on deck. Very tense. There was fear. You have a lot of great minds working together but you just never know about some things. I kept thinking of the MTBF (Mean Time Between Failures). We calculated all that stuff. It wasn't pretty but it all worked out. I'll never forget it." Between the AEA and the DEDA and the great leadership at the Command Center a potential tragedy was averted. And Larry and his team were a big part of it.

For his work, Larry was given a commendation by Jack Sweigert, the Command Pilot of Apollo 13. He also received the "Silver Snoopy" pin (a big deal at NASA!) for his contributions. That honor is bestowed upon only 1% of those individuals regarded as among the best in the business. The letter of commendation and the "Silver Snoopy" are currently on display at the Kansas Cosmosphere and Space Center in Hutchinson, Kansas. All this for the gentle and unassuming man sitting across from me at Elmer's Restaurant. I wanted you to meet him.

Larry went on to work for TRW for thirty years. He mentioned that he later designed the oil pump for the Bomarc missile. I asked, half jokingly, "Did it work?" He said, "Yes, it did. I designed it." His comment was not a boast; it was pride.

A few days later we called Larry with a question. We couldn't get ahold of him. He was at choir practice! Music is still a big part of his life. "The Singing Engineer of Apollo 13." I like it.

Was space travel experimental aviation? Yes, in a big way. And it still is. Larry is but one of us, only on a bigger scale. The whole world was watching.

17

AVIATION LEGACY

Jack Briggs and I go a long ways back-- in magazine years, anyway. What does that mean? This: my first words in this magazine were published in *April 1999*. Tom Poberezny put my story about teaching my son to fly in his column. He titled it "Memories to Cherish." It generated a lot of letters. One of those letters was from a man named Jack Briggs. He wrote, "'Memories to Cherish' is a classic. Thanks for sharing it with us. Funny, I had the same problem with my eyes (watering) but I couldn't blame the wind as it was calm in my recliner." As is my custom with letters, I answered and thanked him. He wrote back and I could just tell that he was a special kinda guy. We began corresponding regularly, eventually met (at the Reno Air Races) and have since visited each other's homes. His wife, Peg, is also a gem of the first magnitude.

Jack grew up in the 1930's in a large family in a little red house on Gingerbread Lane in Ashburnham, Massachusetts. It was quintessential Americana. His mother was a homemaker and his father a master machinist. There was not a lot of money but there was always a lot of love. All the kids learned the value of hard work at an early age. And they made their own fun, Jack's dad often clearing out the kitchen for boxing lessons. He also was a Scoutmaster for many years, helping hundreds of boys earn their Eagle Scout badge. (Still in the family is a handmade bench given to Jack's dad with the names of the Eagle Scout boys on it.) What did the community think of Jack Brigg's father? They named an elementary school after him, "JR Briggs Elementary School." It exists to this day.

Then WWII happened. Jack and his brother Dick entered military service. Dick went into the Army Air Corps, flew B-25's, once brought one home with severe battle damage, and earned the Distinguished Flying Cross. Jack considered the Army Air Corps but, on the day he went to sign up, the line was around the block. The shorter line was at the Navy recruiting office so he went there. He took all the tests and was accepted and then sent to Navy flight school. He earned his Navy wings on *April 11*, 1944. He did so well they kept him at Pensacola as a flight instructor in the SNJ. He said, "I wanted to do more but that's what I was assigned to do so that's what I did." He always coveted the F4U "Corsair."

Jack was still instructing in the SNJ when the war ended. That experience imbued him with a lifelong love of flight. Like so many WWII veterans, he came home to work, marry (his beloved Peg) and raise a family. He worked in retail sales for many years for Sears Roebuck. Along the way he stayed involved in aviation, conducting ground schools and flight instructing at the various local airports. And he became involved with the EAA early on, conscientiously serving as a Flight Advisor for many years. That culminated with him building an RV-4 which he loved, flew, and shared the magic of flight with many.

Jack passed in late 2014 at the age of ninety-three. Before he passed, he sent me his CAA Student Pilot Certificate, dated February 2, 1943, and a set of his gold Navy wings. They sit on my desk. Thing is, Jack Briggs was special: so very humble, passionate about aviation and family, and ingrained with work ethic and patriotism. Others who have written about him used words like "kind," "gentle," "giving," "integrity," "generous," "gentleman." One wrote, "I have never known such a large heart." Another said, "He gave off a golden light." And, "He was wise in word and deed, with a positive nature. Many are better today because they knew Jack Briggs." He was that kind of guy. He also had a lively sense of humor. We corresponded almost weekly all these 'magazine years,' mostly e-mail but he'd also write an occasional letter because that's what you did back in the day. We talked much about things aviation-- and he was always spot-on with his analysis --and family and sports (he loved the Boston Red Sox), a little about the weather and a smattering of politics. I miss those chats.

Jack touched so many with the power of his character. And as I think about it, that is the beauty of his legacy: Fame and fortune fade; character lasts. He *cared!* And people knew that about him and were drawn to him. Patrick Barrett, who Jack took for a ride in his RV-4, said, "I like to use the word 'trajectory' when talking about Jack because he set my life on a different trajectory just from knowing him." Patrick is now a corporate pilot.

Another person…among many…. that Jack touched was Chuck Cavallaro. Chuck's father also served in WWII, as a waist gunner on B-17's. He had to bail out two times. He was the oldest guy on the crew: He was twenty-one. So Chuck bonded easily with Jack, "He was my other father figure. He was truly an inspirational guy, not just in aviation but in life itself." Jack gave Chuck his tailwheel training in a Champ. Chuck later purchased that Champ, serial #123. After Jack built his RV-4, Chuck figured he wanted to build an airplane, too. So he did, a Lancair. And Jack helped him. On Chuck's first Lancair flight, Jack flew 'chase' in the RV-4. Chuck's wife was pregnant at the time and wasn't feeling well that day. Jack also watched over her. Three months later, when the baby was born…on *April 11, 1999* ….Chuck and his wife named their new son after Jack. Sixteen years later….on *April 11th* of this year…..Jack Cavallaro soloed the family Piper Arrow from Oswego County Airport (FZY), he being the third generation in the family to fly that airplane, which has been in the family since 1980. Chuck said, "I knew…could feel it….that my dad and Jack Briggs were on each wing….supporting and cheering."

Jack's RV-4 resided, and still resides, in Chuck's hangar. Just sitting, it's a little more forlorn now but still proud. Chuck says, "I try to wipe the dust off from time to time. I can just kinda feel Jack's presence when I do that. Thing is, everyone around here *still* feels his presence." *That's* true legacy. One of Jack Brigg's sons, Mike, is a pilot, although non-current at present. But Mike has a son-in-law, Jerome, who is current as an Air Force pilot. Jack always wanted the airplane to stay in the family. It will…in due time. Meanwhile, Chuck Cavallaro is generously caring for it.

Several of Jack's many loyal friends reminded me of what Jack used to say when you asked, "How ya doin'?" He'd always say, with great gusto, "Never better!" Or, "Never had it so good!" That's just how he looked at life: His glass was always full.

Life marches on. That seems to be how it works. But you don't march on without memories and a whole squadron of us are sure glad we have memories of Jack Briggs. His is a lasting legacy of character and caring.

18

LACEY LADY

It has been an iconic landmark in Milwaukie (near Portland), Oregon for over sixty-five years. "It" being a B-17G (44-85790) that sits on Southeast McLoughlin Boulevard. Okay, it sits on pedestals but, still, it's on a very busy city street. It's the centerpiece for what was a gas station/café and is now a restaurant called, appropriately, "Bomber Restaurant." Over the years it has become quite the legend. It seems almost all the directions given in Milwaukie revolve around the B-17: "From the bomber, go two miles east and then turn left." The public generally loves it and some city officials generally do not. But, after sitting outside in the Oregon weather all these years, the airplane is showing its age. Still, the love for it goes on.

Is there a story in all this? You betcha. And that's where you and I are going right now.

It starts with a fellow named Art Lacey and the year is 1947. Art had been an Engineer for the Army Corps of Engineers during WWII. He now had a gas station business on McLoughlin Boulevard. And he had a civilian pilot's license. At his birthday party in 1947-- perhaps, it is rumored, having a few adult beverages --he said he was going to put a B-17 over his gas station for advertising. A friend told Art he was goofy and could never pull it off. Art bet the man $5.00 that he could. Art then turned to his friend, Bob, and asked, "You got any money on you?" Bob says, "Yeah. How much do you need?" Art says, "$15,000.00." And the guy had it on him and handed it over. (I'm told Portland was pretty 'wide open' in those days, gambling, booze, etc. Evidently so!)

Punky Scott, Art's daughter, says, "You have to understand, Art was a pretty crazy guy. He was just one of those people who would do anything. Mom just rolled with it." Ah, a character! I like characters; they are the spice in life. But more than being just a character, Art was an outgoing, personable sort of guy. He was very easy to talk to.

So, with $5.00 riding on his bet, Art got acquainted with a guy who was the head of Altus Air Base in Oklahoma, where surplus B-17's were being stored after the war. Art traveled to Altus and bought a B-17 for $13,500.00. After the sale the guy said to Art, "Go back into town and when you and your co-pilot come out in the morning, I'll have it ready for you."

Art was down to just two problems now: 1) he didn't have a co-pilot and 2) he'd never flown a B-17. But Art was Art so he borrowed a mannequin from a seamstress, dressed it, and then propped it up in the airplane as his co-pilot. He then went to the office and got an airplane manual for the B-17. He went back to the airplane, crawled in and, with some help from the mechanic ground crew, got the airplane started. He then taxied it around the airport for a bit. And then he took off. He might have gotten away with his deception except that when he came back to land, the landing gear would not extend. He flew around for a while but eventually had to make a belly landing. And, in so doing, hit another parked B-17. Scratch two B-17's.

Art wasn't hurt in the mishap but he did have to walk back to headquarters and admit that he'd never actually flown a B-17 before. His friend at headquarters took pity on him. The friend turned to the office secretary and asked, "Have you written up the bill of sale on that B-17 yet?" She answered, "No, not yet." He then told her, "Worse case of wind damage I've ever seen." And then he sold Art a second B-17 for $1,500.00. Remember, this was early post-war America, pretty giddy times. All of this rather worked out for Art. The B-17 he'd crashed had seen some serious time during the war. The one he ended up getting was a newer B-17G, with but fifty hours on it, that had never seen combat.

This time around Art called his wife, Birdene, and asked her to call his old flight instructor and also a former B-17 crew chief he knew and ask if they might come to Oklahoma. They said they would. And then Art added, "And send a case of whiskey with them." With the whiskey, Art made a "deal" with the local fire department in dry (prohibition) Oklahoma for them to siphon fuel out of the two wrecked B-17's. And that's what the fire department did. Then they put that fuel into Art's "new" B-17. The next morning, Art and his assembled crew took off for Oregon.

Their first landing was in Palm Springs, California to get gas. Art didn't have money for gas so he wrote a bad check and away they went again. (Art covered the check when he got home.) Enroute they hit a snowstorm and got lost. Art flew lower and lower trying to see landmarks. They finally flew over a town and on a rooftop was written "Fall River Mills." They found Fall River Mills on their chart; they were one-hundred miles off course. Then they found a railroad track and followed it to Klamath Falls, Oregon and landed. A little later they took off again for points North, found another snow storm near Bend, Oregon, managed to cross the Cascade Mountain range, then circled a relative's place near Monmouth, Oregon (south of Portland) and then flew to Troutdale, Oregon and landed. Home! Mission complete! Well…almost.

Okay, a bit of 'urban legend' in this story? Perhaps. But, ya know, it's just crazy enough to be believable. I say again, it was 1947 and things were a *lot* different in those days.

But we're not done with Art yet. He still has to get the bomber to the gas station to win the bet. Art and some helpers dismantled the B-17 and put the parts on trucks for the trip to the gas station. And then he applied for the permits required to make the move. City officials said, "Nope. Too high; too big; too wide." Was that the end of that? You know the answer to that; we're talkin' about Art Lacey here.

Art hired a motorcycle escort, like they use for funerals. And then he had a couple teenagers drive along beside the convoy, telling them, "If the cops show up, you guys burn rubber in another direction and the cops will follow you." Then they all set out in the middle of the night heading for the gas station....with a B-17 I guess they figured no one would notice. Art also told the truck drivers, "You guys just keep going. I'll pay any tickets. Just don't let 'em stop you." Turns out the cops didn't stop them but a drinking driver nearly did. Seems the drinking fella left the bar and was coming down McLoughlin Boulevard (then a two-lane road) in the opposite direction when he sees a B-17 approaching. He hurriedly swerved into a ditch. He later said, "I thought I'd driven onto an airport!"

The convoy menagerie made it to the gas station but the whole thing wasn't exactly a secret easy to keep. Local officials wanted to fine Art for not having the proper permits. The Oregon Journal newspaper wrote an article lamenting "local government tries to keep bomber from final resting place." Patriotism was still running high in 1947; the people favored the B-17. The city eventually fined him $10.00. The bomber has been at that location ever since. Art christened it "Lacey Lady" in honor of his wife.

Art passed away in 2000. But here's the deal: From what I know now, if I had met Art Lacey coming down the street, I'd just empty my pockets of any money I might have and give it to him and then I'd ask, "Okay, what are we doing today? Whatever it is, I'm in." Art, as you might imagine, was a fixture at the restaurant, helping many people over the years and was known to bring his three-string guitar and sing an off-key 'Happy Birthday' to the kids. I like Art Lacey.

But everything has a time and after sixty-some-odd years it's "Lacey Lady's" time. For what? Removal, storage, restoration and *flight*. The legacy of Art and the B-17 still shines bright in the Lacey family. Jayson Scott, Art's grandson, and his wife, Terry, have formed the B-17 Alliance as a 501(3)c non-profit. You can join; you can donate; you can help…hands-on. Jayson and Terry are busy people, running the Bomber Restaurant and a catering business. They also curate the next-door museum dedicated to preserving war time memorabilia. Jayson says, "We're working hard on planning. This is new ground for us but we're dedicated to doing it." There's that word all EAA'ers understand: "dedicated." Jayson goes on, "I've learned there is a lot more behind the plane than just the actual physical structure. It's really more about the people and their experiences and trying to do something to help preserve those memories and their life experiences." Art Lacey would be proud to hear that.

Here's the other part of the story that I'm liking a lot. After searching around for a suitable airport for relocation (you know, one that recognizes passion and puts it a bit above the almighty dollar) they settled on McNary Field, Salem, Oregon. My airport! I can see their hangar from my hangar. That close! It's like the biggest deal around here since Mt. St. Helens blew, and that was in 1980. Salem is the capitol of Oregon so it's a bit of a government town, kinda sleepy except for the mostly predictable political spats. So, hey, I'm going to join the B-17 Alliance and hang around and help out. My buddy, Tom, down Dallas, Texas way, lives where there are lots of old airplane opportunities, mostly with the Commemorative Air Force, and he regularly takes advantage of it. I envy him that. But I'm not quite willing to travel that far; after years of traveling for a living, I'm a "homebody." So a B-17 in my backyard is like a "bird nest on the ground" (one of my Oklahoma-born Mother-in-Law's favorite sayings). I'm excited about it. And so are all the EAA Chapters in the area. To paraphrase a famous movie line: "If you bring it, they will come.

I was talking to a local resident about the B-17 coming to Salem and he said, "Yeah, I went and watched them bring some of the stuff in. Just looks like a bunch of stuff to me." That statement rather illuminates the difference between "other people" and "homebuilders/restorers." "Other people" see stuff and "homebuilder/restorers" see opportunity, challenge and passion. How much work is there to be done? Lots. A monumental amount. Maybe ten years' worth. But hey, we all know the formula: perseverance, time, and money. Some things are a part of who we are as a nation and a people. "Lacey Lady" is one of those things.

And, no, I could find no record of the guy paying off the $5.00 bet to Art. I'd like to think he did. I mean, good grief, Art covered the bet in monumental fashion. But, no matter. I think Art would consider "Lacey Lady" being returned to her original glory as payment in full.

19

THE ART OF THE JOUIRNEY

General aviation passengers don't often get to express themselves in aviation magazines. But they are very much a part of the 'aviation equation.' I know this because when my bride and I co-wrote "Small Airport America" about our first RV-8 flight to AirVenture we received the most letters ever, mostly about Kay's words, from passengers saying, "Bravo! 'Bout time we had a say!"

So, I asked my favorite passenger (and bride of fifty-two years) to pen some more thoughts on the subject. I also asked her because she's by far the better writer in the family. I'm a plodder; she actually has talent.

THE ART OF THE JOURNEY

Kay Lyn Paine

The day dawns with mellow warmth, sunshine flooding through the windows and seeping into my sleepy brain. It is going to be one of those mornings when there is every reason to go flying. Bright blue paints the sky, calm smooth air rides under the wings and the valley floor is alive with springtime growth in its colorful dance. All I have to do is quietly murmur…"Let's go fly". And before I know it, we are on our way to the airport in the little red '64 VW Beetle…the first leg if our journey.

Riding in the Bug is not merely transportation. When you open the doors and climb in, you are transcended to another time; slower, simpler, a roll up window and a pushout side vent, a radio that only gets an "oldies" station. People smile at you. People wave. People shout, "What year?" You smile back at strangers and you feel happy. It doesn't matter where you're going. Two lane roads are the best. You don't really care where you end up. The little car is taking you on a journey, showing you the scenery you don't usually even notice and you are smiling. It is like a safe little carnival ride. But today we are going to the airport to go flying. In our world, the bug and the airplane are equal. They are simple, mechanically sound and pleasing to the eye. But most of all they are trustworthy. They look good together. There is great harmony in a simple world.

The airplane, our RV8 has been waiting for us. She likes the sunshine glinting off her wings. Like a red tail hawk, she circles the fields in a purposeful scan of the beauty below. She begins to shudder a little as she comes to life, reminding me of her power. I adjust my headset and settle into my rear seat. I snug my shoulder harness, always mindful that tight is right. My senses begin emerging from their laziness. Everything is in clear focus. I hear the air traffic controller, the wind through the prop, feel the warmth of sunshine through the Plexiglas canopy, and feel the bump of the wheels rolling over the taxiway.

I like my view and pretend I am sitting atop a giant bird that is going to show me the world from its perspective. Forward is the rear of my pilot's head. I am comforted by his suntanned neck and his favorite flying baseball cap and his skill and gentle touch of the controls. He is one with this airplane, knows every square inch as only a builder can. To my left I can see the river that winds through the emerald green countryside. To my right I can see the snowcapped string of pearls that make up the Cascade Range and define our valley. The fields below are the greenest of spring green. The Pacific Ocean is just visible beyond the coastal mountain range. Above the roar of the engine, there is ultimate peace. We are again transcended to another time and life takes on another dimension. Simplicity. I am lifted above myself. I am flying.

This is not just another day. This is a journey. I see a giant arrow on the ground. It is pointing south. I remember that people used to create these arrows for the mail pilots who made their way in all kinds of weather to deliver their cargo. I see a 150 year old flour mill that straddles a creek that powers the giant turbines that ultimately grinds the flour the farmers have grown and delivered to the mill. I see the tiny towns and farms that quietly go about their business. And there's the steam powered logging mill that is still running and is a true piece of history nestled up against the mountains. I try to put these visions into my mental diary to recall and savor on a wet windy winter day in the future.

My mind often drifts as I fly along to adventures in the air others have experienced. I think of those mail pilots and the freezing weather and zero visibility they experienced, determined to deliver their cargo and get up again and do it the next day. I think of the young crewmen during war that fought from the skies in daring dogfights and came home victorious…or didn't come home at all. I think of the early pioneers who used their skills for navigation and sheer instinct to accomplish incredible feats that paved the way for pilots today. I consider all the pilots who enjoyed the great adventure of flying to OSH, the mecca for all things aviation.

They are all journeys of adventure and skill and heroism and determination.

We return to the airport and float above the runway and the wheels gently touch the earth. We roll back to the hangar and the little red Bug is waiting. We push the airplane back into its nest and close the hangar door. I wonder when another perfect day will come along and I will get to feel the exhilaration of being above the world and all of its complexities.

This day was touched by magic. And it all had to do with a journey. It started with an aging little car that allowed us to slow down. That is where the magic lies. Sometimes the world is too fast and too busy and too complicated. I think about how lucky I am to get to experience this feeling. And I wish I could share it with others. I think about what it could do for young people who have never experienced flight. That is why Young Eagles is so important. Sharing the magic.

I promise Lauran will return next month. After all, you read this magazine because it is written by many interesting and experienced aviators and people with great expertise in the field of flying and building. But we wanted to share what I get out of flying. I am not a pilot and have had to overcome some anxieties when I go flying. I have friends who are afraid to fly and can't imagine going up in a "small" plane, let alone a homebuilt. And I admit the day has to "feel" right, there has to be smooth air and few clouds and great visibility. I'm just picky that way. But I have my great adventure of flying to OSH and I will never forget the exhilaration of landing there and having people cheer as we taxied in to our homebuilt parking space. We dealt with weather issues and holding patterns and landing in the middle of cornfields in the Midwest. And I may or may not have kissed the ground when we landed back at home.

I have no great desire to experience loops or rolls or anything but straight and level. But I go. And my life would not be the same if I didn't. So, I share my thoughts to encourage others who might consider going along for the journey. Because I promise…it is one!

20

BAD VECTORS

Some aviation stories stay with you a long time. Some are a little scary; some are odd; some are, in retrospect, kinda funny. This is one of the 'kinda funny' ones, although at the time it was quite serious.

I was in the US Air Force, in my mid-twenties, with maybe a thousand hours of flying time. I had made the mistake upon graduation from pilot training-- in deference to my parents as a sole-surviving-son --of selecting to fly multi-engine airplanes. That turned out to be a huge mistake; fighters were who I was. So I volunteered for years for any fighter assignment to Viet Nam. No dice. The Air Force is funny that way: Once you get going down one track…multi-engine…it's hard to get off. In frustration, I submitted my paperwork to leave active duty at the end of my commitment. But, since I had a year left on that commitment, the Air Force said, "Alrighty then, we're gonna send you to Korea for a year to fly the C-47." I thought, 'Oh great, flying an old airplane hauling rubber dog do-do.' But, much to my surprise, I came to appreciate the history of the airplane and bonded with its rugged simplicity and the beautiful loud roar of the big round engines. And we worked the old girl, flew nearly every day to the various bases and outposts supplying food, mail, beer and various other deliveries (like whipped cream for the strawberry shortcake of a general who was pheasant hunting on some island). We landed on pavement, grass, and beaches in all manner of weather. My golly that airplane was tough and capable; it never whimpered; it just did what you asked it to do. You couldn't help but bond with it. It didn't go very fast but it demanded to be landed with prior planning and finesse. Screw it up and she was quite capable of bouncing you to the moon in protest. I and the C-47 became rather lost in aviation time; I could just as well have been a TWA Captain flying the line in 1939….except for the grass strips and beaches.

One place we flew supplies and mail to was Paeng-Yong-Do. ("Do" means island in Korean.) We just called it P-Y-Do. On the island, eighteen square miles, was a US Air Force radar site for early warning of enemy activity/threats. Also on the island was an orphanage run by a Catholic priest. Unofficially, we slipped them some supplies, too. (So sue me; those were the cutest little brown eyed-kids you've ever seen.) Often, when the kids saw us coming, they would come running down the hill and bring us homemade bread. It still makes me feel warm-and-fuzzy, even when I think about it forty-five years later.

Here's where P-Y-Do gets interesting. There was no runway; we landed on the beach….at low tide. Part of our weather briefing was the tide tables: We could only land at low tide and had to be out of there before high tide. And there was, as you might imagine, always a strong crosswind, either blowing inland or out to sea. The approach and landing demanded your attention, a curving visual to a beach cove. If you needed a reminder to be vigilant, there was a crumpled Korean C-46 pushed up against an embankment on the beach. Too, and here's the 'sticky-wicket,' the island was in international waters but above the DMZ (38th parallel). The North Koreans, to put it mildly, were not exactly enamored with our presence there. Thusly, on occasion, they would interrupt our radio transmissions during our approach to the island. We were briefed that, ostensibly, if they could lure us into their airspace by mistake they could use the "provocative" international incident as an excuse to take over P-Y-Do. Okay, whatever! I was in my twenties and bullet-proof (in my own mind, anyway) and if my mission was to deliver supplies I was going to deliver supplies. But not without some special procedures along with some good old fashioned American (GI) ingenuity.

As we approached the island we were handed off to the P-Y-Do radar site for vectors to the visual approach. We always went in VFR but there were often scud layers and there were also a bunch of other little islands up there, many with gun emplacements. You had to be *sure.* With our flight publications, we were also issued a small secret book of codes; the P-Y-Do controller (think radar intercept controller, not FAA-type controller) had the same book. When we initially checked in with the controller we'd go to the proper page in the book and ask him to authenticate "Charlie Whiskey." The controller would then have to give the proper response back, say, "Juliet Tango." Okay, now we're talking to the right guy. He'd give us headings to keep us clear of North Korean airspace and we'd follow them until we got the good visual. It was a good system for keeping us out of trouble except, sometimes, after you'd get a heading of "one-three-zero" you might get another one shortly thereafter of "continue left to one-eight-zero." Thing is, the voice sounded *almost* the same, and with no discernable accent. But we had a heightened awareness about such things so we'd ask for another authentication. It was a narrow corridor we were threading. P-Y-Do did have a TACAN so, with timing from experience, we also had our own pretty good idea of where we were. We *had* to have that. The 'vector game' would continue-- sometimes you could tell it was a different voice (I found myself envisioning North Koreans auditioning for the part) --and it sometimes became a little tedious. Still, we didn't relent in our vigilance; we didn't want to be the headline in the morning papers back home.

Now get ready for some good old fashioned GI ingenuity! You may not have been vectored for an approach by John Wayne or Jimmy Stewart but I have. One controller did an excellent John Wayne; another did Jimmy Stewart. "John" would say, "Waa-haa, Pilgrim. Ya better turn now to two-three-zero or I'll knock you to the next county." Jimmy might say, "Say, ah, ah, say, you know, turn to two-three-ah-zero, yeah, that oughta do it, and look for the airport at, ah, well, ah, ah, twelve o'clock." When that happened, we knew we were talking to Americans; the North Koreans had no answer for that. (I imagined North Koreans with raised eyebrows.) Cold War cat-and-mouse is what it was and ingenuity beat subterfuge.

After my Korean tour and after getting off active duty I was able to get a pilot slot with a National Guard unit, flying single-pilot, sitting on an ejection seat with a control stick between my knees. I was back in my happy place; I did that for the next sixteen years. But I never forgot my time in the C-47. It holds a soft spot in my heart. Too, old John Wayne and Jimmy Stewart movies always help bring back the memories.

21

AVIATION LIFE LESSONS

I am fascinated by the many ways aviation blends with life. People, at some point in their lives, grab onto aviation and then aviation grabs onto them. Know what I mean? Aviation becomes a thread in their life forever and the variety of those journeys is amazing….and almost always heartwarming.

I have to tell you about Ron Ochs. Ron is a retired rancher living in Madras, Oregon (think central Oregon). He and Laurice have been married fifty-eight years and raised four boys and two girls. He's presently in his 80's and dealing with cancer. He sold the bulk of his ranch in 1996 but kept the same house, the use of the grass airstrip that is surrounded by alfalfa just across from his house, and the hangar, in the barnyard about one-hundred yards away, that shelters his N3N. He and Laurice have worked hard and done well; they deserve everything that is good. But, of course, there's more to the story.

Ron grew up in Portland, Oregon. He and Laurice were in the fourth grade together. I asked Laurice if he was cute. She said, "Oh, I put my finger on him right away. Wasn't able to throw him down and hog-tie him until seventeen years later, though."

While in school, Ron got a job at a golf course. He loved it: the planting, the growing, the grooming, everything about it. Especially the being outside with nature part. That experience imprinted him. He decided early that he wanted to be a rancher. And that formed one of his philosophies of life: "If you decide early enough and work long enough you can achieve what you want." While working in Portland he remembers seeing a Stearman spraying, saying, "He was so low I could see the pilot's shirt sleeves blowing in the wind." And he remembers watching a P-39 takeoff, adding, "It sounded kinda funny and must have had a bad engine 'cause the guy turned right around and came back and landed." He saw those things……but he wanted to be a rancher.

Ron went on to college and eventually graduated from Oregon State University with a degree in agriculture. And then he got a draft notice from the US Army. He asked a friend who had flown B-24's in WWII, "What would you do?" The friend said, "I'd fly." So, in 1952, Ron signed up for duty with the US Air Force. He passed the tests and entered the Aviation Cadet program. He described it as being "the lowest of the low." He had his work cut out for him.

Initial flight training was in a Cub, the military's way of determining flying aptitude before letting the cadets fly the more expensive-to-operate airplanes. He had taken some "pre-lessons" from a civilian flight school so did well with the military Cub flying. Then it was on the Bartow, Florida for training in the T-6. He said, "I almost flunked instruments. I met a board and they asked if they gave me six more hours could I do it. I said yes. And I did do it." Then Ron went to Bryan, Texas for T-28 and T-33 training. Upon graduation he was awarded US Air Force wings and a commission as a 2nd Lieutenant.

The new 2Lt. Ochs was then assigned to Del Rio, Texas for gunnery training in the F-84 (commonly called 'the straight-wing eighty-four'). Then it was to Luke AFB, Arizona for training in the F-84F (commonly called 'the bent-wing eighty-four'). He said, "It was still a pretty new airplane so there were lots of glitches still being worked out. I only got about ten hours in it." Next was Clovis, New Mexico for training in the F-86H. He said, "The Migs were out-climbing the -86's so the "H" was designed with 30% more thrust. But it had a bunch of glitches, too, so I only got another ten or eleven hours."

Next stop was Korea. It was 1954. Ron was twenty-four years old. His squadron commander was Bud Anderson. (They still correspond.) Signing in, they said, "Oh, you've flown the -84 and -84F, too. Oh....wait....you haven't flown very much!" So Ron began learning his trade, on the job, in the Korean theater. He did not shy from the task; he's a proud man (and still is).

Ron began with, "In dog fighting, we'd go out and this guy would wax me every time. I finally figured out what he was doing and eventually got him a couple times. Then we finally got to the point where it was always a stalemate." This led to another of Ron's axioms: "Flying is so much a function of experience." In gunnery, shooting at the tow target, Ron was missing. One of his squadron mates told him, "Roll-in on the cable and work your way back." So he did and hit the rigging holding the target and blew the whole target away." Another axiom: "Sometimes you just need that right piece of information."

Another time, a squadron mate (a former crop duster) said, "Ochs, I'm getting sick of your join-ups. They stink. Match lead's speed and fly, don't wobble, your way into position." Ron took that to heart and the next time they flew, he did just that. He said, "I could see lead's head looking around for me. He looked to his left and there I was. His head appeared to jerk in surprise. And then he gave me a thumbs-up!" Sixty-years later and Ron remembers-- and is justifiably proud of –that thumbs-up. Lt. Ron Ochs was an F-86 fighter pilot in Korea. He named his airplane "The Portland Rose." Today he says,

"I felt privileged to fly with those guys. They were competitive; they were good; they were fun; they were patriots." And with that, Ron's year in Korea and military commitment were up. He came home to Oregon.....to be a rancher. But don't think that he was done with aviation.

Ron married Laurice (after Laurice hog-tied him) in 1957. She was now a school teacher. Ron took a job that allowed him to travel; while traveling he'd look for ranches. While he was working in Madras they learned of a ranch for sale. Ron says, "We figured we had enough money to run a ranch but not buy it. They wanted $17,000.00 down. We didn't have that." Enter a wealthy businessman from Portland who knew the ranch was prime bird hunting so offered, "I'll make the down payment if you'll give me hunting rights." Ron said, "Okay, but we're paying it back." The business man said, "Okay, but at no interest." Those were still the days of honor and handshakes.

So Ron was now the rancher he dreamed of being-- raising hay and cows. Hard work; good work. He and Laurice raised their kids. All attended Madras High School. All the boys wrestled. Then tragedy. One son, Nels, perished in an auto accident as a teenager. He was the one child who had shown an interest in continuing on the ranch. In Nels' honor, the Ochs sponsored a high school wrestling tournament every year for thirty years. Laurice said to me, "He was a good boy." Of that I have no doubt.

Ron returned to his love of flying. He bought and flew-- off the ranch airstrip, of course --a Cessna 180. And then a Cessna 185. Then he found a N3N in Wyoming, a duster with a 450 hp engine. Being a duster, it had a lot of modifications. Ron spent the better part of seven years restoring it. He then sold it and bought a stock N3N with a Wright 760 on it. He still has this airplane today. It's a beautiful piece of history.

Ron started having a fly-in at his ranch airstrip. That stopped when the ranch sold but rather continues to this day at the Madras Airport, eventually morphing into the Madras Airshow in conjunction with the Erickson Aircraft Collection (think flyable WWII aircraft). Ron volunteers at the airshow, as well as serving at the Reno Air Races. He also donated a Nieuport 24bis (replica) to the Western Antique Aeroplane and Automobile Museum, Hood River, Oregon ("Plane Talk," Jan '15, SA).

From working on a golf course to fighter pilot to successful rancher to family man to giving back, that's a life well lived, with character and aviation running through it. As you can imagine, just sitting, the day of my visit, at the big farm table in the old farmhouse and having lunch with Ron and Laurice and daughter Barbara was an….honor.

22

AVIATION COURTESY

Fair warning, this isn't going to be a warm and fuzzy column. Instead, it's a column about some things that need to be said. We're all in this aviation thing together so sometimes we need to address that which, well, needs to be addressed. So that's what we're gonna do. We're all big boys and girls and can handle it.

It all started innocently enough when I attended an aviation safety seminar this spring. It was hosted by Willamette Aviation, Aurora, Oregon (UAO). Willamette Aviation is very proactive in sponsoring seminars, ground schools, learning sessions, all that good stuff. This particular seminar was 'geared' toward aircraft homebuilder safety. I love the interaction with the other attendees. A topic comes up and all kick it around, offering advice, experiences and solutions. Good stuff! Scott, who works in engineering for Van's Aircraft, talked about aircraft inspections. Many accidents are the result of inspectable items so, of course, those items are important to discuss. Scott also had photos of cracks and flaws and such found during inspections, many of which I wondered if I would have picked up on if it were my airplane. They were photos to make you think. And he also talked about something as simple as the inspection light you use: Use a good one! With all the nifty LED lights out there, there's no reason not to have one.

Then Van (Dick VanGrunsven) spoke. I've said it before and I'll say it again: When he speaks, I listen. And so does everybody else. The thing is, he not only has so much knowledge about experimental aviation, he also has sincerity, humility and passion. He talked about pilot loss of control, the cause of a lot of accidents. He believes in the new stall warning systems for experimentals and that they can help save lives. And he spoke of 'stunt flying.' You know the kind: low level passes over the local runway and steep pullups, that sort of nonsense. That pilot may impress the uninitiated but seldom impresses his peers. It's just hogwash (my words, not Van's). One attendee suggested having a place on-line where pilots could report egregious flying. Hmmmm…the peer pressure concept. There's a quote in my book of quotations, "If Airplanes Could Talk," that says, "Impromptu airshows for friends or relatives often result in death." I still stand by that quote. I'm reminded of the time when I was in US Air Force pilot training that at T-37 instructor pilot was doing cloverleafs, unauthorized, over his grandparent's family farm and ended up crashing, 90 degrees vertical to the ground, in front of them.

Another quote from "If Airplanes Could Talk": "If you do something during a flight that you haven't thought about before the flight, risk increases exponentially."

Have you ever met a pilot who says he's dangerous? Probably not. It's like you've experienced a lot of bad drivers in your time but you've never had one tell you that *they* were a bad driver. It's *always* the other guy. Well, I'm going to tell you about a dangerous pilot. This came to me in a letter from a reader. The reader is retired military and has a J-3 Cub that he absolutely loves to fly. Nothing not to like about that; flying a Cub is about as aviation-pure as it gets. Then he went on to say this:

"I would like to tell you about a Supercub fly-in I flew to this last weekend in northeast Oklahoma. Shortly after arriving I invited another pilot to fly to a different airport for fuel.

We took off and were flying over the river at about 500' when from below and to our right an RV streaked perpendicular across our path not thirty yards in front. Wham-bam! We immediately hit his wake as he flew up and to our left, where he turned and flew down to a few yards above our left wing. I'm sure he thought he was hidden by the wing but my co-pilot in the front seat could see him in the skylight.

My co-pilot friend was visibly shaken. (He is a high-time commercial, multiengine, instrument, CFI.) All the way back he kept saying, 'Damn RV drivers, I hate them! They're all like that!'

When we returned to the fly-in after fueling I had made up my mind that if the yellow RV was still there, I was leaving. I was honestly afraid of what I intended to do to the pilot if he was still there. He was there and I packed up immediately and flew out.

Twenty-years ago my co-pilot lost a good friend and mentor and his wife when an RV pilot making a similar strafing run plowed right through the middle of their airplane. Four killed. The day before that same RV pilot strafed my friend when he was on final for another airport. Instead of making an issue out of it, my friend decided to shrug it off and say nothing. Twenty years he has been blaming himself for what happened that next day.

This time my friend found and confronted the Oklahoma RV pilot. The guy was unapologetic and laughed it off, acting a total jerk. After the confrontation, my friend and his wife packed up their airplane and left the fly-in as well.

I know from your column that you fly an RV. I wanted to ask, do you fly strafing runs like this guy? Reading your columns, I can't believe you do. But it's obvious that RV drivers have questionable reputations.

I fully intended to make some stops and fly to Oshkosh in July for the first time. But if this is the type of crowd a Supercub/EAA fly-in gathers, I want nothing to do with it."

I don't know about you but reading about the errant RV pilot got my dander up. (And my answer to the reader's question was, "No, I don't strafe unsuspecting pilots. Never would I do that!") There is absolutely no place for crud like that! It's bad for you; it's bad for me; it's bad for everybody. And the reader is not a guy who scares easily: he served in the infantry in the Army in the rice paddies and jungles of Vietnam in 1968……you don't do that unless you have character and courage. And the fact that the RV guy just 'blew it off' makes him a dangerous pilot. Presumably, he's still out there…..and unsafe. He knows who he is but it's unlikely he'll read this because the jerks are generally not the ones who attend safety seminars.

Want to dogfight? Attend an air combat course, where they fly like airplanes. Fancy yourself a low level aerobatic pilot? Earn your low level aerobatic waiver. Want to fly formation? Attend a formation clinic. Do not….do not!....bounce a fellow pilot in a slower airplane who's out enjoying the scenery. That's bush league.

To the jerk RV pilot: There are a lot of warbird pilots who could do the same to you. But they don't because they are professionals.

Every airplane has its rights. Back in my airline days I used to chafe when we'd be at some big airport and a Cessna 172 would taxi by and a youngish First Officer would derisively say, “What’s he doing here?” (Never mind that the First Officer was flying the same type airplane a year and a half ago before he got his airline job.) Airline cockpits are no place to start a fight so I’d usually just say, “He has every right to be here.”

Some things to think about, my friends. Aviation courtesy *is* a safety technique. Bottom line: we can’t be our own worst enemy and survive.

23

HIS FATHER'S STEARMAN

He was imbued with it at an early age: flying. That interest was fostered by his father and the memory of his father, with substantial encouragement from his mother. One airplane was particularly motivational: Stearman NC5057N. Rather, I should say, it was a picture of NC5057N that captured his soul. "He" is Pat Carpenter, airline captain, and his story follows.

First, however, I have to mention the story comes to you almost by accident. Last February my bride and I flew commercially to Maui, Hawaii to escape the Oregon rain for a bit. On board the flight, a Flight Attendant introduced the captain as Pat Carpenter. I said to my bride, "I know him. He used to be a co-pilot of mine." It being a full flight (aren't they all these days!) I wasn't able to catch up to Pat until, at baggage claim, I saw him walking by with his crew. I walked up to him and stuck out my hand. He said, "Well, son-of-a-gun, Lauran Paine. You used to try to drill stuff into my thick skull." Our meeting was pretty brief given that our bags were on the carousel and his crew van was waiting but, as we parted, he said, "I found my dad's Stearman." Actually, I don't think I ever knew his dad had a Stearman so I hollered back at him, "I'd like to know more about that." When Pat got home, he called some of our mutual airline buddies and got my number. We talked and I got the rest of the story. It's a good one.

Like many young men at the time, William F. Carpenter, Pat's dad, came home from WWII after fighting a hard war in the Pacific. He came home ready to get back to his life and his dream of flying. Using the GI Bill and armed with a strong work ethic he enrolled in the Spartan School of Aeronautics in Tulsa, Oklahoma. His best friend, Dave Gauthier, also home from service in the Pacific with the Navy, enrolled too. (Dave later retired from Northwest Airlines as a Boeing 747 captain.) While at Spartan, Bill and Dave learned of military surplus Stearman's for sale: The ones with less than 250 hours flight time sold for $500.00; the ones with more than 250 hours were $250.00. Armed with savings and some borrowed (from family) money, Bill and Dave and two other youthful Spartan buddies showed up at the auction at first light. They picked over the line of airplanes to find the best engine and prop combinations with the least damage. They found three to their liking....of the $250.00 variety....and flew them home that same day. The fourth buddy drove the car back to Tulsa. The story is a little murky on who got what N-numbers and why, but Bill eventually ended up with Stearman NC5057N. It was painted bright yellow with a maroon bomb burst on the top wing. How'd it get to be so fancy? Also murky. But that paint job played a big part in its fate.

In 1950, Bill sold NC5057N to help support his growing family. He sold it to a young crop duster in Argusville, North Dakota (near Fargo) named Warren Walkinshaw. Warren paid $800.00 for the airplane, buying in to add to his fleet of dusters.

During the 1950's, Bill Carpenter worked as a mechanic for Northwest Airlines while also flying for KSTP TV in St. Paul, Minnesota. He was also doing some test flying for a new short-takeoff-and-landing airplane (STOL), called the Helio Courier. With all the test flying he did with that airplane, he was dubbed the "Daddy of Helio." That experience eventually led him and his family to Peru to fly for a mining company. The Helio was 'just the ticket' for the short, high-altitude strips there.

Then tragedy. Pat lost his father to his love of flight. In the late 50s, Bill perished in a flying accident, long before his family was ready to say goodbye. Fortunately, the kids were blessed with a strong and loving mom who raised the four of them with a good sense of where they came from. Invariably, her stories were intermixed with flying, about their father's character and his love of flying. Friends and relatives added to the William F. Carpenter lore, saying things like, "He was someone who could put a smile on our face." And there was "The Picture." It was a picture of a yellow Stearman....NC5057N.....soaring above the clouds. Except that it wasn't exactly that: The picture was of Pat's dad in the Stearman, engine running; then that picture was laid next to a blue background with painted clouds and that combination was photographed from inside the top of a hangar. No matter the circumstance or the methodology, that picture provided Pat with dreams and motivation....and still does. Everyone in the family has a framed copy of it to this day.

Pat decided early on, "If flying was good enough for my dad, it's good enough for me." He pursued aviation, building model airplanes and by joining the Civil Air Patrol, eventually having a rag-wing Cessna 140 and entering the US Air Force, becoming a crewmember on the F-4 Phantom. From there he got to where he is today: in the left front seat of an airliner.

But what of the fate of NC5057N? Pat pondered that question often. Unknown to Pat at the time, Warren rigged the Stearman for spraying but then came up with a different idea. He decided NC5057N was "just too pretty." (The paint job, remember!) So he used it to build his business as an 'ambassador airplane,' demonstrating spraying (using water) in front of crowds at state fairs. He also gave rides. And he used it for teaching spray pilots, many of them now retired airline pilots. He often quipped, "I shoulda charged Notrthwest for all that training." Then the airplane was used to celebrate North Dakota's Centennial Celebration in the 1980's. Warren's daughter, Helen, flew the airplane throughout the state, airport to airport, making celebratory mail deliveries. Warrens' fleet eventually grew to sixteen airplanes, twelve of them Stearman's, one a "pretty one." They called the fleet "Walkinshaw's Warriors." Warren is an inductee into the North Dakota Hall of Fame.

Curiosity finally got the better of Pat and, armed with an N-number, he queried the FAA's registration branch. NC5057N was registered to one Warren Walkinshaw in Argusville, North Dakota. Still! Fifty years later! Pat phoned Warren and explained to the answering machine that he was inquiring about his dad's old airplane. In his excitement and haste, Pat neglected to leave his return phone number. With no answer immediately forthcoming from Warren, Pat moved on to other things.

Then came Christmas day. Pat's wife, Kathy, gave Pat a book titled "Pat the Pilot." In it were pictures of Pat's Civil Air Patrol days, his Air Force days and so on. On the last page was "The Picture." Opposite the picture was an invitation from Warren Walkinshaw to come back to Argusville and fly NC5057N! You see, Kathy had followed up on what Pat had started. There's a word for what Kathy did: love.

The logistics of the two family's meeting took some time to arrange. Complicating the reunion was the fact that Warren, now in his eighties, was heading to the Mayo Clinic in Rochester, New York to have his thymus removed. But destiny eventually overcame obstacles and they all gathered in Argusville to reunite with NC5057N.

It was a cool October day when the families met. There were a lot of greetings and hugs befitting the longstanding connections. In the background stood the yellow Stearman, a little dusty but still very, very proud. You can imagine the emotions. Helen, bundled up for the cold, took Pat (and his brothers) for rides. It was something that can't adequately be described; it was something that you can only *feel.*

A week later, Pat was flying a new generation Boeing 737 from Anchorage, Alaska to Chicago, Illinois and passed over Fargo. His thoughts drifted to Argusville and NC5057N, the airplane that shaped him and has meant so much to his family. Aviation connections are magical.

24

THE MCGEE CUMMUNITY

It's unavoidable. When you meet with pilots to talk about a story you get a lot of peripheral stories, too. But, hey, I love it. That's what pilots do: talk. And laugh. And that's what we did when we met at Scott Chamber's house. You see, I had received information from two different pilots about a fella named Fred Frederiks. Fred is a neighbor of Scott's so I invited myself to Scott's house to find out more. And there is this: Scott is a former co-pilot of mine. Scott mentioned to Rick Doherty that I was coming and Rick said, "If he's coming, I'm coming, too." (Rick is also a former co-pilot of mine.) And Tim James stopped by, a friend and talented serial builder from Aurora, Oregon. He's a story unto himself but photographing him is like trying to take a picture of Bigfoot on a moonless night. He darts! Anyway, before we could get to the subject....Fred....we probably told seven-hundred stories. What one doesn't remember, another does. Yammer, yammer, laughter, more yammer and more laughter. That's the cycle and it's grand! Too, there's a whole lot of, "What ever happened to so-and-so?"

Scott went so far as to open his logbook and found some pages where I had given him, a new co-pilot, Initial Operating Experience (IOE). He had dutifully logged the things we had done but, on the last day, he wrote "a really fun day." That was probably twenty-five years ago. And I remembered flying with Rick and him telling the story of when, right after he got his Private, he offered to take his dad, an Eastern Oregon wheat farmer, for a ride. His dad responded, "Ain't got no use for it." That's okay; he was about raising wheat. You do what ya gotta do. And there were lots of pictures of beautiful grass strips in the Idaho back-country that are made to order for the large-tire Cubs that Tim fancies. Talk about pictures of a bunch of happy/smiling pilots: that's real flyin' right there!

Now here my buddies are, Scott flying for United and Rick for Alaska. It did this ol' pilot's heart good to see them "all growed up and doin' well." I laughed when they said, "Yeah, when we were flying with you, you were probably fifty years old and we thought you were older'n dirt. Well, now we're fifty-ish and it don't seem so old." Nice that they had good memories of my working days....made me feel good.

Now back to where I was going with all this: Fred. Several years ago Scott got the itch to make the move to some farm property. He found "McGee" (67OR). It was a home on forty acres located in Willamette Valley agricultural land....and had a grass airstrip! Bingo! Jack McGee was the owner but he had perished in a crash. His two sons...one a pilot.... took the farm over and tried to keep it up but eventually put it up for sale. Scott made the deal. There was much work to be done but Scott dove in, hammer and shovel in hand. One day he was walking along the fence line and happened upon his new neighbor, Fred Frederiks. Fred is a retired veterinarian, of Dutch ancestry, who remembers his folks talking of when the Nazis took the family farm. Scott introduced himself and mentioned that he was a pilot. Fred said, "You're not going to fly off the strip are you? We've had nothing but problems." How's that for an opening by your neighbor regarding your newly acquired dream airstrip? Scott took the high road, saying, "Let me know how to be a good neighbor." That was a good decision. Scott asked Fred, "Ever been flying?" Fred said, "No. McGee's never invited me." Scott continued with,

"Would you like to go for a ride someday?" Fred wasn't immediately forthcoming with an answer but a few days later he mentioned to Scott, "Maybe I would like to go for a ride someday."

Now here is where Scott's aviation community of friends kicked in. Scott, at the time, had no airplane (except for the RV-8 he was feverishly working on) so asked his friend, John Fitzgerald (yet another former co-pilot of mine), if he'd give Fred a ride in his Cessna 185. John said, "Sure." After John took Fred for a flight, another friend, Jerry Trimble, took Fred for a helicopter ride. Fred liked the rides!

So then what happens? One day Fred mentioned to Scott, "Ya know, I might like to learn to fly." Scott is a friendly and caring type of guy; that's all he needed to hear to 'get the ball rolling'. He sent Fred to Aurora Aviation at Aurora Airport (UAO). There his CFI was Sadie (who my oldest son once instructed with, her dad a former F-16 pilot). Fred flies with Sadie for 10 hours then stops by one day and says to Scott, "I think we ought to buy an airplane. What kind should we buy?" Scott's thinking...besides 'wow!'....something basic, like a Cessna 172 or a Cub (secretly mostly thinking Cub). So the 'community' puts their heads together and eventually finds a Husky in Arizona. After a pre-buy inspection Scott and John went down to pick it up. Fred gave John a signed blank check. A blank check! For an airplane! Scott wrote the check and then he and John flew the Husky to its new home at McGee and parked it in Scott's hangar.

Now Scott really had to spring into action because he had let his CFI expire. He set about to renew it with examiner Mary Crittendon (yup, another former co-pilot of mine). She put him through the paces and renewed him. And then the real work began. Scott taught Fred ground school in his hangar and then began the flight instruction in the Husky. Scott said, "It was like teaching family. You don't want to leave any stone unturned. He was a friend and neighbor and you're going to be watching him fly regularly. You wanted to get everything right." And he did. Fred soloed and later got his Private certificate. He has over 400 hours now and has flown the Idaho back country, the San Juan's and many other interesting destinations.

So digest all that a bit: Scott meets his neighbor who wants nothing to do with airplanes flying off the strip adjacent to his property; Scott takes the high road of 'good neighboring' and Fred ends up buying an airplane and Scott teaches him how to fly....with the help of a willing and supporting airport community of friends. It'd be great to see the story repeated in other locations across this wonderful land.

All this happened a few years ago. Fred is seventy-five now and winters in Mexico (where he volunteers at spay and neuter clinics, to give you a glimpse into the character of the man.) Scott has since purchased the Husky but Fred still flies it when he comes home; Scott is happy to honor that agreement.

During the day of storytelling I learned something I did not know: Scott's dad, Dwight, was a Marine helicopter pilot in Vietnam. I always knew Scott was a patriot; now I know why. His father's Marine memorabilia is proudly displayed in the family room. In his spare time Scott raises filberts and he and his bride, Judy, also raise Labradors.

To me it's a heartwarming story of airport community and Fred, a guy willing to try something new. The visit was....... to paraphrase a friend of mine....."a really fun day."

25

AVIATION BY OSMOSIS

(paragraphs in italics are my bride's)

My best friend and bride-- one and the same person --has flown with me many times over the years. She's not an avid flyer but she goes. I respect her feelings; a lot of people don't like being off the ground. But, still, she goes. Since she doesn't have a lot of interest in flying, she doesn't ask many questions. She often takes a book to read. And she doesn't like landing; she looks down during landings. You get the picture.

Over the years of flying with me, however, it can't be avoided: aviation learning takes place. It just does. That was brought home to me during a recent cross-country we flew to visit an Air Force buddy (and best man at our wedding) in California. He has a cabin on Buck's Lake that has been in his family since 1953. The nearest town/airport is Quincy, California/Gansner Field (2O1). It's nestled in the hills at 3419' field elevation and is 4100' feet long. Nice enough. It's a little less than three hours to fly there from Salem, Oregon (which beats a two day drive, which was my selling point for flying). The weather for departure was basically good: nice day, clear and warm. But there was a lot of haze due to some recent forest fires.

We took off into the smooth morning air. On climb out, bride asked, "Are you gonna call those people?" I replied, "Those people???" She answered, "Yeah, you know. The ones you talk to while we're flying along." She was talking about flight following and, "Yes, I will call them." I was duly impressed that she was thinking about that! Ya see, she remembers from our first trip to AirVenture, with the airplane just "finished," that I had yet to install a transponder. Which was fine, as far as I was concerned, since we just went from small airport to small airport. So the only traffic we saw, which wasn't much, was traffic we *saw*. Somewhere along the way she found out other people had "transponders." And she found out what they did. It was then suggested to me that we install one. When we got home from OSH, I did that. She loves flight following.

I love flying. Just not all aspects of flying. I love going on a trip with my pilot buddy at the controls, looking out at the incredible Northwest scenery and looking down at the windy truck clogged freeway. I may appear to be reading, but I am very tuned in. I do like those people who follow us. They are my friends. They track us and get very concerned if we don't make it. I listen to every transmission and have come to pretty much understand the lingo. Especially Experimental Two One Four Kilo Tango. That's us.

Basically, on this trip, we headed south (with flight following) and then took a left at Red Bluff and headed toward the Sierra-Nevada mountains and Quincy. Airport in sight, we began our letdown. The AWOS reported winds light and variable with a very warm surface temperature. Then, just below the hilltops.....wham!!.....turbulence. A big ol' sudden-hard-bump. Bride said, "My iPad just jumped off my lap!" I said, "Sorry." But the bumps continued. On the downwind there is a small hill between you and the airport. In the pattern, bride asked, "You see that mountain in front of you?" I said, "Yup. We're getting ready to turn base now." On base she said, "You see that other mountain in front of you?" I said, "Yup. Turning final now." It was hot and jerky/bumpy so we got a couple crow-hops on landing. From the back seat came, "Whew!" I added, "We're here."

I love lifting off and straight and level and smooth air and no bumps. And let me tell you, those mountains offered up some BIG bumps. My iPad literally flew up to the canopy. Then there were those pesky mountains coming at us. I am usually very quiet on landing, appreciating that the pilot is busy up there. But hey, we had to wiggle between two mountains and it was slightly uncomfortable heading straight for them. I knew he knew what he was doing, but it couldn't hurt to be like one of those screens on airliners that say, "Pull up, pull up" or whatever they say. Then we had about a 3-bouncer landing and he was talking to the plane, "come on baby, come..." I hoped she was listening.

Later, on the ground, bride asked, "Should I have said anything about those hills?" I said, "Absolutely. If you have a concern, bring it up. We're in this thing together." She gave me her knowing nod.

The visit was grand. My buddy and his bride are great hosts and the cabin welcomes you with the patina of many previous family gatherings of fun and happiness. We dented their supply of steaks and adult beverages and they didn't even care.

A couple days later the weather was much the same for the trip home: clear, warm and hazy. Except there was solid cloud cover reported over our destination, but it was forecast to break up before our arrival. (There's a quote in my aviation book of quotes: "Remember, a forecast is a guess.") On climb out my bride asked, "You gonna call those people?" I said, "Yup. Just getting ready to." I called them, they were nice and we were on our way.

Enroute I kept checking the weather and the clouds at home were not breaking up. (I'm a day-VFR experimental; *very* VFR, no attitude indicator at all.) Soon it became decision time on the weather. Bride was reading. I spoke up with, "We're gonna land up here pretty soon before we get into the hills and low clouds and wait for the weather at home to clear." She looked down and spotted Siskiyou County (KSIY), 150 X 7500, uncontrolled and inviting. Bride said, "Okay, let's land there." I think she wanted to get on the ground and get everything sorted out. We landed-- another dang crow-hop (I was getting tired of doing that!). We parked in front of the old, decrepit building where I took my first airplane ride from (SA, July '12). It was all locked up, except for one unlocked and clean room: the bathroom. We wandered about for a couple hours finding a white, concrete block building that said "EAA" on it and, under some brush, a very long-eared jack rabbit. We talked about the time we had to wait-out a thunderstorm in Nebraska during our last trip to Oshkosh. Bride doesn't much enjoy such deviations but she understands them.

I knew weather was becoming an issue. I was looking to the east and could clearly see we could swing in that direction and likely get under the cloud layer. Plan B gave me some comfort. I also knew that if we ducked under the clouds too soon, we would be in the mountains around Roseburg. Heightened awareness. It was hot and we bounced again, this time narrowly missing a large bird tumbling around underneath us. We were marooned at an old abandoned terminal where Lauran had his first ever airplane ride. Rather romantic, don't you think?

The weather at home finally reported broken clouds so we launched again. The nice…flight following….controller said, "You got a lot of cloud cover ahead. You may want to get under it early before you get to Salem." Bride said, "That was nice." She wasn't reading now; she was into it. I didn't want to get down too early because there are lots of mountains until you get just south of Eugene. Still, I appreciated the controller thinking ahead with us. Just south of Eugene I spotted a big hole and got underneath the 3500' layer. It got bumpy again but we were in the valley with home just ahead. We landed…..I finally got a good one!......and bride spoke with, "I may or may not kiss the ground." I don't remember if she did or not but I do know she was glad to be home. So was I.

We slipped down through the clouds and skimmed along under them at 3500'. It was a bit turbulent but bearable. My job is to watch for traffic and I happen to be a very good spotter. Self-preservation. I may not be a pilot but I am a half decent copilot. I even take the controls occasionally when my pilot is checking charts. Briefly. Okay, for a nanosecond or two. It's what we do, always have. We have been a team for 49 years. Call me lucky.

The thing is, what we did, what we had to do, is just normal, everyday run-of-the-mill VFR cross-country flying. Pilots do it every day; decisions are a part of the process. But here I was: tired. That bothered me a bit. Of course, the trip was just a few weeks after my Achilles surgery. And I don't like talking about it but I am getting older. I like my life simple; I like my flying simple. I ain't done but I am picking my battles. Still, it was a great trip to see great friends and I'm forever grateful for flight and, mostly, for my bride.

26

STEAM VISITS GLASS

Okay, this story comes with a caveat. I visited Advanced Fight Systems, manufacturers of those fancy flight instrumentation systems, commonly called "glass panels." But this is not an info-mercial. There are other companies also supplying amazing instrument panel products. This is the story behind the story: the people at AFS.

I visited because 1) my buddy Nel told me to (I seldom do what he wants but, sometimes, if I comply he buys lunch) and 2) they are just up the road from me in Canby, Oregon and 3) I am kinda the "anti-glass" guy, preferring round dials, commonly called "steam gauges." So my visit was innocent, devoid of any commercial intent. But I do enjoy meeting good and hardworking people and that's exactly who I met at AFS.

I'm familiar with glass. I flew it during the last years of my airline career. It's pretty magnificent stuff: When you're going into LAX or DEN at night in the middle of winter you want all the bells-and-whistles and glass gives you that. But when I'm flying day-VFR in my homebuilt I want to look outside, enjoy, and not push one dang button. I've been flying my airplane for ten years now and not once have I regretted my decision to fly "steam." Oh, I know, I'm a relic swimming against the tide but, hey, as they say in this day and age: whatever. Anyway, that's my disclaimer.

Advanced Flight Systems is owned and operated by Rob and Jenny Hickman. It is a successful business that has grown exponentially but is not so big that you can't sit down at the break room lunch table and munch donuts supplied by a friend, Ishmael Fuentes, and casually converse with Rob and Jenny. I asked them not much about their products; I asked about their journey. And I emphasize *them.* They built AFS together and each knows it inside and out. And all the while raising a family and being faithfully devoted to experimental aviation. Bottom line: they are really easy people to like.

Rob is the engineer/tinkerer/pilot. Jenny is the receptionist/business person (with an accounting degree) and also the voice, i.e., "check oil pressure" and "angle, angle, push" for the AFS product line. The story how they got to where they are now has, of course, some zigs and zags but is one driven by talent, hard work, doing the right thing and.....family. Rob's dad was in the foundry business. His dad needed an electrical engineer so Rob attended Oregon State and Portland State and got his degree. While at Oregon State he got "the flying bug" and joined the OSU Flying Club. When Rob eventually went to work for his dad, Jenny was also working for his dad. I didn't ask about the sideways glances that must have happened in the work place but.....they later married. They're a handsome couple.

Then the economy took a downturn and the business was sold to new owners in Alabama. By this time Rob and Jenny had their first child, Jeffrey. So off they went to Alabama with all their worldly possessions. They were there for four years and two more children arrived, Brian and Kelsey. While there, Rob found an RV-4 tail kit for $500.00 and thus started his experimental aviation journey.

Rob and Jenny both wanted badly to return home to Oregon and did so in 1996. Rob drove what Jenny described as "the biggest rental truck you could rent" and Jenny followed with the three kids and towing a trailer with a partially completed RV-4 in it. When Jenny was telling the story I commented, "You've paid your dues." She replied, "I *have*."

Back home in Oregon Rob went back to work. He finished the RV-4 and first flight was on 9-9-1999 (by Jerry VanGrunsven). Along the way of building, Rob wanted an engine monitor. He thought to himself, "I can build that." And he did, using one monochrome screen. Another builder noticed it and said, "I want one of those." As happens in the experimental aircraft community, notes are compared, tools and ideas are shared and friendships are made. Rob became a member of what was then called the "Home Wing," to which the VanGrunsven's belonged. The "Home Wing" is now EAA Chapter 105, Portland, Oregon. Jenny is the Treasurer, and has been for some time now.

Back to the engine monitor. You might call it the birth of a business. Rob and Jeffrey flew the RV-4 to Oshkosh for the first time not long after the plane was completed. They didn't have a booth; they just took the monitor and showed it around. By this time the monitor was now full color with several new functions. Dewey Conroy of Pacific Coast Avionics had seen it, too, and told Rob, "I can sell that." Later, an article appeared in Van's Aircraft newsletter, the "RVator." Jenny said, "I remember the day. The fax used to have an order every so often but then, after the article and such, here came an order. And then another. And another. Suddenly there were twenty of them." You can imagine their excitement: A business was born. But, of course, in the electronics business, you can't hang your hat on one product for long.

Rob went to work on other things. He explained some of the technicalities of doing so and I smiled and nodded but understood little. I'm technologically challenged. But the gist of it all was that he was taking his engine monitor to new levels, as in an EFIS (Electronic Flight Instrument System). But he needed an AHRS (Attitude Heading Reference System) to take it to full instrument panel level. Crossbow Technology made them but they were large and expensive. Over time they became smaller and less expensive and Rob was able to work a deal with Crossbow. Then came synthetic vision and mapping combined with the EFIS. And then a partnership with Dynon so AFS customers could order a complete instrument panel package…including radio, intercom, transponder, etc. With all that technology joining together, installation could sometimes be a challenge. Rob's answer was to offer full instrument panels as "plug and play." Tell him what kind of airplane you have and what you want for instruments and radios and he'll build the complete panel and wiring harness for you. You have but to install the panel and plug it in. Voila! Technology that works….and makes you smile.

One story I really enjoyed was the one about the development of the electronic angle of attack/stall warning system. They're life savers in our experimental aviation hobby. Jim Frantz is an engineer/pilot who flew for Northwest Airlines. He developed an electronic angle of attack indicator for general aviation. He knows Jerry VanGrunsven, who also flew for Northwest. Jim wanted to retire so offered the system to Rob. Rob was thinking, "Man, I got a lot on my plate right now, don't know that I need to be spending any more money." Jim then invited Rob and Jenny to his place in Minneapolis. They went. Over the kitchen table they worked out a deal that was good for all, sketched it out on a piece of paper and signed it, shook hands and a deal was struck. Right then. Right there. At the kitchen table.

The Hickman kids? Jeffrey got his electrical engineering degree, is a pilot and works for the business. Brian, the middle child, is working on his engineering degree at Oregon State and is also interested in aviation. Daughter Kelsey is a business major at Oregon State. Jenny gushes about her kids, "They're great kids. And part of that is because of all the great people they've met in experimental aviation." Just me talking but I'm thinkin' Rob and Jenny had a lot to do with it, too.

I toured the Advanced Flight Systems facility and understood little of the technology behind it but was impressed by all of it. I did find an actual altimeter gauge sitting on a table. I held it up and asked Shawn, the all-around tech support guy, about it. He said, "What is that?" (He was kidding.) Shawn's wife is pregnant with their first child, a girl, and is due soon. I wished them well but did offer that Shawn is in for some new low-tech learning.

No, at the end of the day, I didn't buy anything. Beat me up if you must but I'm happy being a relic. But, also at the end of the day, I was very impressed with the people behind the business and their journey. They're a shining example of what can happen in our experimental aviation community. Work ethic, talent, hard work, family, passion, honesty, and all wrapped in a great sense of humor. They are very much one of us. I'm proud to have met them.

27

AIRPLANE PERSONALITIES

Airplanes have personalities. We know that. But I'm not just talking about mechanical and aeronautical personalities; I'm talking about *who* they are when we fly them. To me, many of the airplanes I flew had personas.

When I think of the first airplane I flew, I think of "honest." It was a straight-tail, straight-back, blue and white Cessna 150. Oh Lordy, it was the neatest, coolest, best, greatest airplane I'd ever seen when I walked up to it. I didn't have anything else to compare it to but, oh well. It was mine to fly and I flew it through to my Private certificate. And it was dutiful. I was told that if I treated it right, it would treat me right. And I did and it did. See where I'm going with this? Airplanes become what you feel they are and, in large part, that's how you fly them.

I know you remember your first aviation experience. Was it a Champ, a Cub, a Tri-pacer, a Colt, a Cherokee? Whatever it was, you still have a soft spot for it, don't you? And it probably comes with some personal meaning.

When I checked out in the Cessna 150's relatives, the Cessna 172 and the Cessna 182, they still gave me that same feeling: honesty. Bigger, but still honest in all respects.

I'm hoping it isn't just me that gets attached to airplanes in this way. Maybe I'm just weird. (You don't have to answer that because my buddy, Nel, for sure will.)

I also checked out in a Citabria after I got my Private. It rolled around in the sky, a whole new aviation experience for me. It's persona to me was "spunky." You had to 'work' through some maneuvers but, hey, the early Citabria's only had 115 horsepower. Too this day, whenever I see one, I still think "spunky" because that's what it was to me.

The Stearman: big, slow, not totally agile, but strong as an ox and with this message, 'Land me wrong and I'll swap ends with you right quick.' As a persona I describe it as "strong but sensitive."

I went from Private Pilot with 100 hours total time to military pilot training. The T-37 was my first jet. I learned its numbers, characteristics, systems, procedures.....all that stuff. And it was heady stuff strapping into an ejection seat and pulling on gloves and helmet. I was in awe. And I loved it. It had jet smoothness, good speed, excellent control response, stick and canopy. But when I walked up to it I always thought of it as "teacher." I learned to fly it, love it, love flying and to know that I wanted to do it forever. It was small, made a whine-like noise (we called it "the 6000 pound dog whistle") and it didn't get a lot of respect but, to me, it was one of the greatest teachers I ever had. A model of it sits on my desk.

And the T-38: we dubbed it "the supersonic ice pick." Before I even flew it, just looking at it, I dubbed it "thoroughbred." And that's what it was. Everything it did was fast: takeoff in full afterburner, climb....60 degrees of pitch and accelerating....supersonic, high roll rate, and final approach, 155 KIAS plus one knot for every hundred pounds of fuel over 1000 pounds. A heavyweight single engine approach was 180 KIAS on final. That sort of thing gets your juices flowing.....and preps you for other fighters yet to come. It's still one of the best looking airplanes around. A thoroughbred indeed.

Then it was on to the military airplanes of duty. The KC-135: to me it was a "jet workhorse." It did aerial refueling, hauled cargo and people, those sorts of things. I never flew the C-130 but that's one I'd call a pure "workhorse." It shot bullets, hauled bullets and supplies and people and landed in the dirt. The -135 was a bit more sophisticated because of its jet nature but it was, still, my jet workhorse.

The C-47 was in a class by itself by virtue of it being a classic. It was low-tech, round motor and a tail dragger. But, boy, did it speak to me: "proud and classy." It could do it all, not fast, but it could and would do anything asked of it. There was no pretense about it whatsoever; it spoke to you with, 'I do what I do the best I can do.' You can't not like an airplane like that!

The OV-1 Mohawk, for all of its angles and abilities, was always to me "mission oriented." It was built for reconnaissance/surveillance and every time you flew it, that's what you were doing. That was its purpose. That doesn't denigrate it at all because, as ugly as it was, it flew like an angel….and totally mission oriented. Always.

And the airliners, they were "businessmen." They were built to carry people and make money. Nothing wrong with that. They were magnificently constructed, with systems to backup systems to backup systems, smooth and efficient and very safe. A fun way to make a living but when I walked up to them they were always businessmen….and that's how we flew them.

I don't get the feelings I've described for all airplanes, only the ones I have flown a lot. I've given a few examples of those that influenced me. I don't know if it's reflection (I'm old) or what. It's just something I do….and feel when I've been through a lot with an airplane.

After retiring and tapering down in my aviation career, I bought a Champ. I don't want to call it a sweetheart but I do want to call it "pure." It's about as pure of flight as you can get in an airplane. When I was growing up I had a Shetland pony named Pancho; he always did his very best to please. And that's what a Champ does; it pleases. It has just enough power and aerodynamics to fly and cruise at 80 MPH and that's about it. But that's all it needs because its purity offers you low-and-slow and beauty, two of the greatest gifts aviation has to give.

And my RV-8: I know all about it because I built it. But here's what that airplane says to me every time I walk up to it: "fun." It oozes it. It goes slow, fast, rolls around the sky, burns 9 GPH, and has super visibility. And fun is a really fine way to wind down an aviation career.

Back to what T-37 "teacher" instilled in me: I still want to fly forever. Come to think of it, "teacher" and "fun" would like each other. They're birds of a feather. (Pun intended.)

I'm sure many of your airplanes have personas, too. My airplanes have guided and fulfilled me all along the way. I'm thankful for that.

28

LITTLE GEE BEE

Most all EAA'ers know the story of George Borgardus and "Little Gee Bee." If not, then we'll just call this 'recurrent training.' The story is about the birth of the homebuilding movement. It is well documented but it bears repeating because it is a tale of passion and grit, two main staples of the EAA.

The short story is that George Bogardus, in 1947, hopped in his homebuilt aircraft and flew from Oregon to Washington, DC and met with aviation officials and convinced them to certify amateur built aircraft as legal to fly. That right there took some grit: fly a tiny airplane across the land meet to with people at "the big house." "Little Gee Bee" vs. Goliath. Good luck with that, huh! But, hey, you guessed it…there's a bit more to the story. There is a whole lot of passion, perseverance and personalities involved, too. And that's the part I like to get into.

But first, a little regulatory background. Airplanes played a big part in WWI so, after the war, interest in airplanes was quite the rage. Tinkering and building and experimenting were a great pastime. Wood, fabric, glue and a motor and away ya go! But, enter officialdom. In 1921, Oregon created a State Board of Aeronautics tasked with issuing pilot and aircraft licenses. For $10 you got an inspection and a license plate with a number that you fastened to the airplane. Presto, you're legal. One of the state officials was quite friendly toward aviation so Oregon homebuilding flourished. Several communities were involved but the largest was located at Bernard Field near Beaverton, Oregon (think Portland, Oregon).

Now enter the federal government. In 1926 the Bureau of Air Commerce was formed and tasked with regulating aviation. In its infancy it didn't have much sway but it later became the Civil Aviation Administration (later to be the FAA) and regulators began flexing some muscle. One of the things that they pretty much left out of their regulations was amateur homebuilding. Their only mention was 'one-of-a-kind' designs could be given a 30-day period for testing. While in testing, they would be designated "NX" for 'experimental.'

But all the while this was going on, back in Oregon, there were active groups of people still building and flying their own airplanes, legal activity according to Oregon law. When the CAA started poking their regulatory noses around Oregon they were either ignored or, it is rumored in some cases, physically removed from the airport premises. This was the wild west of aviation! Oregon pilots said, "We're regulated by the state." The CAA said, "No, we do that and we don't certify homebuilts." So there you have it: regulatory purgatory. You can imagine the fur that sometimes flew! (There was, of course, a lawsuit but it's boring and was eventually dismissed.)

The group in Beaverton kept flying and became known as "The Beaverton Outlaws." And they were proud of it. Ya gotta love it, by my way of thinking. If they had just folded their tents the movement would have been set decades back. One of the ringleaders was Les Long, pretty much recognized as "the father of homebuilding" in these parts. After experimenting with different wing configurations, he built a nifty little low-wing, 30hp airplane he named "Wimpy."

Liking that airplane, a man named Tom Story built a very similar airplane. But then an international impasse occurred: the Japanese bombed Pearl Harbor, much of civil aviation was grounded and America went to war, including many of "The Beaverton Outlaws."

***

The war concluded, Americans were eager to get back to work and to what they were doing before the war. Aviation was no exception to that attitude. After all, the advances in aviation during the war were incredible. Back home in Oregon, aircraft homebuilding was as passionate as ever and the "Beaverton Outlaws" were eager to band together again and experience some of the freedoms they had been fighting for. However, the CAA presence seemed to loom even larger now. The "Outlaws" were as passionate as ever but now they *had* to deal with the CAA.

Right here is where I have to interject a personal note. In 2003 a gentleman wandered into my hangar and stuck out his hand and said, "Howdy. Name's Buswell. Myron. But everybody calls me Buzz. Most everybody knows me. Probably more than I want them to." He was right, everybody does know him, me included. We'd never been formally introduced (that's seldom necessary among airport bums) but I knew Buzz had flown forty-two B-24 missions in the Pacific. *And* he was a "Beaverton Outlaw" before and after the war. I was meeting and listening to history; it was a happenstance that I treasure to this day. He talked about the B-24. He was proud of his service…as he should be. And he added, "Learned a lot of what I needed to know about airplanes from the "Outlaws." We learned stuff about flying because we wanted to and we had to. We were kinda villains, really. Oh, it was a fun time. Lotta passion and sharing. We were doing what was right, promoting aviation." He knew Les Long. He knew Story,

Bogardus and a bunch of the others. He actually owned and flew "Wimpy" in the late 1930's! So when I write about the "Outlaws," Buzz's vignettes about them are included. That's what I mean by this story becoming personal to me.

After the war, George Bogardus acquired Tom Story's airplane. He put a 65hp Continental engine on it, added a canopy and named it "Little Gee Bee" (the GB for his initials). Les Long passed away in early 1945. In October of 1945, the CAA published Safety Regulation #194. It stated that aircraft used for air racing and exhibition would be eligible for experimental certification. The amateur homebuilder was still left out of the equation! George Bogardus took up the homebuilding cause in earnest. He wrote letter after letter to state and federal officialdom. He put out a newsletter and formed the American Airman's Association (AAA). No doubt due to his letter writing persistence, a man named John Geisse, an assistant for personal flying development at the CAA, invited Bogardus to visit him in Washington, DC. Early in 1946 and not having a legal airplane to fly outside of Oregon, George drove his 1937 Chevy to Washington, DC. *Drove*: two-lane roads, manual transmission, no air conditioning, no GPS, 50 mph. Maybe an AM radio?? Along the way he met with aviation people and garnered support for his mission. In Washington he met with officials and stated his case for airplane homebuilding. Respecting what he had to say, officials asked that he fine-tune his ideas and return the next year.

In March of 1947, the CAA published Safety Regulation #236, allowing CAA officials to issue airworthiness certificates to homebuilts. Yay! But it gave no real guidelines how to do it and it wasn't permanent. Still, it was *movement*. Then, in May of 1947, George was issued his NX number with this caveat: he had to fly his airplane fifty hours before going cross-country. Those hours completed, George left Swan Island Airport (Portland) in "Little Gee Bee" for, again, Washington, DC. Cross country in a homebuilt! He arrived in late August proving his point: amateur homebuilts are safe to fly. Talks went well but the wheels of government grind slowly. George made another trip in 1951. Finally, in late 1952, the CAA published Civil Aeronautics Manual #1 allowing for the certification of amateur built aircraft. It defined them as an 'individual group,' built for educational and recreational purposes. Those principals stand today.

George's "American Airman Association" never gained much traction but in 1953 a fella named Paul Poberezny founded an organization called the Experimental Aircraft Association. (Buzz had a two digit membership number, if my memory serves me.) George was initially wary of the EAA but that thought was fleeting because when he passed on in 1997 he left the bulk of his estate to the local EAA Chapter.

After George passed, "Little Gee Bee" fell into neglect. In 2007, Dick VanGrunsven (yes, Van of Vans Aircraft) and a loyal band of volunteers from Chapter 105, including Tom Story's son, Mike, restored "Little Gee Bee." It now has an honored place....fittlingly....in the Smithsonian Air and Space Museum in Washington, DC.

Look at that airplane for a minute and think about it. Imagine from whence it came; imagine what it represents. Imagine a six-foot tall George Bogardus climbing into it, 19' long, roughly 220# empty weight, flying across the US at 100 mph (on a good day!) with 65 hp, no GPS, eight instruments, no radio, rudimentary weather reporting, driven by the notion that amateur homebuilding had a rightful place in American aviation. In the air, cramped and sometimes cold, he had a lot of time to think about it. And he did it twice! We're glad he did.

What if George hadn't done it? If the "Outlaws" hadn't been such a pesky and dedicated bunch? I'm not going to speculate. The fact is that he *did* do it and, in large part, is why you and I are members of the EAA today. We're honoring the passion.

***

(Thank you to Stan Loer, EAA 22047, of Grants Pass, OR for suggesting we rekindle the story of "The Beaverton Outlaws" to keep the history alive. "It's important," he says. I agree.)

29

THE BIRTH OF HOMEBUIDING

We have, of late, been rekindling the story of the early Oregon homebuilders, more widely known as the "Oregon Outlaws." And thank you for the letters about those columns, by the way. You get it; you appreciate the history. Those "Outlaws" were the genesis of the homebuilding movement we enjoy today. And, of course, our friend Paul Poberezny took it to the next level.

One of the letters I received was from Carl Bogardus. He's the Editor of Chapter 555's newsletter. He started his note with, "As with any Bogardus, I am a distant cousin of George. My dad, who learned to fly during the depression by helping build an airport in San Diego, was a founding member of Chapter 555. Dad got the attached letter from George or one of our chapter members." Between the letter and sleuthing in the Oregon Aviation Historical Society archives, my journey of historical discovery became personal and rewarding.

From my perspective the letter is fascinating. It's the story, in George's own words, of his solo flight across the USA in a homebuilt aircraft to visit the big CAA in the big house....Washington, DC.....to successfully petition for homebuilding to be a legitimate and legal hobby. Of note, as you read the George's letter, notice how he credits so many other people with helping. Without his letter, a lot of the names he mentions would be long forgotten. Helping others in their aviation endeavors was a hallmark of the day. And, in and around the EAA, it still is! That's a connection to cherish.

George wrote the letter (I had to paraphrase parts of it for space) in 1986 as follows: *In 1929 the first Home Built Flying Manual was printed. I brought home a copy from Hood River and read it that night. I was in pig heaven. Immediately a plane was started and I went down to Swan Island airport and started flight instruction with Les Meadows.*

In 1930 I finally got out to Beaverton to meet George Yates. At the time, George was building a Geodetic fuselage with ¼ inch tube to be brazed at the joints. This plane was being built for Elmer Stipe and later was of white color and called the Stiper. Les Long at Cornelius built the wing. This plane had a Martin engine and the landing gear was from an Auto Gyro. George was to teach most of the homebuilt pilots at Beaverton in it. George Yates had a forced landing on Charlie Bernard's south forty and soon they were friends. George was to talk Charlie into building an airport. After all, it was poor land, wasn't it? This was the start of Beaverton which became a haven for home builders from the Portland area. Most people don't realize the contribution that Yates did for our movement. He was a staunch Federal government antagonist. Perhaps because of his Navy service. Anyway, all during the 1930's and into the 40's, he was after the boys to keep flying under our state aeronautic rules and disregard the attempted interventions of several Federal government inspectors. Finally, in 1941, the Federals took the home builders to court in Portland. The judge threw the case out of court for constitutional reasons. And then WWII started.

***

George returned to Portland after five years in California working on many airports. He worked on redesigning

"Wimpy" for Les Long, getting Les reinterested in the homebuilding movement again. And then he went to work for George Yates. Since George was at Les' place a lot, they teamed up to start another aviation organization. Bernard and Yates egged them on because they all felt something would have to be done after the War. Les became ill so George took over and with the help of Roy Fry formed the American Airman's Association. Roy was George's confidant in making the decision to go to Washington, DC.

***

April 1946, a wire was sent to Washington, DC for an appointment. A return wire was received and we were off in the 1937 Chevy. We had two proposals with us that Fry and I had drawn up. These were to expand to a total of four by the time I got to Washington, DC.

I had a passenger to Minnesota which helped on the gas. Harry Thalman had the club in Salt Lake City give me all their funds. Alan Rudolph of Wisconsin had left money for me at Pietenpol's. In New York City, William Winter, Soaring Clubs of America, and at Elmira, Paul Schweizer wrote letters in our behalf to the CAA. Jack McRae of Long Island, who was working at Republic as a stress engineer, made his home our base.

We met with the CAA who passed judgement that such a program would be legal. We were turned over to the engineering division, namely Geise, Rider, Marsh and Vollmeeke and I thrashed out the details of our proposal. Fortunately, they accepted the most generous of the four I had. Also the head of inspection was called in so that we could tell him what to expect.

The next March, Russ Stewart and I were the first to be certificated under this program, which was on a temporary six month basis. I knew this would be unsatisfactory as the program could be canceled at any time. Arrangements were made with Jack McRae to see Associated Press for publicity.

***

It was this second trip that George flew "Little Gee Bee" (or, as he wrote it, "LilGB") across the country to Washington, D.C.

***

The flight was made in three days with maps and compass and a cruising speed of 96 mph. Jack McRae flew in formation to Washington, DC to meet with the same CAA engineers. This was all a stroke of luck as the engineers were astounded to see a homebuilt that flew across the Rockies, that had some indication of being engineered, and has an engineer present that could talk to them on their terms and who also was building the Driggs Dart.

Direct result of this flight and Jack's help was the permanent system of certification that we have today. What most people don't realize is the effort of other people that helped. Besides the first flight, I also flew to Washington, DC in 1948 and then met with the same engineers in Seattle in 1949 at their request. In 1952 the last flight east was made and at this time I felt we had the program concreted. Our organization had accomplished what we had set out to do. It was decided to stop our activity at this time and did not run out of steam as one author was to write a letter. I still put out an occasional newsletter as I was testing printing presses.

Almost 1200 hours was put on LilGB up to stop flying it in the late 50's.

I took in about $1,000 in subscriptions. The other $9,000 spent, came out of my pocket. This is why American Airman's *was so successful. Someone paid the bills even if the pants got thin in certain places.*

George Yates egged me on. Roy Fry and Les Long led me along the way. Walt Rupert filled the gas tank. Charlie forgave the hangar rent while I was gone on trips. Cliff Krumm and Freddy Shepard helped with parts and work. Lee Eyerly and son Harry Eyerly let me have the parts to finish LilGB. Tom Story built most of the structure from plans I had furnishd Les Long.

I never regretted the time and money I spent on this though as I look back, I wonder how I got both of them as the only cash I had was what I had earned during the War.

In getting this program through, we were lucky. The old guard was out of the CAA. There were a lot of aviation people back from the War. An aviation bubble was expected after the war. The time was right and a few years later would have been too late.

***

George closes his letter with a heartfelt sentiment.

***

I only ask of the boys to build and fly your airplanes so that I can watch you. That is what I have done most of my life.

George W. Bogardus

***

A reader friend of mine, John Pike (EAA #), sent me a note telling me of some research he did in Paul Poberezny's library at AirVenture. There he found notes from an early meeting where they discussed the new experimental certification process that would allow them to build their own airplanes. And the rest, as they say, is history.

Okay, one more thing. The Oregon Aviation Historical Society (www.oregonaviation.org) has a four DVD collection titled "The Pilots and Airplanes of Bernard Field in the 1930's." It was painstakingly put together by a man named John Patton from oral histories he compiled from the living "Outlaws" in 1978 to the background of historical photos. And it's twenty-measly-bucks ($20.00) which includes shipping and goes toward funding the preservation of aviation history. The DVD's are delightful! You get to sit back and watch experimental aviation being born with the story being told by those who made it happen.

30

WIND IN YOUR FACE

My friend John Pike is an interesting guy: big, friendly, honest, hardworking and passionate about aviation. He owns and operates Big Sky Stearman (www.bigskystearman.com) in Sandy, Oregon. I've told you a little bit about him in previous columns. He likes old airplanes....mostly of the fabric kind....and loves restoring them to their original splendor. Along the way of doing that, he meets some really neat people and gets involved in some great adventures. He was involved in the restoration of a 1929 Bellanca that Hawaiian Airlines now flies on sightseeing tours; he recently restored another 1929 Bellanca that is still serving regularly in Alaska. But the adventure I want to relate to you now is about him and his son, Johnny, delivering a 450hp Stearman from Oregon to Houston, Texas. That type of distance flying......in an open cockpit, stick-and-rudder, and a round motor....just isn't done much anymore. I can relate to it because I once owned a Stearman; it was my therapy from airline flying. You know, wind in the face, low-tech, pure flying. It humbles you; it re-charges you. It makes you keep a firm grip on your charts. It's just the way it used to be on an everyday basis. Not now. Now you're all enclosed, air conditioned, maybe even pressurized, with every gadget known to mankind, twelve radios and thirteen backup systems (*maybe* I'm exaggerating a little). So I want to put you in the seat of that 450 Stearman on a cross country to re-kindle the greatness of pure flight.

First, of course, you check the weather. You're checking it not so much as we do now, i.e., minimums, etc. You're checking it to AVOID it! You choose the Salt Lake City, Utah through New Mexico to Texas route. That route can have some pretty severe weather (as do a lot of routes) but once you get out of the high country you have flat ground which makes it easier to pick your way through or around the nasty stuff.

You're comforted by having 450hp. A 'stock' Stearman, usually 220hp, could make some tough spots even tougher. The Pratt and Whitney 450 burns roughly 25 gph and the airplane only holds 46 gals., so, yeah, lotta short hops. Lots of landings, keeping in mind that a Stearman is no slouch to land. You gotta be straight and consider the poor forward visibility while being on-speed and you'd best stay with it from touchdown to parking. Got it?

Trip wise, we're taking roughly 1750 nm with mostly 1 ½ hour legs. Oh, and no electrics so non-towered airports only; you do have a handheld but it's a little spotty. And stay away, over or under the high-falutin' airspace. And don't forget sandwiches. You still in?

We will give you this: ForeFlight. John's not so much into the fancy stuff but Johnny is. John says, "That stuff makes navigation ridiculously simple." A little 'modern' once in a while ain't all bad.

You leave Portland and have a 30 knot tailwind…..one of the few you'll have the entire trip, it turns out. Your first stop is in The Dalles (KDLS), Oregon, a short leg to check fuel burn. The wind is 24kts right down the runway. Your landing is straight and short. So far so good. Then you head to LaGrande (KLGD), Oregon. There you see thunderstorms ahead. Then to Caldwell (KEUL), Idaho. You squeak in as the storm passes to the west. Then it's on to Burley (BYI), Idaho. There you cough-up a $65.00 call out fee. You're tired. That 95mph wind in your face all day wears on you. You have a big steak for dinner.

The next morning you strap right back in your dutiful beast and go at it again. You stop in Skypark (KBTF), Utah. There you find a leaking mag seal. It's a mess, doesn't seem to be affecting oil burn but you'll have to wipe it clean every day. It's just a nuisance. Or at least you hope that's all it is. Given the high terrain, you land at Provo Spanish Forks (KSPK) field before heading to Price (PUC), Utah. It's always better to have more fuel rather than too little fuel. After Price, you fly over Canyon Lands National Park……impressive terrain!......and BANG!! "What might that be??" you ask yourself as your heart settles from your throat back down to your chest. Next fuel stop you discover it was the prop spinner. It's missing. No other damage…luckily! But somewhere in a canyon there lies a Hamilton Standard prop spinner.

Next fuel stop is Monticello (U64), Utah, elevation 6966', DA approaching 10,000'. Winds are 15kts. gusting to 29kts but at only a 10º to 20º angle off the runway heading. You're tired but you gotta suck it up and put it on the ground right. You do. Then you leave for Farmington (KFMN), New Mexico. It has a tower but your radio ain't that great. You call Farmington on your cell phone before departure with, "Radio's not the greatest. We may need a green light." The winds were reported as 240º at 21kts. with gusts to 32kts. That works okay for runway 25. But there are thunderstorms about and the winds are becoming unpredictable. Approaching Farmington you hear a scratchy blurt on your radio about traffic switching to runway 07. Winds are now from 140º at 21kts. gusting to 29kts. That's 70º off runway heading. YIKES! The Big Sky Stearman four-aileron modification is nice to have at a time like this. Wing down, keep the airplane straight….KEEP IT

STRAIGHT!.....bang, bounce, swerve, wiggle-wiggle-wiggle the rudder pedals and WHEW! Good one! You never did see the green light. End of day two.

You having fun yet? *This* is aviating!

The next day is on to Grants (KGNT), New Mexico. Then Alexander (E80), New Mexico. Then Sierra Blanca (KSRR), New Mexico. Land, unstrap, fuel, potty break, strap back in, fly. It's a routine but it's not an easy routine. Sierra Blanca is 6814' field elevation, winds gusting to 29kts. Taildragger pilots *know* where the wind is from…they have to. DA is 10,000'. The 450hp. super-charged Pratt and Whitney seems to shrug it off. Nice! From KSRR you pick your way between two cells enroute to Lovington (E06), New Mexico. Later that day those cells explode to 47,000' with hail, lightening and high winds. You pass Hobbs, New Mexico and next thing you know, you're in Texas! Now you just want to get into Texas as far as you can. You stop in Big Spring (BPG), Texas (where your humble columnist attended USAF pilot training) for fuel. Then it's on to Sweetwater (KSWW), Texas: home to the Women Airforce Service Pilots (WASPS). That's a story of bravery and perseverance. You feel like you're persevering, too.

On day four, continuing southward into Texas, it's like you're over 'wind turbine central.' Hundreds of huge wind turbines are everywhere, like locusts. On to Comanche (KMKN), Texas, skimming under a lowering overcast now. You have to watch carefully for those dang wind turbines! You fuel at Taylor (T74), Texas, and then you are on to Lane Airpark (T54), Texas to fuel and knock the bugs off the airplane. Grant and Logan Lane, father and son, have a beautiful airpark and are very hospitable. Logan's grandfather founded the duster airstrip in 1946 after serving in the Navy during WWII, flying the Dauntless and Corsair's. Good history! The customer and new owner's airport, Pearland (KLVJ), Texas, is next. You land your rugged and loyal Stearman there……victory!..... where it joins a stock Stearman and two Staggerwings. A very good home!

The score? 1747nm, 487 gallons of gas, 24.9gph, 19 flight hours, four days. You fly home the next day on Southwest in four hours. What's the fun in that?

***

I want to thank John and Johnny Pike for the story. I put you in the seat because it makes it more real: the wind in our face and down the back of your neck; a lotta landings in an airplane with really poor forward visibility and narrow, stiff landing gear; weather and wind; parts flying off; and various and assorted other challenges like eating on the run and resting as best you can before doing it all over again the next day. Real-deal aviating!

Hat's off to John and Johnny. Well done!

31

AIRBORNE GAS STATION

I was talking to an EAA chapter a while back and somehow we rather morphed into talking about aerial refueling, something I did while in the US Air Force. There just seemed to be a real interest in it. The interest kinda surprised me but then I thought, 'Ya know, unless you've participated in it you probably don't know much about the intricacies involved.' Air refueling is accomplished high above and only seen and experienced by the participants. But you know pilots, if it has to do with aviation they are generally interested. And, for sure, the air refueling mission is vital: it's how you get bombers and transports and fighters over long distances in the shortest amount of time.

Early air refueling was one Jenny dangling a hose to another Jenny. Crude by today's standards, perhaps, but it was a beginning. We evolved from that to KB-50's and KC-97's. But the new jets having to hook up to an airplane going piston-speeds, well, it just was not a good fit. So along came the KC-135, built around the Boeing 707 airframe. The KC-10 has been successful, too, but the mainstay is the KC-135. (I understand there is a tanker replacement on somebody's drawing board but it has been a long time coming.) I tell this story with this caveat: I flew KC-135's in the late 60's and early 70's. Pilots had ADF, VOR and TACAN; the navigator had charts, a plotter, Doppler, celestial tables and a sextant. The KC-135 has been upgraded since then, most noticeably with bigger engines, a new fuel panel and upgraded instruments. But 'back in the day' we did stuff manually. I liked that; I'm old school, don't ya know.

The basics of the early KC-135 are a max static gross weight of 303,000 lbs. That's with a 200,000 lb. fuel load. Max takeoff weight was 297,000 lbs. On nuclear alert, during the Cold War, you burned 6,000 lbs. of fuel on takeoff so you lifted off at 297,000 lbs. If it ended up being more that, nobody quibbled. An alert launch meant war. Ground roll was in the vicinity of 10,000' -12,000' with water injection.

In peacetime and in Vietnam we seldom operated at max gross weight. We carried what we needed for offload and to get home. The exception was Alaska were it was cold. There we did heavyweight takeoffs because we had 100,000 lb. offloads over the North Pole to RC-135's. ("R" meaning reconnaissance.) In the nuclear war scenario we were required to give a bomber whatever amount of fuel it wanted. If we offloaded all the fuel we had, that left us with about twenty minutes of what was called "slosh fuel." Desperate times sometime require desperate measures.

Okay, the above is sort of a refresher. I wrote about refueling some ten years ago. Here's the part I want to get into: the things that pilots never seem to forget about certain airplanes they've flown. I will always remember that in the T-38 you added one knot to final approach speed for every hundred pounds of fuel you had over one-thousand pounds. And I can still remember the OV-1 engine EGT start limits: over 675C for five seconds or 760C maximum (L-701 engine). A USAF pilot training buddy flew the F-111. He can still recite the different flap settings for the angle of sweep selected on the wings. Another flew the C-7 Caribou and said, "I'll always remember 'flaps full, sixty-two.'" He added, "That's just what we always said on approach to short fields." I wrote my buddy Ed and asked him of the sight picture while flying wing formation in the A-4. He wrote back immediately with, "Align lead's wingtip light with the joint connecting the front and back fuselage halves while sighting down the wing's trailing edge." Bingo! From forty years ago. Etched in his psyche forever. Why do such things stick in your mind? Not sure. But I know you know what I'm talking about.

One airplane system that has always stuck in my mind is the fuel panel on the KC-135. It was impressive, sometimes befuddling but quite a marvel, too. I swear, the engineers designed it first and then built the airplane around it. The fuel system on a Van's RV is left tank or right tank. In a Cessna it's on/off. And so on. In the OV-1 and many of the fighters, you might have to manage the 'drop-tanks' but, still, not a big deal. In the KC-135, aka 'The Flying Gas Station', you had *ten* fuel tanks to deal with. I used to say the fuel panel looks a lot like a pin-ball machine. In any case, nothing about it was automatic; it required your attention. And that, really, was part of the challenge and fun of it.

Imagine a picture of the fuel panel. Let's start with the #'s 1, 2, 3, and 4, framed by the shape of a jet engine. Each engine has its own respective tank to feed it. Each engine fuel tank has two fuel pumps to feed it, one primary and one alternate. Something else to note: the forward body and aft body tanks are the ones you off-load from. You had to have them configured for the scheduled off-load before the receivers arrived. In the middle of the panel is the center-wing tank. You could drain it into the forward body tank as needed by turning the two transfer valves to the vertical position. You could also drain any of the wing tanks into the aft body tank by turning each respective wing tank fuel transfer valve to the vertical position. Or, with the boom transfer switch (bottom of the panel) in the horizontal position, you could direct the fuel in either the forward or aft body tank to your engines. Got it? Oh, and all the while, you must stay in CG and save enough after offload to get home. We had a slide rule to determine CG. After a while you just looked at the position of the trim wheel and pretty much knew where your CG was. I don't want your eyes to glaze over but this is pilot stuff.

Note the two switches over the forward and aft body tank. Those are the offload pumps. Different receivers used a different number of pumps. All the big airplane types took all four pumps. That transferred about 6,000 lbs. per minute. Fighters generally took one or two pumps. When offloading, the boom transfer switch is in the vertical position and you get a light when you're hooked up. There is a totalizer, bottom right, to record your offload. Too, the boom operator in the back is telling you what is going on via interphone.

Some easy stuff: when there was room in the #1 and #4 engine tanks, you merely drained the #1 and #4 reserve tanks (far left and right) into them. Ditto the upper deck tank (bottom, left center); when there was room, you drained that fuel into the aft body tank. Total fuel quantity was depicted on the lower left panel gauge. Top right is the fuel dump switch. That was used in an emergency to jettison fuel if you had to get down to max landing weight. Flip the switch and you jettisoned approximately 6500 lbs. of fuel per minute. It's not a pretty procedure but the fuel mostly evaporates. Only had to use it twice: once when the cockpit filled with smoke right after takeoff and once in Vietnam when the receivers didn't show up and we had to get home but were above max landing weight.

Now that you're fully qualified on the fuel panel I have to tell you about one other panel variation: the KC-135Q. It was for refueling the SR-71.....the only aircraft that came *down* to refuel. The SR-71 used a different fuel than the KC-135. So the forward and aft body tanks were filled with SR-71 fuel and the forward and aft body to engine manifold transfer valve was removed all together. No mixing allowed!

In a nutshell, you burn fuel, transfer fuel and offload fuel. Something was *always* moving on the fuel panel. Fun, huh!

Know this, I can almost guarantee you that at this very moment there is a refueling going on somewhere in the world. You kinda have to see it to really appreciate the skill and dedication involved.

One more short story: I remember one night refueling a B-58. After the -58 got fuel it pulled over to our right wing and lit all four afterburners. It was an impressive sight. Freedom on parade. And then it pulled away from us like we were standing still.

32

HISTORICAL PRESERVATION

There were 1400 American fighter aces during WWII. There are thirty-two left. One man of late has taken on the task of recording on video all the remaining aces that he can. He is Lew Adams (EAA##). He lives in Texas, owns and flies a motor glider and has a lot of experience in the movie business. And he has a lot of passion about the work he is doing today. His wife, Louise, also a pilot, works right beside him just as passionately. They're an impressive team.

Lew wrote me some time ago, specifically about a couple of columns I did on the "Beaverton Outlaws," the first serial homebuilders in the nation. He wrote, "What a neat story." We corresponded for a bit and then he sent me a DVD that he recently completed titled "Heroes of Old Hickory." It's about a National Guard unit that served heroically during WWII. It is very well documented and….emotional. Then Lew called. It was an easy conversation; we have much in common, including our age. It became obvious to me….as he described what he does and how he does it….that he "thinks visually." I think in "words:" I get an idea and it bounces around in my head until I have to splat the story down on paper. Lew gets an idea and thinks in terms of creating the story for you visually. I found it an interesting dichotomy.

Lew and Louise are presently traveling the country, with the support of The American Fighter Aces Association, to interview and record the remaining aces. It's quite a task but they are up to it. It turns out one of the surviving aces lives in a retirement center right in my home town of Salem, Oregon. Lew invited me to that interview.

Our initial meeting in Oregon, however, was at the Oregon Aviation Historical Society in Cottage Grove, Oregon. Lew is intensely interested in early homebuilding history and OAHS has it. Oregon is where it began! There we met with Cassandra Washburn and Tim Talen, two wonderful mainstays (along with a terrific band of volunteers) at the museum. We visited the restoration of "Wimpy," one of the early homebuilts and saw the Geodetic design of George Yates. It's amazing stuff to see and lay your hands on.

Our next meeting was at the retirement center where Bruce Williams, US Navy WWII fighter ace lives. New to me was the set-up of all the required recording equipment: it's a lot of "stuff" and it has to be set up correctly and tested before beginning. Then Bruce was brought in in a wheelchair. He's ninety-nine. He had recently suffered a small stroke so listed to the right a bit and some of his speech was slightly slurred. But he remained proud and dignified and graciously agreed to this December 2018 interview. First thing Bruce did was proudly proclaim that he was going to be one-hundred years old on January 19th. (As Lew says, "It's a race against time. All these guys are getting older by the day.") Through all the initial hub-bub Lew and Louise are incredibly patient and respectful. They love these men….and it shows.

The interview began. Lew asked Bruce why he went into the Navy. It was 1941 and Bruce was in his first year of law school at Willamette University. He said, "Well, at the time I felt the war was inevitable. I had an inkling to fly. I'd just seen a John Wayne movie and I thought I might meet some pretty girls." With that he was off to the rapid sequence of events that was the norm for wartime training: First was Corpus Christi, Texas where he was put into "the cadet pool," then to Pensacola, Florida for "primary" in the Stearman, then the Vultee; then the SNJ. Occasionally, during the interview, Bruce would slow and drift off the topic, struggling with his memory of events. I get that. He instructed for a short time in Corpus Christi and then was selected for fighter training and carrier qualification in the F4F "Wildcat." That was in Sanford, Florida. Then he was off to Hawaii to Navy fighter squadron VF-19 and the F6F "Hellcat." Here Bruce paused and spoke reverently of the Hellcat, "Terrific to fly." It took him "there" and always brought him back. Then the unit was assigned to the USS Lexington (CV-16) as part of Task Force 38.

Their first mission was a strafing attack on Guam. They lost two pilots. This was war. Bruce said, "The anti-aircraft was murderous. It was hard to get in and out." During a raid on Luzon, they engaged some Kawasaki Ki.61 "Tonys" (the Allied code name). Bruce said, "There were fifty of them and ten of us. It was a melee for survival. I got two Tonys that day." During an attack on Formosa, Bruce shot down a Mitsubishi A6M5 "Zero." A week later they were assigned to attack some Japanese ships off the Philippines. He recalled, "I strafed one without accomplishment. The next time I came in at fifty feet and hit some, two were camouflaged barges. They must have had ammunition on board because they went up, the ships went up and so did I. I was bleeding from the glass that hit my face. All that was left was me and my plane. It was so hard to keep the wings level I had to take my belt off and tie it to my leg to help me hold the stick. I got back to the ship, no flaps, airplane crooked and caught the last wire. It spun me around and then I ran out of gas." All this was spoken matter of factually. Three days later he was back in the air.

Bruce was back in the US training on the F8F "Bearcat" when the war ended. VF-19 was credited with 155 aerial victories, seven of them credited to Bruce Williams. He was awarded the Navy Cross, three Distinguished Flying Crosses and the Air Medal. He came back to Salem, finished law school and practiced locally for fifty years, always engaged with his community. He never flew again: "Too many battles, too many friends lost." Lew asked him what it took to be an ace. Bruce replied, "Oh, it's pretty much right place at the right time." And that, in his mind, was that.

Except that Bruce had one more story he obviously wanted to tell. Without prompting he said, "Only two people in the fleet had size eight helmets: Admiral Halsey and Bruce Williams." And then he laughed. A warm laugh of a warm memory.

So, yeah, stories like this need to be told, saved and seen/revisited. This great country of ours didn't just happen in some permissive vacuum; it was created on the backs of good, hard working and brave men and women. We must never forget that.

Offhandedly I was thinking about the preservation of our EAA home building history. Okay, the story is not on the same level as WWII heroism (although most all of the "Outlaws" served in WWII) but it is important to our aviation culture. To have it unfold in visual story form would be amazing. I asked Lew about that. He said, "Oh yeah, that could be done." And then I could see his mind go "visual." He said, "I'd have a scan picturing the magnificence of AirVenture then transition to a wooden hanger on a grass strip (there is such a place in Oregon) with the door slowly opening and a single ray of sun would shine on "Wimpy." That'd be the genesis. Then we'd use old airplanes from around here and families of the "Outlaws" and some reenactors and tell the story. It's eminently doable."

But.....of course...it does take money. Not like the extravagant budgets of Hollywood, by any stretch of the imagination, but some. Usually it comes from foundations, corporate sponsors, and individuals. I know little of such endeavors; I'm usually too shy to ask anyone for a dime. Some money is recouped through DVD sales but mostly it's a project of passion and preservation. The more you spread that which is good the more likely you are to sustain good.

One more thing. Sadly, ten days after the interview, Bruce Williams passed away. Ninety-nine years and eleven months. A life well lived, of honor, bravery and service to country and community. Fortunately, Lew and Louise and the American Fighter Aces Association are working to preserve his story and the stories of others as we speak. Lessons learned; stories not to be forgotten.

33

GOODWILL BARNSTORMING

We all know about barnstorming, right? Back in the 1930's pilots clambered into their Jenny's, flew over and around a town then landed in a field nearby and hung a sign saying AIRPLANE RIDES - $5.00. Those were the days. Pilots doing whatever they had to do to make a living flying. Days gone by? Maybe. Maybe not. Recently my bride and I were driving north on an Oregon coastal highway and spotted the silhouette of a biplane, hugging the coastline southbound at about 1000' AGL. It wasn't a Stearman. Maybe a Fleet. Couldn't be sure. But it had all the earmarks of an airplane hopping rides. Sure enough, shortly thereafter, alongside the road there was a big sign with red letters proclaiming BIPLANE RIDES. We didn't stop but I had the thought, 'Good for you, buddy. Doing what you want to be doing in a fun way.' Little did I know at the time but I was soon to experience a barnstorming immersion....in grand fashion. I *have* to tell you about it.

Meet the Puget Sound Antique Airplane Club. (Think Pacific Northwest, Seattle area.) Just another flying club? Hardly. They've been in existence since the early seventies. John Tomlinson (EAA #) told me they have about eighty dues-paying members but his e-mail list is one-hundred seventy and he says, "Nobody tells me to take them off the list." Dues are a whopping $20.00 a year and that entitles you to a picnic in June. They meet about five times a year. Members come from several airports around the area but mainly from Crest (S-36),

Evergreen Sky Ranch (51WA) and Pierce County (KPLV). As the name implies, they like old airplanes but they do not discriminate. They welcome all airplanes. There is a lot of socializing and a lot of flying. One of their missions is to bring aviation appreciation to outlying communities, kinda like the barnstormers of old. Except they 'step it up a notch' from the barnstormers of old: They go as a group. They have various 'fly outs' during the year but their big event, held every other year, is what they call an Air Tour. It lasts about a week and it's a big-fun-deal. I'll tell you more about the tour in a minute but first I need to tell you of the airplanes involved so you can get a feel for them, maybe even hear the big radials in your head as you read.

Here is a sampling of the airplanes they bring to the tour: Some Stearman's, a PT-18 Kaydet, an A75 and a B75 Kaydet; from the Naval Aircraft Factory, two N3N-3's and one N2S-4, and a big, beautiful Howard DGA. Oh, and some Interstate Cadet's, a Taylorcraft BC-12D, several Cubs, PA-11, PA-18 Super Cub and a PA-15 Vagabond. And throw in a Bellanca Cruisemaster. And Cessna's, C-140, two C-195's, two C-180 Skywagons plus Skyhawks and Skylanes. And a 5/8 scale Hawker Hurricane, a Wheeler Express, and RV-4, 6, 6A, 7 and 12. And while they don't have a Partridge in a pear tree they do have a Bonanza G-35. It all adds up to quite a beautiful menagerie of airplanes.

The Tour goes kinda like this: a starting point is chosen and that's where members first come together again to get re-acquainted and briefed. It's loosely organized but it's well organized. There are no pressures put on anyone. There is plenty of opportunity for input but, of course, tour organizers are named so there is some final authority when issues pop up. And a person is assigned to each airport to gather and disseminate information about that airport, facilities, any special procedures, where to stay, where to eat, things to do, etc. Tour participants pay a $100 fee up-front to register for the tour. When the tour begins they pay another $150. That money goes to provide food at each lunch stop and also covers incidental expenses. Participants pay their own motels, evening meals and of course, avgas. Think of it this way: It's like going on vacation for a week……except it's with a bunch of airplanes and a bunch of fun people. Since it's every other year, people have time to plan for it. Many members are retired so are free to go anytime but some are still working so take the time as vacation. Something else really stood out to me: There were a lot of couples. People who stick together, play together, adventure together, it's been my experience that they form a special bond. I don't want to overstate it but the camaraderie, the fun, the good will, the friendliness are, well, palpable. And they spread that spirit/goodwill everywhere they go.

I need here to add a quick note about Tom Jensen (EAA#). He was the Puget Sound organizer for the Grants Pass stop. He's a tall, lanky, N3N guy. He's friendly and commands a presence for his positive energy and aviation knowledge. I also met his wife, Marian, who was wearing a Naval Academy shirt. I asked her about that. She said, "My granddaughter goes there." I said, "You can be proud of her." She replied, "I am." Tom, it so happens, is a boyhood friend of Hal Bryan, our very own Senior Editor at *Sport Aviation*. They grew up together at the same airport, Evergreen Sky Ranch (51WA). I asked Tom how long he has known Hal. He held his hand out, palm down, about three feet off the ground and said, "Heck, I've known him since he was this tall. His dad still lives at the airport. He's ninety-four. We took him out for his 90th birthday."

This year's Tour began at McMinnville (MMV), Oregon. It's the location of the Evergreen Air and Space Museum which houses Howard Hughes' "Spruce Goose" and a bunch of other neat airplanes. It's also the home of the Wings and Waves Water Park, where a Boeing 747 sets atop a building. Inside the building you climb one-hundred-forty-four steps to the inside of the 747 and then you jump out the airplane exits onto a water slide. (Not sure how many Air Tour participants took part in that.) The Tour airplanes were scheduled to arrive between and 1 and 4 PM. And that's what they did, trickling in at a nice pace, each displaying their unique personality, until they were all there, the previously mentioned impressive menagerie.

Upon arrival, all participants were treated to a catered lunch. The food was good and the banter rolled. At the table where I was sitting, I spoke with Melanie Jordan, recently retired from the Pacific Northwest Aerospace Alliance, an organization that promotes youth in aviation. She was passionate about that, saying, "The Air Tour is the opportunity to have children sit in the aircraft and be inspired toward an aviation career." Melanie was flying with her friend, Dick Migas, in his C-172, "Miss Lucy." "Miss Lucy?" I asked. He said, "Yeah, I was walking around an airport and saw a FOR SALE sign on this Skyhawk. I called and it turns out it belonged to a lady named Lucy. She had owned the airplane for twenty-six years. She was eighty-one and used it to fly from Phoenix to Denver to visit her daughter. But she was having some medical problems and decided to sell it. But she said. 'If I get well you have to sell it back to me.' Okay, deal." They've called the airplane "Miss Lucy" ever since. Stories abound at such gatherings. I love it. Indeed, youth in aviation is a centerpiece for the Puget Sound group, too. At meetings they sell raffle tickets and use the money to build a scholarship to fund flight training for deserving youth. Everyone on the Tour is conscious of encouraging youth in aviation.

At lunch, tour packets were handed out. Stay the night at MMV, breakfast and brief the next morning, fly to Green Trees Ranch (OG28) for lunch then to Cottage Grove (61S), Oregon for dinner and an overnight stay. Cottage Grove, you'll remember, is the home of the Oregon Aviation Historical Society Museum, where the very first Oregon aircraft homebuilders are honored. It's 'real-deal' aviation history. The next morning the schedule called for flying to Grants Pass (S38), Oregon for more barnstorming goodwill and lunch and dinner and overnight stay. The next day they would fly to Gold Beach (4S1), Oregon for a coastal tour then back to Grants Pass for another overnight. The next and final day it's on to Creswell Hobby Field, (77S), Oregon for lunch and then to Bend (KBND), Oregon for the final banquet. That's the big picture. Notice the airports: small to medium size friendly towns and no control towers. All cities are sent press releases announcing the arrival of the Tour. I'm told that works as long as someone in the information chain takes up the cause and reiterates it to their public. No matter, somehow you have to believe that the staggered arrival of thirty airplanes flying over your small town and then landing at your airport would bring a lot of interest. And, yes, it generally does. It takes a pretty calloused town to ignore all that. One pilot told me that two years ago a whole town came to the airport! Ideally kids would ride their bikes to the airport, as in days of old. (I like to think that still can happen, anyway.)

The morning briefing at MMV was a view into the soul of these people: fun, good and spirited. Like life is supposed to be! The briefing was right after breakfast and held in the lobby of the motel. To the regular guests, walking into a lobby filled with 50 to 60 people all talking with their hands gave a bit of a fright. But they managed to muddle through the crowd with looks of "what the heck!" on their faces. The briefing was typical, weather, special procedures at Green Trees, stuff like that, and all questions were answered. There was a young man in the room....young faces stand out; there aren't many.....and the t-shirt he was wearing said "Capt. Molly – 40 years of flying the friendly skies of United." I thought to myself, 'I'll get to the bottom of that later.' And then the talk turned to the Binky. "Binky?" That's what I asked Tom. He put two fingers to his lips and made a sucking noise. I asked, "You mean like a pacifier?" He said, "Yeah. Binky." More to the point, the Binky is an award of dubious distinction. It is awarded daily for the duration of the tour. If you are found guilty of some infraction, you are awarded the Binky. It comes with a lanyard and you have to wear it around your neck all day. At the start of the next day the Binky awardee gets to pass it on to the next person who is judged to have made an infraction. Binky-worthy transgressions are freely passed on to the person with the lanyard so that he/she may have material to re-award the Binky. This day the awardee was deemed to have done something in the pattern, it wasn't exactly clear to me what. He objected in his defense but then...don't ya know....the cell phone cameras came out. He said, "Ah, those things are all just smoke and mirrors." And then he hung the Binky around his neck. A fella standing next to me leaned over and said, "Heck, I got it once for leaving a gas cap off for a minute and I wasn't even going anywhere."

Back to the airfield we went and I found the kid with the "Capt. Molly" t-shirt. He was polishing a blue and yellow Stearman. I asked him about the shirt. He introduced himself as Ben and said, "Yeah, Molly is my mom and she just retired from United and came on the Tour with us. She's in that Cessna 140 over there." Then he added, "You may know my dad, Keith Littlefield. He's right over there by his Cub." I said, "I do know him." We once worked for the same airline; I didn't know him well because we were in different airplanes, but I did know him. I went over and talked to him and we had a great conversation discussing old memories. So that's the Flying Littlefield's, all on the Tour, Molly in the C140, Keith in the Cub, and Ben in the Stearman.

The band of friendly barnstormers gradually took off and headed for Green Trees Ranch. It belongs to Geoff and Jan Stevenson and defines the word "idyllic." It's a turf runway atop some low rolling hills. The unofficial photographer for the Tour was Tim Heneghan. He uses a drone and gets some spectacular shots. I think his pictures of Green Trees does it justice. It's beautiful. The group was treated to lunch.

Next stop was Cottage Grove Airport (61S). There they were greeted by the Oregon Aviation Historical Society Museum, housing a treasure trove of Oregon aircraft homebuilding history. It's always special to lay eyes and hands on what the "Oregon Outlaws" did to give flight to homebuilt aviation. The Tour spent the night at the Village Green resort, just across the road from the museum.

The next day it was off to Grants Pass, rather a key stop on the Tour. Parking was meticulously planned by airport staff and EAA Chapter 725. The local newspaper put the Tour on the front page and that worked! The people came, roughly a thousand of them! Car parking was difficult. Luckily, the very nice people at Chief Aircraft Supply allowed for some additional parking. Almost everything at the airport is on one side. The other side has the Dutch Brothers Coffee corporate hangar and that's about it. Still, Grants Pass did itself proud, opening both their doors and their hearts. It was symbiotic; you could feel it. It rather centered on the FBO, Pacific Aviation Northwest, Inc., a full service FBO ably run by David Traeger. Larry Graves is the airport manager and he's a force for General Aviation. I hate to say it but some airport managers tend to somehow disappear during events. Not Larry. If it has to do with the airport, he's there…..participating. In front of the FBO was a band: DD214. It was made up of all veterans. (Veterans know that the DD214 is the form given to them as a record of their service.) That was a nice touch. The band declined to take donations, telling Tom, "We're doing this for YOU." She later got a ride in Tom's N3N for that comment. They also held a drawing for more airplane rides. I saw one boy, who when he learned he'd won a ride, clenched his fists, pumped his arms and jumped up and down. He'll never forget his adventure! The Southern Oregon Air Academy was in session while the Tour was there, too. Jenny Jackson is a key person, ably helped by a lot of volunteers, in the program. She described to me how they take up to twenty kids at a time for a one week camp during the summer and they do that three times to accommodate different kids in different schools. They teach aviation and the kids like it a lot. It's really a neat program. I saw many of the kids in a classroom in the back of the FBO. Another key person in Grants Pass is Stan Loer of EAA Chapter 725. He works with the kids, he worked with the Tour, he's a Board member of the Oregon Aviation Historical Society and probably a lot of other aviation things I don't even know about. He's a good guy to have around and he asks for nothing in return. He did say, "The Tour was one of the most fun activities I've gotten involved in in quite a while."

Walking the ramp at Grants Pass my bride and I met Marlo and Susan Jones, tour participants, standing by their Cub. Very nice people. They were talking to Fritz Gemeinhardt, who was in his wheelchair. His ball cap read USMC on the side; the front read WWII-KOREA-NAM-CW. (I took CW to mean Cold War.) In talking to Fritz he said he served for thirty-six years and was ninety-seven years old. When asked about flying he said, "I jumped out of them." My bride bent over and shook his hand and said, "Thank you for your service." Fritz shook her hand and winked at her. Somewhere in the conversation the Binky came up. Susan casually mentioned, "Yeah, I found that on the ground at Chelan. I picked it up and put it on the table." And the rest, as they say, is history. The Binky that day went to someone who was in the airplane ready to go except a tie down rope was still tied. The Binky recipient objected with, "But it was on my wife's side." His objection was overruled.

The next day many on the Tour flew to Gold Beach Municipal (4S1) on the Oregon Coast for some salt air and seafood. There they had another great community turn out. Returning to Grants Pass, that evening they took a four hour, thirty-six mile jet boat ride on the Rogue River, which includes dinner at the Hellgate River Lodge. Imagine a jet boat full of pilots. Don't ya know the pilots wanted to do some 'wifferdills.' The boat driver did not disappoint with 360's, wake crossings, etc. All got soaked and loved it. You get the idea these people know how to have fun!

The next day it was fond farewells and the Tour launched for Creswell Hobby (77S). Creswell is a delightful general aviation airport. The local EAA Chapter 31 hosted lunch. It figures. I've visited that chapter and they are a really nice group of people. After that is was over the Cascade Mountains to Bend (KBND) for the final evening of the Tour. The Bend EAA chapter pitched in to help with transportation to and from the airport. It was a banquet full of friendships, stories and hugs. The final Binky was "awarded." (The winner has to keep it until the next tour.) Then one of their own on the Tour entertained with his guitar and patriotic songs. You don't just measure success; you feel it. And all felt it after this Tour.

The next day they launched for their respective homes. Except for a few that went to some other fly-ins. As they say, "It's the flying season!"

How to wrap this up? For me it's by admiring what the Puget Sound Antique Airplane Club accomplished and how they did (do) it. What a group! They showcased aviation magnificently, brought goodwill and friendship and provided motivation everywhere they went. To the Puget Sound group: nicely done and……thank you.

34

MYSTERY AIRPLANE REVISITRED

In in Chapter 14, I began the story with, "You and I have been on a few journeys in this column over the years." The story was about a DC-3 I spotted in a farmer's field from my RV-8. The title was "Mystery Airplane." Ringing any bells now? Well, guess what! That story has sprouted new legs, or 'new wings,' so to speak. Our journey continues.

Remember Kevin? He owned the DC-3 on the farm. And through hook-and-crook I found him and got most of the story about it. Had to dig a little; he's not a big talker. He bought it, flew it to the farm and there it sat. He had a DC-3 and that's kinda the main point. He drove by it every day enroute to operating his excavation business. For fourteen years the airplane has been sitting. It's a little weathered but still proud; DC-3's are like that. Hey, how many people can say they have a DC-3 in their barnyard? I'm good with that logic.

You have to know that a lot of other pilots in the area know of Kevin's DC-3, too. I mean, it rather jumps out as you fly by. It's a bit of legend. One of those pilots is Paul Bazeley. He's the boss of Aerometal International in Aurora, Oregon. Aerometal restores, maintains and gives flight training in DC-3's. Paul is in his 40's and has 3500 hours in DC-3's. He loves them and knows them and it shows in his work. Suffice it to say that he's known Kevin for quite some time. And, for the better part of the last five years, has tried to buy Kevin's airplane. The answer was always, "No."

Now enter Basler Aviation. Yeah, the Basler Aviation at Wittman Field in 'our very own town' of Oshkosh, Wisconsin. They buy, restore, lengthen the fuselage and install turbine engines on DC-3's. And the airplanes are very much in demand. They're practical, hardy and classic. Don't hardly get much better'n that. So Basler is always looking to find DC-3's; the market is hot. And, hey, there just happens to be one sitting in a barnyard near Corvallis, Oregon.

So Paul, checking now for Basler, made another offer to Kevin. "Nope." And, awhile later, yet another offer. Still, "Nope." Then another. This time Basler 'came up' and Kevin 'came down' (a little). Kevin said, "Okay." Why the change of heart? Don't know. Only Kevin knows and, remember, he doesn't talk much. I guess it was time; he had his fun. At any rate, 'why' and 'how much' are none of my business. Kevin 'do-what-he-do' and that's good enough for me.

This particular airplane was purchased surplus after WWII by Cummins Diesel Corporation. They 'fancied it up,' corporate-like, and installed speed mods: tighter cowling, prop spinners, wheel well doors, wing root fairings, retractable tail wheel, and a modified hydraulic system. With the passage of time the corporate glamour of the airplane faded and N84KB became a 'freight dog.' Still proud but a little tattered here and there with the badges of heavy use.

Now Paul has a DC-3 that's been sitting in a barnyard for fourteen years to get airworthy. Not a job for the timid. For the next three months Paul and his crew would load up his van with what they figured they needed for the day and make the drive....about an hour each way....from Aurora to Kevin's place and work on bringing the DC-3 back to life. In lesser hands it might not have happened; in Paul's hands the challenge was met. Think about it for a bit: years of condensation cycles, old fuel and decaying hydraulic lines, clogged screens, old wiring, rodent nests and pigeon visits. You get it. So did Paul. He attended to all of the above plus replaced a carburetor, boost pumps, hoses and hydraulic lines, the elevators and recovered an aileron. He also did a gear swing. Then they started the engines, ran them up, taxied the airplane and then did it all some more. Imagine bringing such a classic airplane back to life. That *has* to be very satisfying.

The day came to fly. Kevin helped ready the farm field. And then Paul flew 84KB off the ground…..after fourteen years *on* the ground. He used 1800 feet of 'runway' and still had 2000 feet of clearway in front of him. Air was under those magnificent wings once again. Kevin was unto his own thoughts; I'd imagine he had to be proud of his airplane. Paul and his co-pilot flew the DC-3 uneventfully to Aurora, landed and pulled it into the hangar. There Paul and his team tended to the airplane all over again to get it ready for its next journey: a 1450 nm ferry flight across this great country of ours to Oshkosh, Wisconsin.

Now enter my buddy John Pike. He's an old-time aviator living in modern times, a rare but magnificent breed. He gets into all manner of interesting things. (I've previously shared some of his other adventures with you.) He was invited to be Paul's co-pilot for the journey east. John's answer, not surprisingly, was, "Yes!"

Their first leg was to Lewistown, Montana (KLWT). 4.3 hours flight time and no problems. They just roared along like a DC-3 does. Plus with a tailwind and the speed mods they had some speeds up to 200 kts., heady stuff for a DC-3. Then it was on to Aberdeen, South Dakota (KABR). 3.5 hours this time. No problems. Piece of cake, right? Maybe. After a day like that they had a big steak for dinner!

The next morning they arrived at the plane early. It was cold. They used a battery cart for engine start. Remember, starting a radial isn't just pushing a button and watching the turbine wind up like those silly jets do. Starting a radial is like building a house: move a lever here and a toggle switch there, count the blades, massage the mixture, waggle the throttle, listen, look and feel. It's an art. Engines started, they warm them and then shut them down and wait for sunrise. The sunshine melts the frost off the wings. Then they start the engines to leave but…hey!....the right engine is running rough. Paul says, "Probably an ignition lead." He shuts down and, when he can, reaches into the bowels of the big Pratt & Whitney and finds an ignition lead that had worked its way off the plug. Not too many CEO's can stick their hands into a radial engine and fix it.

Airplane fixed, they launch for Oshkosh. It's smooth with a tailwind. Uh oh! Smoke! They smell smoke. Paul hands the airplane over to John and goes back to find smoke wisping through some center section flooring. The smoke smells electrical. They do a 180 degree turn and head back to Aberdeen. There Paul discovers an electrical accessory hydraulic pump has overheated. He pulls the circuit breaker. Problem solved. (By now you know that Paul's an experienced, licensed mechanic.) The airplane doesn't smell too good but it's ready to fly again.

They launch for OSH again, 2.5 hours planned with the tailwind. Life is good. Then, well into the flight, the airspeed drops from 150 KIAS to 125 KIAS. Huh? Paul looks out to see the gear hanging down! Hydraulic failure in a hydraulic airplane: brakes, landing gear, cowl flaps, wing flaps and windshield wiper, all hydraulic. Stock DC-3's trapped some pressure; this modified airplane did not. Lose pressure, gear comes down. Paul says, "Okay, let's think this through." He's exactly the guy to do that. At OSH the wind is from 300 degrees at 30 knots. Runway 27 is 6000 ft. long. (Remember, no brakes.) But Paul has brought spare gallons of hydraulic fluid. The plan is for Paul, just before landing, to go back and pour hydraulic fluid in the reservoir hoping it will be enough for braking. He did that then came forward to take over the airplane that was bucking in the turbulence. Just before touchdown he called for John to turn on the hydraulic pump. Then Paul touches the airplane down like the pro he is and uses light braking…the brakes work!.... to bring the airplane to a stop on the centerline. Then he shuts down the engines. They are puking hydraulic fluid all over the runway. Basler comes out to get them. Just another day at the office. DC-3's all have individual personalities but they're also tough as nails.

Now 84KB will get a complete rebuild, be made longer and have Pratt and Whitney PT6-67 turbine engines installed. And it will be rechristened a BT-67 (Basler Turbo with -67 engines.) But at its heart it's still a DC-3. From barnyard to OSH with high flying adventures, nice job Kevin, Paul (and his team) and John. An airplane with the heart of a lion, this story could go on for a long time. And I hope it does.

35

FULL CIRCLE

How often is it at age 17 that you get your first ride in an airplane….a *historic* airplane, a 1942 Meyers OTW? Then you end up thirty-five years later owning that same airplane? Not very often. That's why I want to tell you the story. It's 'full circle' unique.

Don Generaux attended Ridgefield High School in Ridgefield, Washington. He then attended Western Washington University and became a high school shop teacher. He loved to restore old Fords and along the way, in 1969, he acquired an airplane, the 1942 Meyers. Unfortunately the plane crashed in 1972 and Don's partner perished in the crash. The aircraft was then rebuilt in the mid-1970's. Don later earned his credentials to become a high school counselor.

During all that time a kid named Jay Haldeman was growing up in Vancouver, Washington. He had a paper route, about half of which allowed him to see airplanes taking off and landing at Portland International Airport (PDX). That part of his route always took him a little longer due to airplane gawking. Unwittingly the 'airplane bug' had bit. Jay later attended Ft. Vancouver High School. There his counselor was, you guessed it, Don Generaux. At some point during a counseling session Don asked Jay what really interested him. Jay said, "I like airplanes." Don said, "I have one. Would you like to go for a ride?" You already know the answer to that question.

Don took seventeen-year-old Jay for his first airplane ride in the Meyers. Jay was hooked. By his own admission, Jay says, "I was just an average kid." But Don saw more than "just average" in him and guided him toward Big Bend Community College which had an aviation program.

About the 1942 Meyers OTW. An airplane is an airplane, right? Not so fast. What captured Jay's imagination was the history of the airplane….a biplane! Old airplanes have stories! The Meyers was built in a competition to be the new military trainer. That competition was won by the iconic Boeing Stearman. One-hundred-two Meyers were built, one-each. To this day, they each have their own personality. Early models had a Warmer Scarab engine; later models (#160 and beyond) had the Kinner R5. Legend has it the OTW stood for "Out To Win," as in the military contract competition.

Jay graduated from high school in 1981 and headed off to Big Bend Community College with an aviation dream and a healthy hands-on dose of aviation history. And, truth be told, that's a good thing to have: learn to fly, yes, but also *appreciate* the history of aviation. Perspective is good!

At Big Bend, Jay earned his Private, Commercial and Instrument. He came back to Vancouver and Pearson Field to finish work on his multi-engine and CFI ratings. Remember the airport where Jay watched airplanes while doing his paper route? He needed a job so he went there one day. He got hired by Horizon Air, a very successful regional airline. But not as a pilot; he was hired as baggage handler, a bag handler with a lot of ratings but not very much flight time. No matter, he was glad to be there. So there he was, working, going to school and earning more ratings all at the same time. Undaunted by the work, he handled bags, became a ramp supervisor and even worked at the ticket counter as a customer service agent. He did it all. And he did it with a smile and a good attitude. Jay was on the company's radar: "We like this kid." (Hint to job seekers: work ethic and good attitudes get noticed.)

One day Jay happened to be at the Flight Operations Center and one of the big-wigs called him into the office. Jay thought, "Maybe it's for a flying job." But.....nope. In college Jay had written a paper about the buyout of Horizon Air by Alaska Airlines. *That's* what the big-wig wanted to talk about. No matter, Jay had made contact; he'd been noticed. As time went on the powers-that-be kicked his name around a bit and began to encourage him with, "Finish your ratings and get some time and we'll hire you." That was all Jay needed to hear. He did as they said and they hired him: Jay Haldeman, airline new hire, 500 hours total time, 10 multi-engine. But with this footnote: "Great attitude, works his tail off."

Jay started his airline career as a First Officer in a Swearengin Metroliner, a nineteen passenger turboprop. The airplane had nine rows of seats. Jay said, "When I first started flying that thing, I was so far behind I might as well have been sitting in row nine." But hard work and perseverance won the day. Today Jay is a Boeing 737 Captain for Alaska Airlines. Welcome to the world of professional aviation: it ain't easy; it ain't always a straight line but it is, oh, so satisfying and rewarding.

Now back to where we started this story: the 1942 Meyers OTW. Into his airline career now, Jay chose to get back into general aviation where it all began for him. He bought a Cub. Then he happened to walk into the Pearson Airpark Museum and there he spotted a 1942 Meyers OTW. Upon closer examination, it was *the* 1942 Meyers OTW that he had received his first airplane ride in! Whoa! Seems Don had developed Parkinson's and chose to preserve his airplane in a museum rather than sell it. Later the museum encountered difficulties and had to cease operations. The Meyers had to be moved. It moved around the airport a bit until Jay put it in his hangar. By then, Don had passed and Jay told Don's son, "I want to rebuild the airplane and honor Don's legacy." Jay bought the airplane in 2015.

Jay is not a licensed mechanic but he dove into the restoration under the able tutelage of A&P Nelson Brown. The fuselage and 'tail feathers' are metal, the wings are wood and it's fabric covered. Jay exalts in the joy of the building process, the discovery and the learning. He says, "I worked in furniture repair in high school. I liked doing fabric work." He found a Kinner engine expert in Dale Krumm, a very humble but extremely knowledgeable man. (Dale's father, Cliff Krumm, was one of the original "Oregon Outlaws" and, in fact, was the only licensed mechanic at the Beaverton field where the Outlaws hung out.) After some work, that original Kinner started and ran…and still runs. It's had some good care along the way.

So really, the story I've told you is just the beginning. Jay figures to have the airplane completely restored and painted by this summer. Then he wants to invite all the important people in the life of the airplane to the first flight. And here's where the character of Jay Haldeman shines: he doesn't want to just own the airplane and give the occasional ride; he wants to use the airplane to "give back" to the aviation community. Here his mind runs free: talk to a shop class; talk to various aviation science programs; talk at the Cascadia Tech Academy. He wants to encourage others, which preserves Don's legacy and the history of one particular 1942 Meyers OTW. *That's* were Jay is; that's also who he is. He doesn't want it to be about him. He just wants to be the catalyst for the airplane in which he had his first ride. Full circle.

36

THIRD GNERATION BUILDERS

I've long said that if more people could experience the joy of aircraft homebuilding the world would be a better place. Okay, I know, I know, that's a massive overstatement. But you homebuilders get the gentler meaning of what I'm saying: The hands-on enjoyment of building something that has a lot of meaning is, well, both magical and immensely satisfying. And that's *not* an overstatement.

I'm sure an engineer gets satisfaction from designing and building a big suspension bridge. As does a craftsman who builds a violin or a spiral staircase. As does the artist who captures on canvas exactly what he wants to capture. The list goes on and I get it: There are many ways to experience "achievement happiness." My way just happens to be aircraft homebuilding; the others will have to write their own columns.

What I wanted to do in life was never a question. I can only remember wanting to be a pilot after I saw a DC-3 fly overhead one day, when I was eight years old, while I was playing with my Collie dog on our ranch meadow. We watched it until it disappeared over the horizon. That night I looked up "airplane" in the encyclopedia (remember those?). My Mom later bought me a plastic model and I got glue on it, me, my clothes, the wall and a doorknob. When it was finished I hand-flew it all around the house. Between farm chores, baseball, my dog and airplane models, I was a happy kid.

The homebuilding thing came later and largely by accident. I was well into my career with the airline, the National Guard and owned a Stearman when my oldest son, Brody, showed me a small magazine ad by a company called Van's Aircraft. It had a picture of an airplane they called an RV-8. Brody, knowing my bias for tandem, fighter aircraft, said, "Hey, it's just up the road in North Plains. Maybe we should go there someday." So we did.....and came back with an RV-8 tail kit rattling around in the back of the car. What did I know about aircraft homebuilding? Nothing. But I knew I like all things airplane and, given time, I could figure mechanical things out. Learned that on the ranch at an early age. And I knew that while I might not be the brightest bulb in the box, I have perseverance in spades. The result of all that is the RV-8 that I built.

And, it turns out, the whole build project was the perfect punctuation mark for my flying career: fly something that I built with my own hands. But the building process isn't just about building. It's about the new knowledge and skills you gain and the personal confidence that goes with that. It's also about the people you meet and the friendships you make along the way. Homebuilders are fun people! It's a package deal and it's a wonderful one.

But I've digressed; I don't want this to just be about me. My tale is illustrative but there are many ways to get "the build bug" and I like them all. The EAA and EAA Chapters are intimately and passionately involved in spreading the word and offering up different homebuilding opportunities. There is Teen Build and One Week Wonder and the Air Academy and on and on. And that's all wonderful especially since aviation is generally (but not *always*) given short shrift in many school systems. Ya see, you can't learn aviation at the feet of a guru; the learning has to be "hands-on." But here's what I've seen: While the mass media tends to focus on all things negative, so many of the kids I meet nowadays are really good kids and want….indeed *crave*….something they can 'sink their teeth into.' Aviation provides that. And bless the adults who are willing and ready to start them down that path. As I tell some of the kids, "Cleco pliers are more fun than cellphones." Sure, I get some "whaaaattttt???" stares for saying that but, generally, a month or so down the road, they'll often say, "Ya know, I really like doin' this stuff. It's fun." And many of them begin to *visualize* a future, as opposed to Google-ing it.

And now, yet another unanticipated benefit of homebuilding: My family is getting into it. And that makes me unabashedly proud. I never pushed my sons into aviation but, of course, never discouraged them, either. What I did push onto them was work ethic, "If you want something, earn it." Oh, we paid for their college educations but that's about it. Everything else they worked to earn. I did buy a Champ but that was for me, even though I did end up teaching Brody to fly it. (Which, incidentally, was the subject of the first essay I submitted to Sport Aviation in 1999.) And both sons chipped in to help me build the RV-8. Today, Brody is flying a Cessna Citation CJ-4 for Life Flight and my youngest son, Darin, just received his Ph.D., is teaching at Texas A&M and also serves with the Texas Air National Guard. (As an aside, Brody, while flying for an air freight outfit, has flown dolphins to the Caribbean, Sno-mobiles to Alaska, one B-1 landing gear from Canada to Texas, a plane load of tractor water pumps from Mexico to New York, and rolls of air bag material from Canada to Mexico. It never ceases to amaze me the amount of commerce that goes on over our heads!)

And now…..and *now*….my grandsons are involved in a build project. That fact warms my heart. When I sold my RV-8 I didn't just roll over into the fetal position; I expanded my aviation interests in several directions. One of those was to buy Brody and his sons, Trystan (15) and Colin (13), an RV-7 tail kit. (They live just a few houses up the street; we've always been very involved with our grandsons…to our delight.) Brody and I once again, twenty-one years after the first time, drove to Van's Aircraft….now exponentially larger and located in Aurora, Oregon….and loaded yet another tail kit. We then brought it to our hangar and spread it out. Later that day I brought Trystan to the hangar. I had him cleco the VS-801PP vertical stabilizer skin to the VS-803PP rear spar and…viola!...we had an airplane part. That is exactly the same thing I did when I brought my tail kit home twenty-one years previous. It's the quickest part you'll ever make. Of course, there's lots more that must be done to it but, boy howdy, it's a fun beginning.

I'm the advisor/helper emeritus on the project. That's a roll I like. I often bring home ribs and such and give them to Trystan and Colin to prep after school. (Trystan wants to be a military pilot; Colin is a math whiz.) Of course, I save a few parts for myself. It just feels good to have a HS-603PP rear spar in my hand. And a HS-708 main rib. Or a HS-706 tip rib. It's in my homebuilding DNA. But it's *their* project. Trystan asked me, "Papa, how many high school sophomores are building an airplane?" I said, "Not nearly enough of them."

Grandkids are different. You don't have to raise and discipline them so much; you just have to love and encourage them. And that is just a way lotta fun. I never pushed aviation on them, either. But it was always around when they were growing up. They went with me to museums and airshows and, of course, rode in the RV-8. The whole scene is very natural to them. Like I said, Colin is the math-whiz (he stopped asking me to help him with his homework after about the first grade) but even I can count to three and Trystan and Colin make it the third generation in the family to be involved in building an airplane. Wow! Time flies when you're having fun in aviation!

37

WORKING AIRPLANE

We all know of the romance and beauty and excitement of flight. But, hey, sometimes its work and today we're going to 'work an airplane.' It's the early 1970's and we're going to deliver freight and mail to some outposts in South Korea. We are going to be 'working' a US Air Force C-47. It's old but it's just right for the job: good for short distances, packs a good load and can handle a variety of landing surfaces. You're in the Air Force; you're young. It's not what you'd call a 'plum assignment' but you're doing work that needs to be done and you're doing it in an airplane that is a legend. But the work has its moments. This ain't fantasyland; this is nitty-gritty.

You show up for work. It's early and cold. You're given a tail number and destinations. The rest is up to you. You walk out to your steed. It's a little tattered but still proud. It's a workhorse. It's not some frou-frou cream puff airplane. Cream puff is for Hollywood and Vine. The cold begins to wear off as your activity increases. You don't just climb into your video game cockpit while people bring you a flight plan and such. Here, if it needs to be done, *you* do it. Today you're going to Kunsan, Cheju-do and Taegu. Kunsan is by the sea; Cheju-do is an island; Taegu is in the mountains in a valley. You flight plan it; you file it; you fly it. The word "automatic" is nowhere in the C-47 flight manual.

You pre-flight. You take a rag. There is oil to wipe; there is always oil to wipe. Streaks, drips and splatters. This isn't a beauty contest; this is a 'get the job done' contest. Your airplane is ready; it's been ready a thousand times before. Now it's up to you and your co-pilot. The co-pilot is a Major; you're a Captain. But he is new to the country so you're the pilot. He previously flew B-58's, a real thoroughbred in its day. It's a quantum leap in airplanes but, deep inside, an airplane is an airplane. You learn their personalities or you pound sand.

You clamber up the rickety stairs through the big aft cargo doors and amble up the fuselage. The ground crew has loaded the freight. There are boxes everywhere. And mail sacks. GI's love mail. On the right side of the airplane the boxes are labeled "Beer." On the other side are various non-liquid foodstuffs. All is strapped down, straps everywhere. Looks a little rickety. You hope for smooth air. You settle into your pilot seat. Worn seats. Very worn seats. Stuffing is coming out of them. A hundred butts have sat in them over the years. You plop down the cushion you brought because it fills the hole in the seat and allows you to see over the glare shield. Right about this time a ground crew member comes into the cockpit and hands you a paper bag, saying, "The general is pheasant hunting at Cheju-do. Last night he didn't have any whipped cream for his strawberry shortcake." You take the bag and give your best "Really??!!??" look.

It's time to start the big, round, oil dripping, beautiful motors. You bond with round engines: they sound good; they feel good; they do good. But starting them, especially first start of the day, can sometimes be dicey. Left engine doesn't want to start: you crank, count blades, prime, wiggle mixture and throttle but all you get is cough-cough but no pocka-pocka-pocka. You need pocka-pocka-pocka. Give it a rest. Start the right engine: do all the switches and levers while the co-pilot counts the blades for you and, bingo, you get a cough, a little smoke and then pocka-pocka-pocka. Victory! I don't care who you are, it's a beautiful sound. Jets start with just one button; that's just silly. You try the left engine again. This time it's jealous of the right engine, so it starts. What instruments you have bounce and wiggle and come fully alive. You feel this airplane; it vibrates right up into your soul. Time to go to work.

Airplane kinda waggles when it taxies. Boxes waggle, too. It's a ballet of gentle rocking and rolling. And those two throttles under your right hand are all yours and it's time to fly. Close your side widow.....no latch, just push it closed. Line up on the runway and lock the tailwheel. Props forward, throttles up and the propellers blur and glint in the sun as those big beautiful engines roar their magnificent symphony and your beast of burden begins rolling down the runway. Yoke a little forward and the tail comes up and the airplane flies off when it's ready. Maneuver the two gear handles to get the gear coming up. You sometimes get a little wiggle as one gear lags behind the other during retraction. Cruise power and you're on your way. No autopilot, no GPS, but a lotta landmarks. One with a great airplane and a job to do, you're living the dream.

Great! Kunsan is reporting some fog. Weather reporting is sometimes Korean, sometimes American and sometimes not at all. Kunsan has an NDB to get you in the area and a radar GCA (Ground Controlled Approach). LAX it ain't. Controller suggests a GCA, saying, "You might get a portion of the runway but it's pretty thick looking out the window." It's clear above but on final you see the ground fog. One two story building beside the runway is sticking up through it. You configure the aircraft for a 'look-see' and maybe a landing. At minimums you're still in the clear but the runway is nowhere in sight. You can't land on what you can't see. Co-pilot says, "Well, I'll be danged. Ain't seen that before!" You go around: Throttles up and then its hands and elbows all over the place getting the airplane cleaned up and under way again. You head for Cheju-do.

Looks to be a little squall-line-type cloud formation ahead. No radar; just eyeballs. Can't go over or around it and under it is just more rain. But it's not one of those huge fisted-ones; here they're generally wet but brief. You go in. It's like ten car washes. Co-pilot speaks, "Why me?" Airplane leaks....right down from the front windscreen onto your lap. You get pretty well soaked. Co-pilot's stare is rather fixed. And then, just like that, you pop out of it.....into the clear. Airplane is washed. This is how life was meant to be lived; the great swami C-47 has delivered you.

The landing strip on Cheju is grass, formerly used by the Japanese in WWII. Submarine pens blasted out of the coral are nearby. And the grass is bumpy. You land, skip, bounce a little, land again and bumpity-bump down the runway, wings wagging like a penguin walks. You pull over and shut 'er down. Boy howdy, what fun. This is where the beer gets off. You figure the GI's got word it was coming because they swarm the airplane. They work fast. Beer boxes are flying into the nearby trucks. You hear the pop-fizz of a few bottles being opened. The landing fizzed them up pretty good. The back of the airplane smells like a brewery. Inappropriate? Work a year of duty in Korea, through their winter, and then tell me you don't need a break now and then. You then hand the paper bag with the whipped cream to a GI and say, "This is for the general's shortcake." The guy takes the bag while simultaneously giving a big eye roll. Whatever.

Another GI comes into the cockpit and says, "Homebase called. Taegu is low overcast and their radar is out. But

Kunsan is open now. Go back there and drop off the mail then come home. You can do Taegu tomorrow." You say, "Yes, sir. Three bags full." So that's what you do....in clear and smooth air. It's C-47 bliss: engines singing their smooth rumbling melody of "job well done." You think, 'Really, how does it get any better'n this?'

Duty in Korea is a one year tour. Co-pilot asks, "How long you been here?" You reply, "Ten months." He says, "Only eleven months for me to go." You say, "You're one lucky son-of-a- gun." He mumbled something unintelligible.

38

AIRPLANE ON A STICK

We've all seen airplanes displayed on elevated mounts (in slang, "on a stick") at various airports. They catch your eye. But never have I much thought about the many things that must transpire for a particular airplane to be put where it is: the acquisition, the permissions, the money, the labor, the heavy equipment required. But now I know more because I recently became involved with the very task of mounting an airplane for display. I wasn't mainly involved, but was partially so. Still, it was quite an adventure, a three-and-one-half year adventure to be exact. I'm talking about the mounting of an OV-1 "Mohawk," an airplane that I flew for sixteen years in the National Guard. And it was being put on a mount to display at my home airport, KSLE. Completed now, we're all pretty proud of it!

Many aircraft displays are funded by government entities, particularly the ones near military bases. But not this one. This one was accomplished by private funding (read: donations) and private gumption. The 'mainly involved' guy is Gary Clark. Many years ago he and I attended U.S. Air Force pilot training together. We even played in a band together during that year, he on a guitar and me on the drums. Then, years later, by pure happenstance we ended up in the same National Guard unit flying the OV-1. Gary felt about the OV-1 the same as I: It was a bit ungainly in appearance but was an absolute sweetheart to fly. And it had the great cat-and-mouse mission of aerial reconnaissance, using conventional and infrared cameras and a Side Looking Airborne Radar (SLAR). The airplane served with our National Guard units (the 1042nd Military Intelligence Company and the 641st Military Intelligence Battalion) from 1972 to 1992. They were proud and decorated units. It was a sad day when, in 1992, the last OV-1 flew away. It was like losing a sports car you've had for a very long time; you know every sight, sound, feel and smell of it. 'Bout all we could do was swallow hard and pat it goodbye.

Several years later Gary picked up the mantel and took it upon himself to see about putting our beloved airplane on display at the airport where it had served so well for so long. It turned out to be quite a journey but he absolutely saw it through to fruition. As difficult as it was sometimes, I think he actually relished it. He said, "Each of our work parties was like a unit reunion."

The OV-1 was produced by Grumman Aircraft (aka "The Grumman Ironworks") from 1959 to 1970. It was initially a joint Marine Corps-Army project for a STOL light attack and battlefield surveillance aircraft. It was twin turboprops, crew of two with ejection seats, with but one set of flight controls. Besides the pilot the other crewmember was the Technical Observer (TO) and operated the surveillance equipment. Three hundred eighty were built. The Marine Corps eventually dropped out of the project so the airplane became solely an Army asset. It first served in Germany and later Korea. It was also used during the Cuban Missile Crisis. I flew some Cuban surveillance missions in the early 1980's when they were suspected of shipping arms to a South American country. Stateside, most were based at Ft. Hood, Texas, Ft. Rucker, Alabama and Ft. Huachuca, Arizona. National Guard OV-1 units were in Georgia and Oregon. It served in combat during the Vietnam War and the Gulf War, among other conflicts. Its forte was that it could gather battlefield intelligence and relay it immediately to the ground commander, no waiting for various other agencies to filter it down. It performed some ground support missions (read: guns and rockets) in Vietnam and did well. It was accurate and could loiter. But military politics entered when the Air Force insisted that fixed-wing ground support was their mission. I maintain that the troops don't care who supports them, only that they *are* supported. But the Army caved so that was that.

The particular airplane that we put on display was tail number 926. It was built in 1967 and assigned to Ft. Lewis, Washington then to our National Guard unit in 1973. It served in our unit for the next fifteen years. Along the way it was fitted with dual controls for instruction and check rides. Most every pilot in our unit flew it at one time or another. It's in my logbook several times. The aircraft was returned to Grumman for updates and enhancements in 1989 and was then assigned to Ft. Hood. In 1990 it was deployed for service with Operation Desert Storm. In late 1991, #926 was returned to Ft. Hood. There it was later decommissioned and demilitarized and left the service in 1994. It was then purchased by Mohawk Technologies, Latana, Florida and used under an Army contract to test new airborne sensors. It operated as an "experimental" until roughly 2005. And then it sat, being used as a 'parts spare' for other OV-1's. And it very well may have ended up being the aluminum Coke can you drank from the other day had not Gary Clark stepped in.

With his vision and desire Gary found #926. It was particularly significant because it had served in our very unit for several years. We didn't need the engines; we didn't need the ejection seats. We just needed the airframe. And that's what Gary bought, had disassembled and trucked to Oregon.

Along the way, he formed a non-profit and began a GoFundMe campaign. And the 'troops' stepped up! Funny looking, rare, unheralded, no matter, if you brushed up against it at some time or other in your career, it touched your aviation soul. #926 had been gone for a while but it had not been forgotten; it was brought home by the people who loved it.

Gary had help along the way and readily acknowledges that fact. He had what came to be called his "A" Team: Milon Whittier, Grant Rush, Jim Brown, Floyd Jones, Paul Pefley, Jeff Lewis and Ken Foote, all willing and able experts. You can't thank people like that enough but you sure can admire them. There was a lot of taking apart, sanding (my job) and putting back together. It was a team effort or, more to the point, as Gary puts it, "A magnificent team effort."

On the left side of the display airplane, near the canopy rail, it reads: Pilot Maj. Stephen F. Hammons and T.O. 1Sgt Richard E. Dearborn. They were honored for their long and distinguished service with the airplane. Steve flew the OV-1 in Vietnam and served as our full-time instructor pilot in the National Guard. He is the highest time Mohawk pilot in the world. Not to mention that he's a good guy, loves country western music and wears cowboy boots. Richard was a full-time technician and TO in our unit, a big, strapping, happy kid. He now has ALS and is being cared for by the Veteran's Administration (which, incidentally, he has very high praise for). He was unable to attend the dedication ceremony but his wife, Nancy, was there and 'face timed' the event to him in his room at the VA. Also remembered at the dedication was SFC Kimberly Jark. She was the first female OV-1 Technical Observer (TO) in the US Army. We didn't give it any thought at the time; she did her job and made no big deal of it. But it turned out to be a pretty big deal-- she paved the way for many other women. She has passed on but her son, Christopher, was there to see her honored.

And there was this: Robert Nopp (pilot), a Salem resident, and Marshall Kipina (TO) were lost in 1966 during an OV-1 mission over Laos. They were listed as Missing in Action (MIA) for many years. I flew in a missing man formation for them. Steve Hammons (Scan 21) was lead, Mike Polansky (Scan 10) was #2 and I (Scan 14) was #3. At the appointed time, Mike pulled up and I left the gap. It was an honor. Robert's wife, Patti, wrote us all notes of appreciation. Fifty-two years later, their crew remains were discovered. Both are now buried at Arlington National Cemetery. Patti was at the OV-1 dedication ceremony. You can imagine her feelings: Her husband died flying an airplane he loved for a country he loved. Now he is honored and immortalized at the display.

That's an airplane story in a nutshell, an airplane "on a stick." But, oh, it's a whole lot more than that. It celebrates the lasting legacy of one airplane for a lot of people. As Gary said, "This was destined to happen." It's not just an airplane on a stick; it's *pride* on a stick. People and passion made it happen.

Airplanes on display have stories to tell!

39

1920'S BARNSTORMING

It's the early 1920's. It's spring and it's barnstorming time. Let's

follow Jim and John. They're a couple of characters and bought a war surplus Jenny and need to fly some rides to make some money. They've been buddies for a long time, went through Army flight training in the Jenny and served in France during WWI. And they badly want to continue making a living flying. But there's a lot of nitty-gritty in doing that. Let's follow along and experience barnstorming from the inside looking out, from *their* perspective.

***

"Hey, Jim, where we gonna go today? The Jenny seems to be runnin' fine. I changed the oil and wiped the belly clean of oil streaks. She's a thing of beauty, ain't she? Got about a quarter of a tank of gas. We gotta sell some rides and generate some revenue."

"'Generate some revenue'? That's pretty fancy talk coming from the likes of you. You trying to make people think you're smart? Good luck with that! You mean fly some rides for dollars, right?"

"Sheesh! We're just getting started and you're already raggin' on me. Nuthin' new there. Gonna be a great day! Let's go to Neederville. I think there may be a county fair going on. And there's a grazed pasture just to the northwest of town. I used it last year and the farmer was a friendly sort."

"Isn't that where you busted the tail skid? Took us most of the day and half of our money to get it fixed."

"Shuddup. It wasn't my fault. The gopher built his mound too high."

John gets a little philosophical. "I can't believe we have this airplane. The Army paid $5000 for 'em and we got this one for two-hundred bucks. You had a $100 and I had $50 and I borrowed $50 from my mom. Bingo....we're in business. Well, hopefully. And, thinking back, what an adventure it was learning to fly them in the Army at Camp Taliaferro in Texas. That was a beehive! Had about a crash a day there, it seemed. But the spirits were high. Youth and adventure!"

And Jim chimes in. "Yeah, and then we went to France. Maybe not as much fun as we thought it would be but you do your duty. People died there, tho. But we got the war over with. Maybe won't have another big one like that, ya think?"

"Hey, let's git goin' and have some fun with this airplane. Lotta people in these parts ain't never seen one. It's up to us to show them. Get the gas can and water bag and some oil and the sign. We'll beg a sandwich off some customer for lunch."

"Sounds good. Yeah, before you know it bread's gonna be 10 cents a loaf. Hiway robbery!"

"Remember how we get there? It's over yonder a bit, ain't it?"

"Yeah, head toward the railroad water tower you'll see after takeoff then follow the tracks south. There's a big church steeple in the middle of town. Pretty big town, maybe five or six-hundred people."

"Put the chocks in. I'll call the switch on."

"Chocks in!"

"Switch on!"

Jim gives the prop a pull. Nothing. He gives it another pull. Still nothing. Maybe a slight cough. Again. Sputter-sputter then a smooth idle. The OX-5, all 90 hp., is a good engine....water cooled V-8.....but it *does* have a personality. Jim pulls the chocks, clambers into the front cockpit, buckles in and pulls down his goggles as John starts the taxi.

John heads into the wind and pushes the power up. They're off. This is flyin' as they know it and they love it. Noise and wind in the face. And a quarter tank of gas. And burning 8 gph. Gotta get some paying passengers.

Soon, Jim points and John finds the town. He circles and then flies right down main street, wagging his wings. Then he heads to the friendly farmer's field. Looks good....short green grass. The two milk cows that regularly graze it are way off in a corner of the field.

A neighbor is burning some trash so John checks the smoke. It's lazily drifting straight up. John lands such that he can easily park in the corner of the field closest to town. Nice touchdown, little skip, then rumble-rumble-rumble over the small bumps and then the tail skid touches and helps the airplane slow. He gets to the corner, swings the airplane around and shuts 'er down. Jim jumps out and gets the sign and drapes it over the fence: AIRPLANE RIDES $2.00.

Jim says, "That was fun. Short and sweet. This is livin'!"

"Hey, I think I see a couple bicycles coming down the road toward us. That's good. The kids are usually the first to arrive. The adults gotta go climb in the car and such and wander on out. We gotta get those first couple rides in to get more exposure in the air and the word out."

"Yup, that seems to be the name-of-the-game, don't it!"

A kid arrives and leans his bike against the fence. He crawls under the barbed-wire fence and shyly walks towards the airplane. His buddy…turns out to be his brother… does the same and follows behind. They both stop about fifty feet away until Jim engages them, "How you boys doin'? Ever seen an airplane before? This is called a Jenny. It's a real good and fun and safe airplane. Think ya might want to go for a ride?" They allow that, no, they haven't seen an airplane up close but, yea, they'd like to go for a ride. But they've never had two-dollars all at once. But….their mom and dad were gonna be out in a bit. Meanwhile, a few other cars pull up alongside the road. Many folks just sit in their cars. You can see them thinking, 'So that's an airplane, huh! Kinda crazy!' A fella on horseback stops by, too, with his barking dog. And the friendly farmer saunters out from the nearby barn and asks, "You fellas need a sandwich? Ya did last year." John's thinking, 'This place is a friendly gold mine.'

The kid's parents show up and don't even dicker about the price, like most do. They plunk down the $2.00 and John tells the boys to climb in the front seat. He straps them in and points to the stick and says, "Don't touch this." He asks the kids where they live and they point in a general direction. And with that, they're off. First ride, never to be forgotten. Off the ground and wind in their face. John watches them from the back seat, heads peering from side to side, big smiles on their faces. He circles their house. They wiggle and point excitedly. This is a very good ride. Fifteen minutes and they're back on the ground. Those two kids stayed the rest of the day and talked many people into going for rides.

After two rides, John gave Jim the four dollars and asked him to go into town and get some gas, "And don't spend more than 30 cents a gallon." And he added, "And, oh yeah, tomorrow you do the flying and I'll be the 'go-fer'." The father of the first two kids gave Jim a ride to and from town. John gave airplane rides for the next four hours. It was an excellent day.

Jim and John bedded down in the farmer's barn.

"What a great day! Traded a ride for a real cooked supper at the restaurant in town and I got $22.00 cash in my pocket. It's warm and the stars are out. And the farmer penned the milk cows up so they wouldn't chew on the airplane. Is this a great country or what! It just doesn't get no bettter'n this!"

"Where we goin' tomorrow? The world's our playground. Do ya ever wonder if this aviation thing will catch on? I mean like so a lot of people can learn to fly and enjoy it?"

"Don't know but I hope so."

40

HOMEBUILDING BENEFITS

Building an airplane is a life changing experience. Okay, that may be a bit of an overstatement. But for many it *is* an experience of significant proportions. How's that?

Where am I going with this? Reflecting, I had a twenty-year experience with both building and flying my RV-8. And here's the deal: I had been flying professionally for thirty years before I stumbled upon experimental aviation. I guess I was just too busy making a living to raise my head up to see what else was out there. I'd owned a couple store-bought airplanes, a Champ and a Stearman. And, as I did in the military and the airlines, I dutifully learned all their particular systems and procedures. Pilot stuff!

But here's what I didn't know that I didn't know: how airplanes are engineered and put together. Oh, I had cursory knowledge but not practical knowledge. But when you build an airplane you really get to know the mechanical stuff because you *built* the mechanical stuff! And that, as it turns out, is 'an experience of significant proportions.'

It's like this: If I had an electrical problem with my experimental, I could more easily figure it out because I knew every wire, its gauge, solenoid, relay and connection in the airplane. I put them there! I could trace the whole thing in my mind. (Okay, many of you will remember the intermittent tachometer that drove me daft for a while. But we did *finally* get it fixed by using shielded wire!) Ditto the hydraulics. And the fuel system. And the instruments. Which, I suppose, is why builders can do their own ‘condition inspections.’ They know every nut and bolt in their airplane. And all that is very rewarding and satisfying.

When I say I ‘stumbled’ onto experimental aviation, it’s true. One day my son showed me a small ad in a magazine about a neat little airplane called an RV-8. It was offered by a company called “Van’s Aircraft” and it was just up the road from us in North Plains, Oregon. With not much else on the schedule that day we drove there, not really knowing what to expect. The business was in a big, old barn-type building. We walked in and there were airplane parts everywhere. And it smelled like an airplane place. Know what I mean? And the people were friendly, like airplane friendly, honest, up-front and fun. What’s not to like about all that?

After a couple hours of touring and talking I’m beginning to think, “Well, for cryin’ out loud. This is doable!” Never mind that I knew nothing of the processes involved. Perhaps it helped that I grew on a ranch and we had to do hands-on mechanical stuff all the time. Not fancy mechanical stuff, just ‘that which had to be done’ stuff. Like when my bicycle chain broke I fixed it. When the tractor broke we fixed it. No money or time to have someone else do it. But I barely knew a rivet from a rabbit. And I certainly knew nothing of torque. On the ranch, you tightened the nut with a big wrench until ‘you couldn’t tighten it no more!’ So I wasn’t particularly knowledgeable but I wasn’t really afraid either.

Next thing I know my son and I are driving down the road with a tail kit rattling around in the back seat. I was motivated, too, by the fact that you buy the airplane in segments. Buy one kit, pay for it, buy the next kit when you’re ready, pay for it and, before you know, you have a ‘paid for’ airplane. We got the parts home. I spread them out and thought, “What now?” I just dove in. I pieced together some scrap aluminum and began practice riveting. Boy, I mashed some doozies on that scrap. (I still have it.) I didn’t attend any build classes; I know they’re great but, at the time, none were convenient for me to attend. I read Van’s instructions, which were quite thorough and good. With no previous airplane building experience, I strayed not from them; if Van said “do it this way,” that’s how I did it. All the while, learning was taking place. Sure, you rivet with a rivet gun and a bucking bar or a rivet squeezer….pretty straight forward….but you learn that a good rivet has a lot to do with ‘gun pressure’ and a sense of timing. It’s a rhythm. And with the squeezer, it’s important to have the gap set just right for the rivet you’re squeezing. Learning by doing; it’s a very motivating process. So I pressed forward to bulkheads and ribs and spars and fuselage parts and fuel tanks and landing gear and canopy and engine hanging. The key for me was to go slow; think about it three times before doing it once. One airport bum said to me, “You do good work but I dang sure wouldn’t pay you by the hour.” And it was on to epoxy and fiberglass. That was a little bit yucky!

Finally, after six or so years of building, I flew what I had built. While taxiing out I was gazing at all the assemblies I had done but once I pulled out on the runway and put the power to it, it became a project no more. It became an *airplane.* And here’s one of the results of all that: It gave me a feeling of confidence that if I could successfully build an airplane I could do a whole lot of other things I had not previously thought of doing. And that’s the point of this column; once you learn new skills and gain confidence, the world is your oyster. You rather develop a thirst for projects and accomplishment. In my book, that’s a good thing. We’re all different so perhaps it helps that I’m wired such that I can’t just sit. I have to be doing something. I’m not a cruise ship type-guy…..not that there’s anything wrong with that......and I don't have to see the Alps or the pyramids. I'm happiest when I'm knee-deep in a project. That's just me. Truth be known, I've met a bunch of you who are the same way. The majority, it seems, are airplane builders. (Perhaps it's the company I keep!) Many are *serial* airplane builders. I get that.

So....I'm now building an RV-7 with my son and grandsons. It's a shared experience that I really enjoy but the process is slower. My son works and the boys are busy with school. They get to building stuff when they can. Which is okay because it's not about a timeline; it's about the project.

Meanwhile, I've taken on some other projects that before airplane building I probably would not have attempted. I restored one of the first tractors we had on the ranch: a 1953 Ford. I love the rugged simplicity of the old stuff. My first car was a 1959 Volkswagen Beetle so when I found a '64 Beetle that was stored in a barn for nineteen years, I bought it and restored it. I even took the engine out and installed a new clutch and oil cooler. I did it the same way I did the airplane: slowly and methodically. And I properly torqued the nuts! Now I've taken on a whole new...to me...concept. I'm building a wooden boat. Didn't want a store-bought boat, wanted a boat I could build with my own hands. Amazingly to me, the kit came with CNC machine cut marine grade plywood. It reminded me of the CNC parts that were in the RV-8 kit. And, initially, you wire the parts together with, get this, safety wire. They didn't suggest it but I used my aircraft safety wire pliers. Bingo! Then you epoxy the parts together. And then you fiberglass the whole dang outside of the boat. That used to be "yuk," remember? Now, not so much. Am figuring it out. The key is the proper "wetting" of the fiberglass.

I've visited a number of hangars across this great land over the years and, hey, almost all of them have other type projects in them. Especially at the more rural airports. Aviation is a passion all its own but it's a passion that lends itself to all manner of other endeavors.

Build an airplane. The benefits will stay with you for life.

41

THE OREGON AERO STORY

We met in the lobby of the big hangar-type building that constitutes the business of Oregon Aero, located on the airport at Scappoose (KSPB), Oregon. You've probably heard of them: headset cushions, headset ear seals, helmet upgrades, aircraft seats and cushions, headset bags, ShockBlocker shoe sole inserts and a myriad of other related civil and military products. Some of it is stuff you may already have plus other stuff you probably want. In aviation, the logo "Oregon Aero" rather speaks for itself: quality. The first things you notice in the lobby are several examples of aircraft seats. More on the "why" of that later. Also, on a high shelf that rings the room, there were…seemingly….about a jillion aircraft models. More on that later, too.

It was in the lobby that we all met, Mike Dennis, founder and owner, his wife Jude, and Gayle Crowder, his assistant. And it was there….with the receptionist's office phone ringing, people coming and going….that we all conversed for the next two hours. You see, Mike doesn't have a big formal office; he's not a formal type guy. His "office" is the building we were in plus the other adjacent buildings that constitute the whole of Oregon Aero. "The business" is his office. Here's the thing: his intellect and his passion for what he does are the driving forces for the entire operation. I asked him of his education. He said, "I have a Ph.D. Translated that stands for 'Pig, Hoe and Dig.'"

About the seats in the lobby, they are examples of what Oregon Aero does but also are for what they call "seat school." I just happened to be sitting in one of the starter seats. It wasn't that comfortable; it was an example of a standard airline seat. It was then that Mike ...slowly and subtly...started me into "seat school." Next to the seat I was sitting in was Oregon Aero's improved version. I moved to that one. *Much* better! And then Mike talked of the technical reasons for that. We got into anatomy, posture, physics, spine compression, fatigue, material composition (a huge factor), and so-on. Non-stop. It was fascinating, the detail, thought and science that he puts into his products. I sat on many a military cockpit seat over the years that was little more than some foam with fabric sewn around it. You "make do" but, boy-howdy what a little thought and applied science can do to make it better! And that's what Mike Dennis does. "Comfort and safety" is his daily motto. How's it working for him? The "jillion" models on the shelf that rings the lobby are all examples of airplanes that use his products.

How did Mike get to where he is today? He slugged his way through the "stuff of life"....the good, the bad, and the ugly. The kind of stuff that makes you or breaks you. It made Mike Dennis, instilled in him perspective and the strength to succeed. You can't beat him down with a problem; he *will* figure it out. That's who he is. And there is also a huge element of family intrigue that drives him to this day. I have to tell you about it.

Mike's father was James Dennis. James' father died of a heart attack at the age of fifty-three in 1941. His mother then left with her youngest son and moved from the Pacific NW to her family home in Norfolk, Virginia. James stayed behind. He was fourteen. In those days fourteen was old enough to work so that's what he did. It didn't take long before he got into some trouble. The judge told him, "You can go to jail or to the Merchant Marine." James chose the Merchant Marine. Not long into his Merchant Marine service……someone, somehow…..singled out James….young and alone….and offered him a "job" to learn German. (He found out later that others with similar backgrounds were offered the same job.) Hmmmm. James was then sent to the Midwest to live with a German speaking family. He learned German. Language finishing school was at Ft. Bragg, North Carolina. There he learned different German dialects. After a couple more schools he was smuggled into Berlin, Germany by the French Underground. There he lived in the home of a baker who was an anti-Nazi spy. Hitler had a sweet-tooth and had a standing order for pastries at Army Headquarters. James delivered the pastries. They called him "The Doughnut Boy." He'd hang around at Headquarters and listen to what was being said and then reported what he heard to the baker. He was a spy! At seventeen! It's kinda hard to wrap your head around that!

James eventually came home to the US but the experiences and a lot of the trauma stayed with him forever. He seldom spoke of it and when he did he never fully answered questions. Mike only got bits and pieces over the years, which always created yet more questions. So the story has always held Mike at arm's length. James passed away in 1977, a retired VA Chaplain. Why is all this important? Because it gave Mike a journey he had to complete; he needed to know some of the "why" of who he is. He began researching. Hint: When someone is a spy their official records are never about who the person really is; they're a paper trail to nowhere. Undaunted, Mike and Gayle did the research and wrote a book about James. It's aptly titled "The Doughnut Boy." It's captivating!

Back to the rest of Mike's story. He learned to fly. His mentor and CFI was Irv Allen who Mike to this day waxes poetic about. An aviation mentor is a good thing in life. Mike also journeyed to Longview, Texas and earned his A&P at Le Tourneau College. He says, "Those two pieces of plastic in my pocket that say 'pilot' and 'mechanic' represent a whole lot of who I am." He also endured a wife abandoning him and their three children. And he had an irrigation sprinkler head repair business he wasn't enthralled with but learned a lot from. And then he met and married Jude. She had motorcycled from Pennsylvania to Oregon in her mid-twenties. Life began to get sweeter for Mike Dennis.

All of the above leads to an Ercoupe flight Mike and Jude took from Oregon to Pennsylvania for a visit. Jude said, "I like the flying but this headset hurts my head. Can you fix it?" A born tinkerer and fixer, he was up to the task. His first idea was padding, but not just more rubber. He went with leather and sheepskin. Soft and natural. And he made it large enough to "spread the pressure." Jude liked it! It wasn't very aesthetically pleasing at first but Jude wore it nonetheless. On a cross-country stop a fella noticed Jude's headset and asked, "What is that?" "A cushion," Mike explained. The guy said, "I'll give ya fifty bucks for it." Two other pilots walked up and one of them said, "You owe it to the world to make that." Mike thought, 'I've had a business. Not sure I want to get into that again.'

However.......Mike started a hobby at home, cutting and assembling sheepskin and leather on the kitchen table. He took the cushions to fly-ins and they sold. Then he hired neighbor kids to cut pieces for 'the fuzzy thing.' All of this was in 1989. That project graduated to headset ear seals; so many of the early ear seals were seriously substandard and didn't fit all ears. So get this: Mike put on a white coat and went to a mall and told passers-by that he was doing a study of ear sizes for industrial ear protection. He successfully measured two-hundred-fifty ears before security threw him out. He then made improved ear seals. People liked those, too. One who liked them was an Oregon Air National Guard pilot. That pilot showed the new ear seals to his Air National Guard Commander saying, "We need these." The Commander called Mike in and asked, "Are you going to make these?" Mike said, "I can't. I need a $10,000.00 custom sewing machine. I have three kids and can't afford it." The Commander then wrote a note and handed it to Mike and said, "Will this help?" The note said, 'The Oregon National Guard is ordering $100,000.00 worth of headset ear seals." It was on letterhead stationery and the Commander's signature was at the bottom of the note. A business was born.

The next order of business on my visit was to tour the other large buildings where the production magic happens. There is foam everywhere-- all manner of foam of various types -- seats, upholstery, CNC machines, materials testing machines, and so on. There are approximately sixty employees. I met Kim at the 'static table' where fabric is cut; Erin who was cutting foam (cutting foam accurately is an art); Alice, a twenty-one-year employee, building seats; and Rose, who was proud and excited she had successfully sewn a difficult pattern at a customer's request. Mike knew all their names and something about them. That speaks volumes to me. He has a good cadre of employees and he's proud of them.

I could go on but you get it. Oregon Aero was born from a man with a passion imbued with the intellect and stamina to ensure success. It's a quality place; it's also a people place. I like that combination.

42

FOR THE LOVE OF FLIGHT

They walk among us. You don't always know it until, perchance, you stop and talk to one. I'm talking about people with some really interesting aviation backgrounds.

We were visiting the Evergreen Air and Space Museum, McMinnville, Oregon. The "Spruce Goose" (a name Howard Hughes hated) is housed there. Docents are stationed at various locations in the museum. They wear green vests, traditionally adorned with various pins and patches indicating their backgrounds. One guy had a set of Air Force wings pinned to his vest. He looked to be about my age (okay, 70's if you must know). I pointed to them and said, "I recognize those." He answered, "Yah, I vas dere." An accent, pretty much a German accent! Another docent, standing behind him, said, "He flew for the Luftwaffe!" I have to tell you his story; it's an interesting one.

Joergen (John) Guenther was born in Berlin, Germany in 1939. Okay, "Germany, 1939" almost immediately invokes visions of Nazi Germany and WWII. Understandable. But to Germans then Germany had come back from poverty and despair to reach a degree of ascendancy. Nazism was the rule but little did they then know what a horrible and horrific rule it would turn out to be. Certainly Joergen didn't. He was born into it.

One of Joergen's first memories was from when he was three years old. The air raid siren had sounded and he and his family and the other residents of the apartment ran to the bomb shelter. There children were crying, women wailing, men were arguing and it stunk. After that particular raid, he went to the bombed-out roof with his father, who was in charge of keeping the roof antennae operable, he being a radio/television expert. After raids, everyone was required to turn on their radios…loud….and hear "patriotic" music and news of German victories. On that night Joergen looked up--he remembers it vividly --and saw searchlights bracketing an airplane above. Then the airplane was hit and began breaking apart with little specks falling away from it. Those specks were people. Three years old! This was Joergen's early childhood, bombs, shelters and fear.

Joergen's father was a talented television engineer. His mother was Danish and there were two sisters in the family, also. As time went on the family's future went from bleak to really dismal: the Russians came. Women and children hid and men were conscripted. Jorgen's father was forced to supervise a group of German television workers. The Russians wanted to know more about how all that worked. His father was sent to occupied Czechoslovakia to continue the work. Later he was sent to Leningrad, Russia, this time to work with Soviet "supervisors." All that, of course, left the rest of the family alone in a badly crumbling Germany. Joergen is now six years old.

Fortunately, with her Danish background, Joergen's mother was able to move the family to Copenhagen, Denmark to live with her parents. There the children found a modicum of peace and the family love of grandparents. They attended school again and learned Danish. Still, Joergen's mother felt the family should all be together so they eventually journeyed to

Leningrad to be with the father. They lived in an apartment and Jorgen went to school again-- this time learning Russian. I asked him of his relationship with the Russian kids. He said, "Tentative. But I carried things they wanted to keep the peace. They valued pencils. My father brought me handfuls of them and I cut them short so I had more and handed them out....as needed." The Russians eventually felt they had what they needed from Joergen's father and sent him back to Berlin, *East* Berlin.

East Berlin was grim. Guenther family ties....what was left of them....were in West Berlin. As were the Americans. Here's where the story gets a little murky....and clandestine. Joergen came home one day and all the furniture in the apartment was packed. His parents said, "Don't say anything." The next day, family members, instructed by their father, took separate forms of transportation (Joergen rode his bike) to a prearranged location in West Berlin. There they were met by a big, black car and told, "Get in!" Joergen says the car drove "all over the place" and they were told not to look outside. Then they were dropped off at a building (read: safe house). Inside, there were Americans who spoke German. (Remember, Joergen's father had a valuable trade.) The next day they were told to pack up again. The big car took them to an airport and pulled up beside a C-47 with engines running. They were told, "Get out and get in." Up the steps they went. They landed at Wiesbaden and were then taken to Darmstadt. This was their new home thanks to...you may have guessed it....the CIA. Joergen was eleven years old. Quite the childhood.

Joergen went back to school and finished high school. When he was 'of age,' he signed up for driving lessons. Happens his driving instructor had a Piper Cub. Joergen had long held a desire to fly. The driving instructor took him for an airplane ride and Joergen was immediately ‘hooked.’ He said, “The instructor would give me a plane ride and sign it off as a driving lesson.”

We’re into the mid to late 50’s now; Joergen is a teenager. He told his father he wanted to fly. His father knew someone at Lufthansa so they went for a visit. The friend said, “We’re full now. You should consider the *new* German Air Force.” So Joergen did and signed up. His military obligation was six years. He first attended basic soldier training, saying, “That wasn’t much fun.” After interviews by the CIA and German Intelligence, he was allowed to attend officer training. And then he was selected for flight training. He soloed in a Cub. He says, “All solo students had a red ribbon tied to the wing strut.” (Great idea, huh!) After more training in navigation and such, Joergen was told, “For two more years of military obligation, we’ll send you to America for US Air Force flight training.” Joergen said, “Yes.”

Arriving in America, the German students journeyed to Williams AFB, Phoenix, Arizona. Along the way they learned of scorpions, Gila monsters and tarantulas……all new to them! Joergen first flew the T-37, which he loved (as I did) for its quality handling characteristics. After that he was awarded his USAF and German military pilot wings. Then it was on to the T-38, to learn the handling characteristics of supersonic aircraft. Then it was across town to Luke AFB for gunnery training in the T-33 and F-84. He enjoyed that immensely. He was in “Hog Heaven.”

Back in Germany, he first flew the T-33 to reacquaint himself with European flying, as in weather and frequent borders. Then he was assigned to fly the RF-84F, the reconnaissance version of the F-84. He enjoyed that mission. I asked, “Did they not let you have guns?” He said, “Up north they had them but in the south we flew reconnaissance.” After about three years, he was assigned to the RF-104....reconnaissance version again. It was an early version and ejected downward: A low level emergency required you to roll upside down and then eject. (Think about that.) That was later fixed. The recce version had but one camera and not much agility close to the ground but it was a thoroughbred nonetheless.

Nearing the completion of his military obligation, Joergen had a former military friend who was flying for Swissair. The friend encouraged him to apply, saying, "It's a smaller, friendlier airline." Joergen did and was accepted. There, domiciled in Zurich, Switzerland he flew the DC-3, DC-9, DC-8 and Airbus A-310, retiring after twenty-eight years.

After retiring, Joergen relocated to California and owned three different airplanes, a Cherokee, a Comanche and then a Beech Travel Air. He hangered them at Corona Municipal (KAJO), a legendary airport. Tiring of population and traffic, he moved to Salem, Oregon (my hometown, which is where we met and he told me his story). He kept his Travel Air at Independence Airport (7S5), home to EAA Chapter 292, until selling it. So, too, he knows "experimentals," having flown a RV-6, 7, 10, and 12.

Now fully retired, Joergen lives with his wife Sandi in their home surrounded by the many artifacts of his life and career and their cat, "Sortie." He's a true gentleman. From the bombed-out rubble of Berlin, to staying strong, curious and positive in life, to following his dream of flight, he has 'walked' a commendable path! For fun, he volunteers one day a week at the Evergreen Air and Space Museum, where his stories are much appreciated. Before I left his house, he got out two small glasses, put them on the coffee table and poured them half full of red wine. He wanted to toast. So we did.

43

THE TWEET

Okay, here's the deal: Sometimes you fly an airplane and you like it but then, sometime later, it dawns on you that "dang that was a really fun airplane to fly!" The one like that I flew I remember for its handling characteristics. Never have I flown an airplane since with such a control feel; it was one of grace and responsiveness at the same time. It was just natural to become one with it. You have your favorites, too, and you may be thinking right now that I'll name one. But probably I won't. The 'favorite memory' airplane I flew was once as common as popcorn…at least in the military….but today, for all practical purposes, is non-existent. When I tell you what it is, you're going to say, "Huh??!!? What??!?"

The Cessna T-37.

I'm going to have to explain that, aren't I! Fair enough.

Yeah, it was small, squat, noisy, non-afterburning, sub-sonic and with the sex appeal of an aluminum pancake, which it looked like. But in the US Air Force it was *your* jet…your *first* jet….so none of that mattered. You bonded with it, no matter its warts. It was a little fighter in sheep's clothing.

Some historical background: in 1952 the Air Force issued a request for proposals for a "Trainer Experimental (TX)." It was to be an easy to maintain, jet, two-seat basic trainer. Jets were the future. Cessna Aircraft stepped up with the "Model 318." (The Air Force later designated it the XT-37.) It was a small, twin jet (J-69's), with straight wing, side-by-side seating, ejection seats, speed brake, hinged canopy, unpressurized, and wide track tri-cycle landing gear. In every respect, it was designed for the mission of training jet pilots. The initial prototype crashed during spin testing. Long nose strakes were added to the remaining prototypes and the tail was enlarged and re-designed. The first T-37A was delivered to the Air Force in 1956 and student flight training began in 1957. A follow-on T-37B was introduced not long after with uprated engines (10% more thrust) and upgraded avionics. All previous "A" models were converted to "B" models. All told, 1269 T-37's were produced. In 1969 an attack version, the A-37, was designed and built for service in Vietnam, with more powerful J-85 engines and provisions for armament. And it did well. It could loiter, stay over the target and was accurate. The last T-37 was retired in 2009. That's fifty-two years of service. Slice it anyway you like, it all adds up to being a very successful airplane.

A few stats: engine, J-69, 1025 lbs. thrust; length, 29' 3"; span, 33' 9"; height, 9' 2" (on its tiptoes); empty weight, 4,056 lbs.; max takeoff weight, 6,570 lbs.; fuel capacity, 309 gals., fuel burn, 150 gph (varies greatly with conditions of use); max speed, 369 knots; service ceiling, 35,000'….limited to 25,000' by Air Force regulations for unpressurized aircraft; 6.67 positive G, 2.67 negative G; no snap-rolls. (Oh, it would do them but fifty-years of twisting g-loads would take a debilitating toll on the airframe so…..no.)

Cutting to the chase now, the T-37 had a plethora of names. Most of the names were derived from the noise the engine made: a shrill, high pitched whine. The Air force toyed with a fix but it reduced power so they stuck with the noise. Noise protection was required within a 100 nm radius of an operating airplane. (Okay, I may have exaggerated a *little* but you get the idea.) In the air, flying it, it was not a problem whatsoever. The name that stuck the most was "The Tweet," short for "Tweety Bird." Other names were "The Six-thousand Pound Dog Whistle" and "Converter" (converts JP-4 to noise). Some unfortunate students dubbed it the "Vomit Comet." Still, it was endearing.

Okay, let's hop in. Remember, you're now twenty-two years old and bullet proof. You suit up. Helmet, mask, gloves, and parachute. You walk the flight line to your airplane. You are so excited you can't even spit. You walk around your airplane, checklist in hand. (It's the 'military way.') It's small but all-aluminum, no paint and strong. You strap in. The ejection seat is a pretty good one but you have to be 200' in the air to safely eject (1966 version). Twin engine failure below 200' required you to land straight ahead....in the soft West Texas desert. Probably not very survivable but I never heard of it happening either.

Time to start engines. You can start on battery power but usually there was a power cart available; cooler starts that way. Boost pump on; boost pump warning light off; left engine start switch – GND and hold; left ignition stitch – on at 5% rpm and hold; left throttle – idle at 8% rpm; left ignition switch – off at rapid EGT rise; left starter switch – off at 25% rpm. Got it? Now check hydraulic pressure, signal for APU disconnect, check the loadmeter, advance power to 60% and start the right engine. Now show the ejection seat safety pins to the crew chief and give the "pull chocks" signal. You will learn to appreciate crew chiefs: they're proud and very capable. Taxi is a 'piece of cake' with nose wheel steering and wide main gear. On the runway now, you push engines to MAX PWR and check engine instruments. That's your 'run up.' One thing, do not push the engines up faster than the rpm gauge can follow: These are 'slow spooling' engines. Then release the brakes and away you go….with a very smooth and steady acceleration. Rotate, positive rate, gear and flaps up and you are being pushed aloft with a hum, feeling rock solid. Magic, I tell ya!

Now fly it. Visibility is superb and control feel is instant. No hydraulics and fly-by-wire hooey, just cables and pushrods directly to the controls. You *feel* the input; you *feel* the responses. Piston fighter speeds and jet smoothness: a perfect match. Once you've experience it you never forget it. I haven't. Roll: up, over and smooth as glass you draw a corkscrew in the sky. Effortless! You do another one the other way. Loop: lower the nose to gain a little speed and up and over you go….the Earth showing wonderfully through the top of the canopy before you start the downhill side. It's like being on top of the world which, at this point, you feel like you are. (On my first solo flight to a practice area I did four loops in a row, lost in joy.) Stalls: straight ahead and honest. But with a straight wing and aerodynamic cleanliness, they added some small spoilers on top of the engine nacelles that came up automatically and disturbed the airflow such that you could feel it in the elevators. Kinda artificial but it got the point across.

Spins: now we're going to experience a distinct T-37 personality trait. Stow every loose object; this isn't going to be gentle. Approach the stall, stick back, at the appropriate moment bottom the rudder, stick in your gut and….WHAM….you are on your back, nose falling. It ends up pointed down and rotating r-a-p-i-d-l-y. Pick a spot on the ground where the spin started; when you see that spot again, that's one turn. For recovery, aggressively apply opposite rudder to stop the rotation…don't be shy. One turn later, slam the stick forward to the stop to break the stall. You are beyond straight down now but under control. Neutralize everything and recover from the dive. Fail to neutralize the stick and you could very well tuck under and then be in an inverted spin. Not pleasant. Often, during recovery, your helmet would hit the top of the canopy. That scratched the helmet; those were called “spin scratches.” They were a badge of honor. Great fun!

Back to the traffic pattern now for an overhead ‘break’ to landing. Straightforward. But for the slow-spooling engines “thrust limiters” were installed such that you could keep the rpm up in case of a go-around but not gain excessive speed on final. Clever. Nice wide landing gear and ‘plunk-plunk’ you’re back on the stupid ground.

The Air Force has other bigger and faster and more powerful and jazzy jets, for sure. But I don’t know that they have one that’s more fun than the Tweet. My two-cents worth, anyway.

My Tweet instructor was 1Lt. Hassen. He was tough but fair; I liked him. But I lost track of him and now can’t find him. He was from the East Coast, Maine maybe, had an accent and a hardy laugh. Named Lloyd Beckwith Hassen. Anybody?

Something else I can’t find? Search the internet for “T-37 for sale” and see what you get. Not much. You’ll have better luck finding hen’s teeth. Oh, there are some in private ownership, but not many. Most all are, sadly, in ‘boneyards.’ Maybe the Tweet doesn’t have enough, you know, visual pizazz? Dunno. But I do know this: For sheer flying delight the Tweet is held in high esteem.

44

SELF-SERVE AVGAS

Okay, can we talk about self-service avgas pumps? I can operate the one at my home airport, having come to an almost friendly understanding with it some time ago, and am now actually able to refuel without swearing or throwing things. Well, most of the time, anyway. But what of those self-serve pumps at the outlying airports? Who designed those things? Einstein? Or Frankenstein? Either way, they look like someone took a control panel off the Space Shuttle and added some stuff from Radio Shack. They're generally not very user-friendly, intimidating even, and sure to implode if you push the wrong button. Plus, with the card receptacle here, the control panel there, and the pump in the next county, you need three arms and must be able to run the one-hundred-yard dash in under ten seconds in order to complete the refueling. But, hey, we're pilots; we'll figure it out.

First you have to chock your airplane. The wooden chocks at the pump have been there for seventeen years. They have been thrown back and forth so much that they now look like two toothpicks fastened together by a length of ¾" rope. But, hey, we're pilots; we'll figure it out.

Next you have to ground your aircraft. The grounding wire? It's a rat's nest that looks like it's been through three hurricanes and two flash floods.....in the Byzantine era. You tug it toward your airplane. This just serves to further tighten the twenty-seven knots that are already in it. You don't have the three weeks available that it would take to untangle the line. You surrender and move the airplane closer to where the rat's nest will reach.

You then confront the control panel. You confront it some more. You then extend your left arm, lean on it and look at the panel real-up-close-and-personal-like, trying to recognize something......anything. You then take a quick glance to check if anyone is watching your befuddlement. They're not. That you know of, anyway. The panel is made up of lights, buttons, bells, and whistles. Behind it are pipes, warning signs, tanks and pumps. You hope the thing doesn't swallow you up and whisk you to Alfa Centauri, where it looks like it came from. You notice a little reader-board above the keypad. It is scrolling a message: "screw this up and the machine will chew your arm off." That's comforting. On the panel you see something that looks like where a credit card might go. You put your credit card in it. The machine pushes it back out. The little reader-board reads "card not accepted." Okay, you rummage around in your wallet and find another card. You put that card in. The machine pushes it back out. The little reader-board then says "remember what I said about chewing your arm off?" You push the button that says "yes." You try your Bed Bath & Beyond card. The little reader-board asks "do you need new towels?" You push the button that says "yes." The machine now seems happy with this arrangement and begins asking you twenty-questions: "What's your N-number?" There are only numbers on the keypad, no letters. You have numbers *and* letters in your N-number. It is time to assert yourself: You punch in three bogus numbers and.......wait. Machine's thinking. But then the machine went on to the next question. You raise your arms high over your head in victory, saying, "Stupid machine! Those numbers are bogus! I outsmarted you!" A small victory but a victory nonetheless. You then look around again to see if anyone is watching. No one is, as far as you can tell. Maybe from Alfa Centauri, but not locally. But you still haven't gotten any fuel so you turn your attention back to The Machine. The Machine asks "have you grounded your aircraft?" There was a button for "yes" and a button for "no." There was not a button for "are you kidding me? with that wad of Byzantine copper you call a grounding wire?" You punch the "yes" button.

Next question was "which pump?" Which pump??? There's only one pump!! You push the number "1." Machine accepts that; machine is toying with you. Then it asks "how much do you want?" You then push "3" and "0." Machine asks "gallons or dollars? for gallons, multiply the square root of seven-hundred-eighty-nine by three and enter that number. for dollars, divide the national debt by four trillion and enter that number." Machine was not going to beat you: You pull out your iPhone and Google "The Machine," which then took you to a website that gave you the answer for gallons (or so you thought). You enter the number. In a few seconds, all manner of pumping and whining noise emanates from The Machine. The reader-board then says "good luck, sucker, and hurry."

You run to the hose, throw it over one shoulder and start dragging it to the airplane. The harder you pull it the more it pulls back. About a foot from the fuel tank you are bent over, both feet and one hand digging into the ground for traction, your chin about one foot off the ground. From this position you attempt to raise the nozzle to put it in the tank. You even remembered to take the fuel cap off. Ten inches to go. Eight inches. Two inches. Then suddenly it gets quiet. Real quiet. The pump had "timed out" and shut off. Silence. Seething. Visions of bad words dance in your head. But, hey, you're a pilot; you'll figure it out.

Back to The Machine. Reader-board says "sorry." Somehow it didn't seem very sincere. You start over: twenty questions again. You enter another bogus tail number (thank Heaven for simple pleasures) and The Machine once again springs to life. You get the nozzle in the tank, squeeze the trigger and fuel is flowing. Victory!! Until 4.3 seconds later the pump shuts off again. You run to the pump and the reader-board says "$30.00. Thank you very much." Arrrggghhh!!! You entered the numbers for the "dollars" question, not the "gallons" question. Do you know how long it takes to pump $30.00 of avgas? 4.3 seconds.

If nothing else, pilots learn, at an early age, perseverance. You persevere.

You once again saunter to the reader board-- you somehow get the feeling the machine is feeling sorry for you --and get it running again with all the correct inputs....you think. You run back to the hose. Somehow it has retracted about five feet from where you left it. It has obviously tired of your abuse or artificial intelligence has directed it to taunt you. You again do the fireman-like drag of the hose to your tank and....voila!.....finally!.....you insert the nozzle into the tank and fuel flows and keeps flowing. Full at last. Only one more tank to go. You almost gloat. But then you glance up at the control tower. You see a lone silhouette of a human. That silhouette is holding up binoculars and looking directly at you. You can't see her laughing but you know she is. The thought comes to your mind, 'So that's how they entertain themselves on the slow days. They get their 'yuks' spying on pilots doing battle with the self-serve pump.' You're pretty sure you're not the first pilot that has entertained them in such a manner. Benevolently, you're glad to be of some humor to them. Privately, you want to get on the radio and say, "Tower, we're a flight of twenty student pilots five south coming in for landing."

Bottom line, it was man vs. machine. It wasn't pretty; it wasn't easy. But, this time, victory belongs to the human. Now you just have to wait and see if you get your avgas bill on your Bed Bath & Beyond statement.

45

FIRST GRADE

There are a lot of things we learned early in life…..like in the First Grade….that helped us to become good pilots. For example:

- Big storms are really scary.
- When you jump out of a swing, the higher you start your flare the harder the landing.
- When you jump from a tree, homemade parachutes don't work very well.
- Blue skies are really pretty and fun.
- Don't be afraid to ask for help if you need it.
- Learning about new things is really fun.
- Hummingbirds can fly really good.
- Eagles can glide really good.
- Flat tires are bad; they make it hard to pedal.
- Go to the bathroom before you go on a long trip.
- Carry snacks.
- Watch where you are going.
- When it's dark, a flashlight is a good thing.
- Flapping your arms doesn't help you fly.
- You can see far when you're up high.
- Have a good battery. Sometimes my mom's car won't start on cold mornings.
- Doing stupid stuff sometimes gets you hurt.

- Loud engines are really cool.
- Learn from your teachers. That's what they do: teach.
- It's hard to stop quick on ice.
- Teeter-totters work best when the weight is balanced.
- You can't lower the high side of a teeter-totter when your bigger, older brother is sitting on the low side laughing at you.
- Goggles are really cool when you ride your bike really fast.
- It's harder to see things when you have bugs on your goggles.
- When snow sticks to your sled runners, the sled doesn't work very good.
- Warm clothes are good when you're doing stuff outside in the cold.
- Propellers on wind-up balsa wood airplanes can really whack your fingers.
- Balsa wood gliders do really neat loops.
- Model airplanes teach you stuff about airplanes.
- Real airplanes are fun to dream about.
- Following the rules, for some reason, is usually is the best way to go.
- Don't hit the person sitting on your right who's trying to help you.
- Don't run into stuff.
- Stay in the lines.
- Know the way home.
- Milk and cookies make you feel good.
- Peanut butter and jelly on white bread, also good.
- Take naps, but not when you're up to bat.
- Clean up your messes.

- Don’t be afraid to say you’re sorry.
- Keep your nose up if you want to see where you’re going.
- Listen before you talk.
- Don’t interrupt.
- The more you practice tricks and stunts, the better you get at them.
- Be aware of wonder.
- Don’t throw things.
- Be careful when ducking under stuff.
- Mud stops you in a hurry.
- Clean clothes are good if you’re going somewhere.
- If you don’t understand something, ask.
- Don’t play when you’re sick.
- Leather jackets are really cool.
- When you’re working on your bike, dirty clothes are good.
- Take care of your bike. It works better and lasts longer that way.
- Grease is good stuff.
- Polishing makes stuff look nice.
- Know where you’re going.
- Eat good food.
- You can’t run fast in soft sand.
- Wet grass is slick.
- Breaking the rules is generally not a good thing to do.
- Tell your parents where you’re going to be.
- Never lose track of your lunch pail.
- Having fun is a lot of fun.

Of course, I grew up in the pre-video game era. If you wanted to do things and have fun you made your own fun. I'm thankful for all that, actually. But, not to be judgmental of a different generation, the video-game-kids are really quite good at mastering glass cockpits. Then there's the other end of the spectrum: I once attended some flight training in the military with some foreign students. They were nice people.....mostly from the privileged class in their country....but had very little mechanical experience. They suffered mightily learning to fly. So, just me talking, somewhere in the middle is probably a good balance, a little bit of playground, a little bit of working on your bicycle and perhaps a few video games and you'll have a good start on your flying career. Then it's just a matter of more learning and acquiring some discipline and judgment. But I go back to my original premise: The good stuff you learned early in life...as early as the First Grade.... served to make you the good person and the good pilot that you are.

46

SOLD

I sold it. Sold what? My airplane, N214KT.

The first question always asked is, "Why??" I'll get to that in a bit.

But first: the emotion of selling a homebuilt. I started the tail kit in 1998; I sold the airplane in 2018. That's a twenty-year relationship with an airplane. A few years building-- a completely enjoyable experience --and all the rest flying. I mean, this airplane was born from parts I assembled; I raised it! So, yeah, the bond is strong. As is the bond of gratefulness from having experienced "the experimental opportunity" that the EAA fosters in this great country of ours. I'm trying….still….not be too emotional about it. After all, it's just an airplane, right? Wrong. It's a part of my aviation soul. I've sold a couple other airplanes in my time but none tugged at me like this one. I'm thinking many of you know exactly what I'm talking about.

Okay, back to the "why" question. Here's where I'm going to fall back on an age old cliché: It was *time!* "Time" is a lot of things: quit while you're ahead; age deficits that slowly but relentlessly creep in; go out on your own terms; times change; things change; other things to do; being at peace with what you've accomplished……yadda-yadda-yadda. So, no one big thing, just a lotta little 'life things' that add up to say, "Okay, it's *time*." And, no, it was not a rash decision; I pondered it for over a year. I've been flying continuously for fifty-three years; my bride has been with me for fifty of those years. We make decisions together, but not this one. She said, "This one is *your* decision." She, of all people, knew the gravity of it.

My friend Jack had to stop flying (pre-basic med) when he "lost his medical." That was a bitter pill for him to swallow. I didn't want that pill. Another friend "hung it up" three years ago, also invoking, "It was time." He passed away last month. Stroke. Another reader/friend, Jim, a former-military and professional pilot, wrote to tell me, "I understand how difficult the decision is. I sold my C-180 last week and have decided to hang it up. I still have the same number of landings as takeoffs and everything I've flown has been reusable. Time to move on." None of what I'm saying here is meant to suggest what anyone else should do. The decision is a personal one. To each his own.

How did the sale go down? Emotionally it was a roller coaster; I knew it would be. Process-wise, it went well. I put an ad in Barnstormers and ten days later had a deposit. I got a few calls of the "you okay?" variety. I answered, "Yes!! Just making some changes." And one saying, "I like your airplane but don't need the aerobatics. Seems like a waste of time." Then this one, "Name's Dave. Am in the terminal in Dallas. Just got off a trip. Just read of your airplane being for sale. Hope I'm not too late to the party but I'm interested in your airplane." That was on a Tuesday. On Wednesday, he got a jump seat to Portland, Oregon, rented a car and drove up to my hangar that afternoon. Good guy, a 'doer.' We bonded right away. He's a Captain for Southwest Airlines; he's a long time EAA member; he served in the Air Force; he's an A&P; he likes old airplanes and airplanes with personality; he's owned a J-3 and has a beautiful Fairchild (now for sale); he's very family oriented. I took him for a flight. We came back and he looked over the aircraft log and said, “I want the airplane.” And he gave me a deposit. And away he went. (Of note, he quibbled not once about the price. I could have sold the airplane for $30,000.00….which I did not…or $250,000.00…..which I did not. The emotional result would have been the same. This was a personal decision, not a financial one. I think Dave knew that.)

At home in Dallas, Dave started all the official paperwork and got transition training. I flew every day of the next week and then did a fresh condition inspection for him. With all the paperwork in order, Dave returned 5-23-18. I picked him up at PDX and he stayed the night with us. The rest of my family came for the BBQ, too. They wanted to meet Kilo Tango’s new adoptive parent. They approved.

Then 5-24-18 came: ‘fly it away day.’ Dave was well prepared; I appreciated his professionalism. We went to the airport and opened the hangar door and pushed Kilo Tango out. I gave him my cockpit rundown. He got in and started the airplane. It was the first time I’d ever heard it run from outside the cockpit. It sounded good. Then he taxied for takeoff. It felt a little like the day our oldest son left for college. Then came the takeoff. I couldn’t watch; I turned my back. But I heard it. Dave didn’t leave immediately. He took the airplane out to get the feel of it then returned for some touch-and-go’s. I watched those; he was in control (you can just tell). His last pass was a fly-by with a wing rock. That was a nice touch. I told my bride, “He’s feeling it now.” A little later Kilo Tango became a speck on the horizon. I teared up.

Feeling a little melancholy, my bride and I took our fun little 1964 Volkswagen Beetle for a drive in the country, down two-lane roads in farm land. That always puts us in a happy place. We crossed the Willamette River on a ferry, the only car on it. Very peaceful. Then, a very short while later, a car at an intersection pulled out right in front of us! I swerved but he still managed to mash the right front fender of our precious, restored fifty-four-year-old car. I said, "Dangit" (or a reasonable facsimile thereof) three times in rapid succession. We exchanged driver information (he admitted fault), I pulled the fender away from the tire by hand and we continued to our planned destination, 'The Flat Tail Brewery' in Corvallis, Oregon. There I had one adult beverage with lunch…and I never do that. 5-24-18 is a day we'll not forget.

Ya know, I never really planned to do a 'last flight.' I wasn't sure what the heck you'd do on something like that. So I didn't. Instead it went like this: the last landing of the last day I did all the flying was a pretty stiff crosswind. One wheel gently touched, then the other….still straight down the centerline….then the tailwheel. I'm not bragging; it's just that it came at a good time for the last time. And that, as it turns out, was that.

What's next? *Something*. How's that? Aviation's been a part of my life ever since I watched a DC-3 fly over our ranch when I was seven years old. That ain't never gonna change. Maybe a partnership with my son, a flying club, renting. Dunno. I'll work it out; it'll be low key. And it will be this: tandem with a tailwheel and a stick. That's my aviation imprint.

(I have to tell you, I called around to three local FBO's and asked of tailwheel rentals. They said, "Yeah, we used to but the pilots kept wrecking them so we stopped." You can draw your own conclusions about that!)

Dave kept us apprised of his journey back to Texas. We cheered him on and his family was glad to see him. Kilo Tango answered the call and now has a new home with new adventures to look forward to. I'm at peace and have a great family of support but I’ll never forget my RV-8 friend, that’s for sure!

47

JOE

It was always in the distance while driving by. In Colorado. Near Walsenburg. We've driven by it many times over the years during our travels. And it always called to me: "visit!" Know what I mean? It's an airport. Not a big airport; a small airport. One runway that I could see and a cluster of hangars. I kinda knew what to expect; I've visited lots of small airports and they're always genuine and friendly. And often there's no one there, just you. They're just kinda magical. So this year.....crazy 2020.....we stopped. It's off the freeway about a mile and a half down a gravel road with one rattly cattle guard. I was excited! We parked and I got out. It was quite warm and there was a steady light breeze. And there it sat right in front of me...the runway....nice, paved and with a bit of a dip in it. Looked to be about 5,000 ft. (Okay, I looked it up for you; it's actually 4700 ft.) Upon closer examination there appeared to be a crossing runway, too. It was turf. Maybe a couple thousand feet long. Looked to be a little rough. (Looked that up for you, too: Says "rough, ruts and bumps. Prior permission required.") I can take a hint! And a "terminal" close by with the inviting cluster of hangars behind it. It was totally quiet. Perfect.

I walked up to the terminal, a small office-type building advertising its identity: "Spanish Peaks Airfield (4V1), elev. 6050." I peeked inside. It was uninhabited. On the top of a table lay a "Sport Aviation" magazine of some vintage. To one side there were some parked cars. I'll leave it to you to pick out the one that is the courtesy car. I then ambled toward the hangars and almost bumped into a yellow sign. It was rather surrounded with weeds and brush. The top of the sign said CAUTION. Under the word CAUTION was a symbol: a snake. I immediately looked down at and around my feet. (You don't fool me; you'd a done the same thing!) Warning duly noted I continued walking toward the hangars…..head and eyes mostly down.

I came to the first hangar row, all buildings of different colors, shapes and vintage but all proud. And each, I knew, had a story to tell. Stories of passion, friendships, flights and maintenance cuss words. It was a very good feeling. Between the rows I found one airplane tied-down outside. One! Transient? Maybe. Maybe not.

I then strolled toward the last row of hangars. In front of them was the self-serve fuel pit. Pretty standard. I turned around to look at the hangars behind me and noted a Quonset-type hangar with its doors partially open. Yeah! Somebody's here! I'm afraid of snakes but I'm not afraid of poking my head into an open small airport hangar, have only always had good experiences doing that. I stepped in the very solidly built hangar. Airplanes: what looked to be a flyable RV-6A and behind it an RV-7A under construction and tucked in nose-first a straight-tail Cessna of some sort. And an old car…Model A, I think….undergoing restoration. Wow! Had I not stopped to visit, I'd a missed this magic! But didn't see any*body*. So, I hollered, "Hello!!" and that echoed quite loudly. From somewhere in the back came, "Hello!" And then out walked a bearded man with suspenders and a hat. He walked up, stuck out his hand and said, "Name's Joe." When you meet somebody like that, they are immediately your friend. It's Americana: genuine and friendly.

I asked Joe, “You’re the only one here. You the Mayor of the airport?” He smiled and replied, “No. But I’m out here a lot.” About that time his cell phone rang. He answered and listened for a bit and then asked, “Is it humming? It’s probably a circuit breaker. I can be up there in about thirty minutes and take a look at it.” He hung up and I asked, “You need to be somewhere?” He said, “Naw. No hurry.” Joe is ‘airport people.’ You can just tell. “Hurry” is not a part of his every day routine. We then discussed the hangar contents: The RV-6A is flyable; the RV-7A is under construction; the straight-tail is a pristine 1958 Cessna 172. He remarked, “Got more time in that than anything else.” (I forgot to ask who owned the RV’s.) And we fussed over the Model A a bit. Yup, pretty sure Joe can do and fix most anything. He probably gets called upon a lot.

I asked Joe about other airplanes at the airport. He said, “Oh, yeah. We got quite a few. Mostly Cessna’s and Piper’s. Used to have a jet here but I haven’t seen it in quite a while.” I asked of airport administration. Joe said, “The county had a guy in charge but he passed away a few months ago. Not sure they’ve named a replacement yet.” Given that Joe had two RV’s in the hangar I asked if he was an EAA member. He answered, “No. Did about twenty-five years ago but let it lapse. I did go to Oshkosh, tho. That was fun.” I wasn’t about to get political but I did say, “They’re a pretty good organization.” He said, “I know.”

I asked of airport traffic. He said, “Oh, we’re not too busy but we usually get some traffic on most days. Doss from Pueblo comes down for training but they don’t stick around.” And I queried about the weather in this high Colorado country. He stated, “Yeah, it snows. Not real often. But when it does it generally really snows.” Hence, I suppose, the solid Quonset construction of the hangar; he doesn't have to worry about the snow.

Then we broke into just general, genial conversation about airplanes, airports, hangars and projects and such. Easy conversation, just like we'd known each other forever. Aviation facilitates that sort of bond. That's a magic I love.

Finally, knowing I had miles yet to go that day, I had to say, "I don't want to keep bothering you." He said, "No bother. You can hang out." And I certainly could have….except that we had a schedule to meet. It's bothersome when the hasty life interrupts the peace and goodwill that a small airport provides. But that's just how the ball bounces some days. Still….we met and it was immensely enjoyable.

There are "Joe's" at most small airports. Stop and visit, you'll see. But here's the deal (and I probably don't have to say it because you already know it): don't bring pretense, big titles, gold chains and braggadocio with you; they don't give one wit about that stuff. Small airports are about "real" and that, exactly, is the beauty of them.

Joe, thanks for the visit. Made my day!

48

THE PEOPLE'S PIET

Jim Markle has a story to tell. But it isn't just about him. It's about a whole lotta other people, too, most of whom he doesn't even know. Jim's beginnings in aviation are fairly typical for a general aviation pilot. It's the middle of the story that is not typical. In fact, it is quite remarkable in a very heartwarming way. We'll get to that part in a bit.

Jim's grandfather was a WWII veteran. After his grandfather completed military service he purchased and flew a surplus Stearman. Neither of Jim's parents were interested in aviation so Jim only got bits-and-pieces of his grandfather's stories. Nevertheless, they resonated with him. He says, "I just always liked airplanes."

Early in his adult life Jim lived in Louisiana and took six hours of flying lessons. But then he ran into the "can't afford it" wall and stopped flying. He later moved to California. There he started flying remote control (RC) sailplanes. That turned out to be an affordable catalyst. He took a ride in a full-size sailplane……and he was hooked forever more. His wife was supportive and he got his glider rating.

The next move was to Dallas, Texas. The nearest glider rentals were an hour drive away. Closer was the Addison airport. He poked around there and found a friendly flight school. He was working in sales now and making more money. He earned his single-engine-land rating and then rented 152's and Warriors to continue flying.

Jim gave some thought to airplane ownership but concluded that was more than he could afford. Then he rather stumbled on some pictures of a Pietenpol Air Camper. He researched it more and read about Bernie Pietenpol. He said, "Wow! He was quite a guy. He just did what he did with passion and perseverance." Then he got to thinking: 'Shoot! I can just go to a lumber yard and buy wood. I can buy what I need as I need it. That's doable!' So that's what he did. He bought plans from the Pietenpol family, bought lumber and started building ribs in his garage in 2002. In his Pietenpol information gathering he learned of the Pietenpol fly-in in Brodhead, Wisconsin. It's held every year the week before AirVenture. So here's what Jim did with his enthusiasm: He loaded his completed ribs into his pick-up truck and drove to Brodhead for the fly-in. His ribs! Only his ribs! That's all he had. But you and I know, that's all he needed. Friendship's formed immediately. The aviation kind: honest, helpful, friendly. You know what I'm saying. Jim was welcomed into "the Piet Community" with open arms. He reveled in it.

In 2006, Jim moved to Pryor, Oklahoma to a place in the country that had a 32 x 40 shop. More room for building! Then he rented a hangar at the Claremore, Oklahoma airport. He later purchased that hangar. The Piet now had a flying home. But no engine. Then, don't ya know, his business took a downturn. A serious downturn. He reached the agonizing decision that he had to sell the Piet. Jim put an ad in Barnstormers and about four hours later he had a buyer…..in Belgium. The guy said, "I'll pay your price. I'll send a crate. I'll pay shipping. Just pack it up and send it." Yikes….so far….so fast!

Now this is where the plot thickens. John Recine, a loyal member of the Piet community, called Jim that same afternoon and asked, "What are you doing??!!??" Jim explained the circumstances. John said, "Okay. Talk to you later." An hour later, John called back and asked, "Has any money exchanged hands yet?" Jim said, "No." John said, "Put the guy off a couple more days." Jim had some rather urgent financial matters to tend to but has great respect for the Piet community so said, "Okay. But I can't go any longer than that." John then quietly enlisted the help of another member of the Piet community who is computer savvy and the word got out fast. The next day, John called Jim again with, "Your airplane has been sold. For more than you're asking. We're selling shares in it." (Side story: one of the Piet community wives was telling the story at the beauty shop and several of the ladies in the shop contributed to the fund!) Jim's head is still spinning when the John adds, "Here's the deal. We're gonna buy it but we want you to take care of it. Finish it. We don't care how long it takes. You fly it. It'll still basically be yours." And more, "Don't think much about thanking us. There's eighty-five of us and all are anonymous."

Okay, wrap your head around that for a minute. Surprised? Maybe a little, huh? But here's what you know: aviation, the EAA, the Piet community, all are made up of a lot of givers. That's just the amazing beauty of it.

Jim used some of the "sale" money to 'right' his business and the Piet then became front-and-center again. He had an A-65 that he had bartered and horse-traded for. But then another A-65 popped up. This one had only one-hundred hours on it and it was for sale for a couple thousand dollars. Of course, it had been sitting for ten years but the seller did say that he started it from time-to-time. Jim bought it. This is the engine that Jim installed on his Piet. It's still there.

In 2020, after and eighteen-year build period, Jim completed the Piet. ("Completed" is a relative term in the experimental word; we're *always* working on our airplanes.) He numbered it serial #1001 and christened it NX1929J. But he had no taildragger time. He found someone who would teach him in a Citabria. Jim paid for four hours of dual. After three hours his instructor said, "You're ready. But here's what I'll do. I'll come to your place. We'll fly that last hour and then you hop into the Piet and fly it." So that's what Jim did. He flew the Piet it took him eighteen-years to complete, helped along the way by eighty-five other people he didn't know.

After the flight, Jim "blasted" (his word) the successful flight on Facebook to the Pietenpol community. He received a lot of responses and congratulations. Over the years many people had heard "the story." His airplane became known as "The People's Piet." Jim had vinyl labels made saying just that. He put them on the tail.

Okay, I'm gonna let-the-cat-out-of-the-bag. But it's Jim's secret so don't tell him you heard it from me. He's going to be at the Piet fly-in at Brodhead this year and he's going to ask 'Piet people' to sign the tail of his airplane. He says, "I probably won't be able to read the signatures but I'd like them to leave their mark on the airplane." Look for NX1929J at Brodhead. And remember, act surprised when he asks for signatures. It's a secret that he's gonna do that.

I asked Jim of flying the Piet. (I've never flown one.) He said, "Low levels, 60-70 mph, goggles, cloth helmet, and handheld radio, as needed. He added, "On one cross-country there were some 3500' mountains. I had to climb to 4,000' to get over them. I took a picture of the altimeter. Highest I've ever been in it." Jim has over two-hundred fun hours on his Piet now. And he's a proud member of EAA Chapter 10 in Oklahoma.

As you might imagine, Jim waxes poetic when talking about the Piet. He speaks openly and freely. Michael Cuy, a fellow Piet aficionado, calls him "The Mayor of Brodhead." Jim says, "Every time I stand back and look at it, I think of the goodness…on so *many* levels…that it represents."

49

TANKER MAGIC

This story is more evidence of what I have come to call "EAA magic." Jim Harris, who owns and flies a Bonanza and a pristine 85hp J-3, knowing I flew KC-135 tankers for three years, sent it to me. It's a 'tanker story.' And here's the deal about the story: It's about a tanker that flew into North Vietnam…very prohibited!....to save a damaged fighter. The story was 'the stuff of lore' in the tanker community. It was told again and again….details sometimes getting skewed in the process, I'm sure. Still, it touched the tanker pilot's soul. Yet never did I know who actually did it or a lot of the other facts. Until now. It was Jim's former father-in-law, Galen Sargent. Jim suggested I call him. So I did. And the conversation was wonderful. In his late-eighties now, Galen is modest, sharp and proud.

Galen grew up on a farm in the panhandle of Oklahoma. He attended college, majoring in animal husbandry and also enrolled in the ROTC program. Upon graduation, Galen was commissioned into the US Air Force and sent to UPT (Undergraduate Pilot Training) at Bainbridge, Georgia as class 56M. There he flew the T-34 and T-28. He still remembers the name of his T-34 instructor, a civilian named Porky Stoner. And that one of his classmates was a fella named Gene Kranz, director of the Apollo missions. (Jim had sent Galen my column about the T-37 and that seemed to trigger a lot of memories for Galen.) Then he was transferred to Vance AFB, Oklahoma where he flew the B-25 and earned his Air Force wings upon graduation. He was then permanently assigned to Vance AFB to be an instructor in the B-25 and, later, the T-33. After that assignment he was shipped out to fly the KC-97 (crews nicknamed it the "tri-motor") and then the KC-135, which he flew for fifteen years.

Now jump to the Vietnam "conflict." Galen was now a very experienced tanker pilot and had led many tanker-force missions. Those generally consisted of four tankers and sixteen fighters. I've participated in them, too, but not as flight-lead like Galen. As you might imagine, there is a lot of planning and precision involved. When all goes well it is a very satisfying experience.

In Vietnam, we had what we called "anchors" (think great big holding pattern). They were named after colors, "orange anchor, red anchor, blue anchor," etc. They were generally located near enemy borders except in the south, where they were mostly over the ocean. A tanker would proceed to its assigned anchor and hold. The fighters, usually a flight of four, would come from their bases, "top-off" refuel and then proceed to their targets. The tanker would stay in orbit to re-fuel the fighters after they came off target. So this is what Galen was doing, waiting for his fighters to return, when he got "the call."

Of note, that day the fighters were F-105's, a big-horse of a fighter (could carry as much load as a B-17). Some were F-105B's, a two-seater version nicknamed "Wild Weasel." The guy in the back seat was a navigator turned EWO (Electronics Warfare Officer). The mission was for the crew to find the anti-aircraft weapons and jam them electronically. Dicey? Very! (Imagine being in the back seat, you can barely see out, your head is in your EWO gear and your body is getting thrown around from the maneuvering G-forces....but they did it!)

"The call" on the refueling frequency was from one of the four fighters that Galen was waiting for. The fighter was pleading for Galen to come and get him; he was battle damaged and leaking fuel. He didn't think he could make it to the anchor point. His other option was to bailout over North Vietnam, a horrible prospect. The F-105 flight leader told Galen that the Weasels had suppressed the SAM's and machine gun fire....for the time being.

It was decision time. The regulations specifically prohibited tankers from "going up North." Too inviting a target: one missile hitting a tanker with 25,000 gallons of fuel would be a "propaganda coup." Galen said the decision took about ten seconds. The boom operator in the back chimed in over the interphone, "Let's go get him." Galen then looked at his other crewmembers up front and all nodded in agreement.

The damaged airplane gave the tanker his position and the navigator plotted a course directly to him. At the calculated time the tanker turned in front of the fighter and the hookup was made. They were about thirty miles from Hanoi. (Imagine being the F-105 pilot in a leaking airplane over enemy territory, adrenaline running high, and then having to smoothly hook-up to take fuel.)

Ordinarily, the "boom" (refueling probe) is held in place by the receiver maintaining position and some spring-loaded latches at the end of the boom. But there is also a procedure called "manual boom latching," where the boom operator can hydraulically lock the latches, thereby allowing for some "towing" capability. A disconnect in that situation is called a "brute force disconnect." When that happens, there is a "bang" and the whole airplane shudders. Manual boom latching is what Galen's boom operator was doing to assist the fighter to hang onto the boom at a greatly reduced (read fuel saving) power setting. He once had to unhook to allow the three other fighters to take fuel but then he got back on for the trip home....being refueled and leaking fuel at the same time. Over his home base, Takhli, Thailand, Galen dropped him off for the landing.

Galen and crew landed after him. As they were crawling out of the tanker the fighter wing commander drove up in his staff car and gave each crewmember a hug and a "thank you." The F-105 pilot they saved was a 1Lt. and a new father. The fighter commander submitted paper work to award Galen and his crew the DFC (Distinguished Flying Cross).

A couple days later, Galen and crew flew back to their assigned base, Utapao, Thailand. About a week later, he got a call to report to the commander's office. When he entered he knew there was a problem. The guy was red-faced! He was holding the paper recommending the DFC. And then he said, "You broke regulations and endangered your flight crew and your airplane." Galen said, "Yes, sir." The commander then...literally!....tore the DFC paperwork in half and threw it in the wastebasket, saying, "There's your medal. I'm sending you home." Galen then asked, "If it was you, would you have left the kid there?" The commander looked at him a said, "Get the h**l out of here!"

Galen went back to quarters and told his crew, "We may be going home early." Two days later they were back on the mission schedule board. They ended up finishing their regularly scheduled tour of duty and rotated home. No medal, no recognition, just a big question mark. They came home and basically never publicly told the story.

But here's the deal. Galen and his crew didn't do what they did for recognition or anything like that. They did it because it was the right thing to do for a fellow GI in distress. Period.

I asked him why he never really told the story. He said, "I didn't want it to sound like bragging." How do *you* spell h-u-m-i-l-i-t-y. I then asked him how he felt about the whole situation now. He said, "I sleep well at night."

Galen retired from the Air Force as Commander of the Strategic Air Command's Combat Evaluation Group at Barksdale AFB, Louisiana. Fitting.

Where do we find such men? They walk among us on the grounds at AirVenture.

We had a chuckle towards the end of our conversation. He talked about when he held the rank of Major that he was Major Sargent. I chimed in that when I held the rank of Major, I was Major Paine. He said, "Whoa! I think you win." I said, "Naw. You win just by being you."

www.ingramcontent.com/pod-product-compliance
Lightning Source LLC
LaVergne TN
LVHW050613100826
845148LV00011B/1569

* 9 7 8 0 9 6 5 7 6 0 7 6 8 *